External Debt Servicing: A Vicious Circle

EXTERNAL DEBT SERVICING: A VICIOUS CIRCLE

Alvaro Cencini and Bernard Schmitt

Pinter Publishers
London and New York

First published in Great Britain in 1991 by
Pinter Publishers Limited
25 Floral Street, London WC2E 9DS

For enquiries in North America please contact PO Box 197, Irvington. NY 10533

British Library Cataloguing in Publication Data

A CIP catalogue record for this book is available from the British Library
ISBN 0 86187 185 5

Library of Congress Cataloguing in Publication Data
A CIP catalog record for this book is available from the Library of Congress

Typeset by Communitype Communications Ltd
Printed and bound in Great Britain by Biddles Ltd, Guildford and Kings Lynn

CONTENTS

Acknowledgments

We wish to express our gratitude to the research staff of the Centre d'études monétaires et financières (University of Bourgogne) and of the University of Fribourg, to our students, and to Adrian Pollock who played a decisive role in improving the style of the English manuscript.

Introduction

In his paper on *The Future of International Payments* (1963), Meade stressed the need for a system of international payments that should

1 allow the deficit as well as the surplus countries to devote their domestic monetary and budgetary policies primarily to the maintenance of domestic full employment, price stability, and economic growth;
2 enable them to press ahead with the removal of tariffs and other obstacles to imports; they must not, that is to say, be driven to restrict imports simply in order to restore equilibrium to their balance of international payments, and
3 enable them to develop an enlarged program of untied financial aid to the underdeveloped countries; they must not be under any compulsion to cut down their foreign aid, or to tie their foreign aid to their own national exports, as a means of putting their balance of payments into equilibrium. (Meade 1963: 305).

Meade's requirements are still the ones that a correct system of international payments must satisfy. They represent a challenge which, so far, has not been met either by monetary theory or by pragmatic intervention. In fact, too often countries see their domestic monetary policies influenced or modified by external factors, and it is not too daring to say that these same factors are a major obstacle in the economic development of most indebted countries. Monetary instability is a sad reality of international economics, and so is the external debt crisis which lies heavy on the population of an impressive number of countries. And if we add to this the ever growing destabilizing impact of international speculative capital, we obtain only an approximate picture of the effective gravity of the problems faced by the actual system of international payments.

Of course, these difficulties have long been known and several attempts have been made to find a satisfactory way of dealing with them. The basic system which has been chosen, following the Bretton Woods conference of 1944 and the American decision of 1971 to suspend convertibility of the dollar into gold, is known as the 'dollar-exchange standard'. Since the American currency is that which is most used in the settlement of international transactions, this expression is still accepted world-wide, even though other key currencies are today increasingly playing the role of international standard. In all cases key currencies must be able to withstand the pressures put on them due to their use as international monies. As was so clearly admitted by Rockefeller, since the dollar is the key currency *par excellence* the main task of the international system is to 'strengthen the position of the United States as an international banker' (1963: 153). According to Rockefeller the measures to be implemented varied from the elimination of the national gold requirement to the elaboration of domestic economic policies capable of reducing pressures due to excessive capital movements. The great similarity between this approach and the more recent attempts to tackle the international monetary crisis is immediately evident. A whole series of measures have been proposed to reduce the American trade deficit and to rescue the dollar from all sorts of strains due to international capital flows. Simultaneously, the substitution of the dollar standard with a multiple-currency standard [1] is part of a programme of reform which includes the coordination of monetary policies and the cooperation against the effects of international speculation.

As for the external debt problem, several plans have been worked out in order to help indebted countries out of the ditch. After Baker's attempt to involve private banks in a project for the re-financing of the debt, the actual secretary of the American Treasury, Brady, is trying out a new set of measures to cure two of the most seriously ill patients: Mexico and the Philippines. In short, the reduction of the external debt is carried out through a discounted re-purchase of the debt itself which the country can partially finance thanks to loans granted to it by the IMF and the World Bank. Besides this official re-purchase, the plan contemplates the conversion of the debt through the technique of debt-equity swaps and the open market sale, again at a discount, of the credits owned by commercial banks.

Yet, the claim that, in the present system, the stability of exchange rates can be attained through monetary policies capable of counteracting the erratic movements of speculative capital is far from being self-evident. The use of credit expansion or contraction, increased monetary reserves and international agreements to avert any threat of impairment to the international monetary system has not proven up to the task and exchange stability seems to be as attainable under the present regime as was water by Tantalus. Economic commentators often argue that this results from the unwillingness of some countries to comply with the rules of the game. Thus, surplus countries do not sufficiently expand their domestic demand while deficit countries are not prepared to reduce theirs. The problem is very complex, of course, and it would be vain to try to establish a complete list of all the destabilizing factors working within the system. Yet, the difficulty in finding a satisfactory solution to the problem of monetary stability should not simply be attributed to facts, for it could well result from an insufficient understanding of reality and not from the hypothetic intrinsic inconsistency of the reality itself.

This assumption is indeed supported by the further observation of the failure of the system to impede the constant growth of international speculative capital. In fact, not only are speculative capital movements an increasingly important cause of fluctuations in exchange rates and stock exchange investments, but they are also incessantly nourished by the system, for which they represent a kind of tumoral excrescence.

And things do not work better from the external debt point of view. Like every other pragmatic approach, Brady's plan tries to tackle the symptoms of the crisis leaving unaltered the causes of the disease which, therefore, can only go on producing its negative effects. Rescheduling, restructuring, rolling over, debt-equity swap or simple repudiation are alternative (or complementary) ways of somehow reducing artificially the amount of external debt accumulated so far. Were they to be successful, the negative impact of the debt would be momentarily neutralized, it is true, but the debt itself would immediately start another expansion stroke. As analysis and empirical observation show, in fact, within the present system of international payments external debt servicing is a self-defeating process, which is independent of the goodwill of both debtor and creditor countries. The anomaly is rooted in the system and, in order to eradicate it, it is first necessary to understand clearly its nature and genesis.

All this justifies the need for a new analysis of international money which, starting from a critical appraisal of the traditional approach, will lead us towards a novel insight into the etiology of the present pathological situation.

Let us avoid a possible misunderstanding. The claim that 'balance of payments problems are essentially monetary' (Johnson 1974: 51) has often been used to privilege the monetary as opposed to the 'structural' approach and to introduce at the international level the well-known dichotomy between monetary and real variables. The analysis proposed here is not a modern version of the neoclassical approach to the balance of payments, and neither does it imply any dichotomous perception of international economics. Thus, the importance of the deterioration of the real terms of trade, which is one of the main arguments advanced by the theorists attempting a structural approach, is not being undermined. Nobody could reasonably deny the existence of great difficulties and inequalities at the real level. Yet, it is likewise certain that these problems can be effectively perceived only through their monetization. And it is here that the necessity and the priority of the monetary analysis of international transactions finds its *raison d'être*. Suppose the actual monetary system to be (as it is in fact) seriously flawed, how could it then be possible to know whether the deterioration in the terms of trade is entirely due to real inequalities or, at least partially, to monetary disequilibria?

The understanding of the disequilibrating impact of international monetary transactions requires a novel approach to monetary analysis, and in this respect the distinction between inter-regional and international payments plays a crucial role. The concept of nation as the set of a country's residents is worth further investigation, particularly in relation to the concept of national currency as spontaneous acknowledgment of debt. Even from a short analysis it appears, in fact, that the monetary homogeneity of inter-regional payments makes them radically different from international transactions in which the use of national currencies as world standard leads to countries themselves becoming indebted in addition to their residents. Now, the fact that the debt of the set (nation) adds up to the debts of its elements (state included) is a striking result which does not seem to have received the theoretical attention which it deserves. Several economists tend to play down the importance of the distinction between one-currency and multi-currency areas,[2] and only a few[3] seem to be aware of the dangers of considering the international payments problems as substantially equivalent to the problems of inter-regional order.

And yet, the specificity of international payments and particularly of external debt servicing can be traced back to Keynes. In his debate with Bertil Ohlin and Jacques Rueff about the payment of German war reparations after World War II, Keynes stressed the fact that Germany could not pay its external debt simply by sending abroad part of its domestic income. Besides having to find the required amount of national saving, it had also to get hold of the international currency necessary to carry out its external payment. The transfer problem — this is the expression chosen by Keynes to define the necessity of converting the domestic money of the indebted country into the foreign currency chosen as international standard — is what characterizes our system of world payments and makes it substantially different from the structure of inter-regional transactions.

What was so clearly perceived by the British economist is that to carry out international payments a monetary vehicle is required and that the use of this vehicular money should not have any negative repercussion either on the internal relationship between domestic money and current output or on the external relationship between national currencies. The plan for the institution of an International Clearing Union advocated by Keynes at the Bretton Woods conference of 1944 was conceived in order to give a satisfactory and practical solution to this problem. Unfortunately, Keynes's arguments were not endorsed by the members of the United Nations participating at the conference who failed to understand the importance of the transfer problem, i.e. of the specific role played by Adam Smith's 'great wheel of circulation' at the international level.

The consequences can be extremely serious if the structure of international payments does not naturally conform to this monetary constraint, which is indeed what happens under the present system. As is shown by theory and fact, the compulsory purchase of what is merely a nominal vehicle hinders positive external debt servicing. In other words, it can be proven that, when servicing their external debt, LDCs transfer abroad, to the profit of international speculative capital, part of their domestic resources. Their payment of external debt is therefore double since they have to part with both a given amount of international money earned through commercial exports and with an equivalent amount of national income. The present situation is thus an irrefutable vindication of Keynes's intuition and of the necessity to rethink the whole body of international monetary theory in the light of the distinction between inter-regional and international payments.

The first chapters of our book deal with a thorough analysis of this distinction and with Keynes's attempt to elicit interest in the specificity of the international debt problem. As for the other chapters in Part I, they are concerned with a critical appraisal of the solutions which were subsequently implemented in order to tackle the different problems of international monetary (dis)order, and with a re-examination of Keynes's proposals for the institution of a 'central bank of central banks'.

After the Bretton Woods conference and the institution of the IMF the world went through several crises which were alternatively attributed to the increasing use of the American dollar as international currency (and, thus, to the persistent deficit of the US balance of payments), to the monetary policy followed by IMF member States, to capital flight, to the constant growth of the eurocurrency market, to the oil crisis (and the creation of OPEC), to the irresponsible behaviour of LDCs and so on. Confronted with this state of affairs economists put forth a whole series of analyses and suggestions which brought convertibility to an end, and which led to the creation of new international monetary assets (like SDRs) and a changing mixture of conjunctural measures. It is often claimed that, despite a host of disparate point of views, a sort of adjustable agreement was reached which granted a degree of flexibility to the system which has so far proven sufficient to avoid a major crisis. In fact, it would be wrong to consider the debt crisis as a minor shortcoming of the dollar-exchange standard and the increasing poverty of the world population as the price to pay to relaunch economic development. The situation is, indeed, too serious to be underestimated. Reality has to be overtly faced, and it has to be acknowledged that both theory and practice have been unequal to the task of their ambitions. 'Along with others, the IMF perhaps underestimated the severity and obduracy of the unprecedented debt crisis. A problem that had been so many years in the making, and that had been allowed to reach such unsustainable dimensions, could not easily be dealt with (even in the medium term) with instruments designed to cope with "normal" balance of payments difficulties' (Nowzad 1990: 13).

This is what we have tried to show in the first part of the book, where both the axiomatic approach of neoclassical analysis and the pragmatic intervention of world bankers and official authorities are critically tested. The result is a rediscovery of Keynes's fundamental principles of monetary theory and some precise indications as to the way international debt servicing must be conceived and, then, consistently carried out.

Based on this result, the second part of our work is concerned with the specificity of the problem posed by external debt servicing. Apart from the disequilibria characterizing the whole of international payments, it can be shown that the servicing of external debt is the source of a peculiar formal anomaly. The intuitions of Keynes, Rueff and Triffin are confirmed, and the pathological double payment of external debt is definitively verified both theoretically and experimentally. Whereas the use of a key currency for the settlement of international transactions (both commercial and financial but exclusive of external debt servicing) does not have any negative repercussion on the exchange market, its use for the payment of external debt is highly disruptive since it implies the net purchase of what in reality is a pure numerical vehicle. In order to service its debt, therefore, the indebted country must earn a positive amount of international income (through commercial exports) and finance a net outflow of the foreign currency chosen as international vehicular money. As will be proved, because of this anomalous purchase of the 'wheel of circulation' the indebted country's commercial surplus required for the servicing of its external debt is bound to remain unpaid. In other words, it will be shown that, under the present non-system of international payments, the indebted country has to run up a new debt in order to service the old one even when its commercial exports are greater than its imports, because the external debt servicing neutralizes the gain resulting from the commercial surplus itself. Hence, the international earnings of the country are diminished not only in the trivial sense in which they are used to pay for its external debt, but also in the far more worrying sense that the payment of the debt causes the very source of these earnings to dry up.

The payments of the indebted residents, which should be the only payments required for the positive servicing of external debts, are doubled by an equivalent loss of the country's international earnings. On one side, the residents have to send abroad part of their domestic incomes, while, on the other side, the country has to sacrifice an equivalent amount of the foreign currency earned through net commercial exports. External debts are thus paid both by the indebted residents and by the country itself. Logically, there should be a unique payment. If the country has to carry this out, then, relative to this particular function, the country acts as a simple intermediary. This means that the payments made by the residents must be to their own country, which would therefore earn in domestic money the exact counterpart of what it loses as foreign currency.

The reform of the present pathological system of international payments must prevent the double servicing of external debt. Hence, payments have to be structured so as to avoid the loss of domestic monetary savings which today adds up to the sacrifice 'in kind' corresponding to the country's commercial surplus.

The elements of such a reform, which is called for by the increasing gravity of the international debt crisis, are briefly introduced at the end of Part II, whereas in Part III we propose a plan for the solution of each individual country's double debt payment, based on the logic of indebted countries' external accounts. The synthetical rules of the plan, which are corroborated by theoretical and factual analysis, are first derived from the general principles of the solution and then applied to three case-studies. At a time when the debate on European and world monetary issues is of paramount importance the specialists have too often opted for a barren, pragmatic approach. Now, the time has come for a reappraisal of the principles of banking and of their application to international transactions. Let us consider the following pages as a modest contribution to this task.

Part I

External Debt Servicing as a Specific Case of International Monetary Disorder

Chapter One

The Dangerous Confusion Between Inter-regional and International Debt

1. Expenditure-flow relationships and asset-stock adjustments: a false dichotomy?

1.1. *The problem*

In economic literature a case is made for the dichotomy between expenditure-flows and asset-stocks. Applied to the balance of payments framework this dichotomy implies a rigorous analytical distinction between 'the determination of the current-account balance and the analysis showing how this balance (surplus or deficit) will be financed by flows of financial assets, in the capital account plus reserve movements' (Goodhart 1975: 264). As is clearly recalled by Goodhart (1975), whereas flow relationships have been investigated since the forties (see Machlup 1943), asset-stock adjustments have only recently been analysed in a detailed way. Mundell (1961), Johnson (1972) and Swoboda and Dornbusch (1973) are among the authors who were first involved in this kind of analysis, which they developed putting the accent on the determination of the equilibrium of money. Around the same period, other economists — like Floyd (1969, 1973) and Tower (1972) — were also working on asset-stock adjustments trying to include capital and non-monetary financial assets into their models, and it is along this line that research on the debt problem is usually carried out. Given the importance of this approach, particularly for the correct understanding of the way international monetary problems have recently been analysed by both the monetarist and the Keynesian schools, it is worth while to test carefully its validity.

Let us examine the dichotomy between expenditure-flow relationships and asset-stock adjustments from the monetary point of view. The simplest example of this distinction can be construed referring to an economic agent *A* whose earnings, expenditures and savings are, respectively, x, y and $z + (x - y)$; where z is the amount of savings accumulated before the period taken into consideration. Obviously, x can either be greater, equal to or smaller than y. If *A*'s expenditures are not greater than his earnings, no particular problem arises, and the stock-flow equilibrium seems easily determined through the constancy or the increase of his savings. Things change when *A* spends more than he earns, since both his flow-account and his stock-account are now negatively out of balance.[1] To finance his current-account deficit *A* has to reduce the amount of his financial monetary assets, an amount which he can eventually restore — so we are told — either by selling financial non-monetary assets or by borrowing on the financial market.

In order to clarify the terms of the problem it is useful to refer to the monetary system as it actually works in a monetary developed economy. As is well known, money is nowadays essentially bank money. From a strict materialistic point of view bank money can be represented by coins, notes and book-entries. According to modern monetary analysis, however, book-entries are, by far, the best representation of a money which, by its own nature, exists only relative to a bank account.[2] Now, if we take up this modern approach to money we can easily see the strict relationship which exists between expenditures and money capital. Let us consider *A*'s earnings first. Being paid via a bank, *A* finds his current account increased by the amount of his earnings which, defining a positive bank deposit of *A*, immediately take the form of capital money. At the very instant *A* is paid, his earnings are deposited and define his positive savings, and, therefore, also the amount of his monetary financial assets. Whether or not *A* decides to change his monetary savings into a less liquid form than his current account (buying any sort of financial assets), it remains true that his bank deposit is positive, and the holding of a bank deposit is in every respect equivalent to the ownership of a financial asset.

If we now pass on to analyse *A*'s expenditures we can easily verify that for every 'flow' of income there corresponds an equivalent adjustment of stock-assets. When *A* spends part of his earnings to pay his economic correspondent, say *B*, he actually asks his bank to debit his account and credit *B*'s. Thus, *A*'s deposits (financial assets) are decreased by the amount of his expenditures in one and the same movement: the payment of *A*'s purchases. How could it still be possible, then, to speak of a dichotomy between the two joint aspects of the same event? The study of the 'determination of the current-account balance and the analysis showing how this balance (surplus or deficit) will be financed by flows of financial assets, in the capital account plus reserve movements' (Goodhart 1975: 264) cannot be kept separate, for if it is true that expenditures can only be financed through monetary asset adjustments, it is also necessarily true that no expenditure could ever take place without such an adjustment. *A* can purchase goods and services in the commodity market on condition that his expenditure of money income be positive, and this implies a decrease of his savings. *A*'s bank deposits are debited by the amount of his purchases and it is precisely because his assets decrease (relative to this operation) that his payment is effective and can be called 'expenditure'. This conclusion is also perfectly justified when *A*'s purchases are greater than his earnings and his previously accumulated savings. In this case, in fact, he has to borrow on the financial market the sum equivalent to his net expenditures. If *A* were not able to find the amount of money-capital necessary to the financing of his net expenditures these would obviously remain on the level of wishful thinking, and *A* would be forced to adjust his expenditures to his own earnings and savings. *A*'s possibility of spending more than the amount of money he disposes of (current earnings and accumulated savings) is therefore limited by the amount of savings deposited within the banking system by other economic agents. Supposing that *A* can borrow part of these deposits to finance his net expenditures, it is evident that his net purchases on the commodity market are equivalent to his net sales of assets on the financial market. Borrowing money is just the same thing as selling financial assets, the sale of which can either define the indebtedness of the agents issuing the assets or the investment of the buyer. In both cases, whether he sells shares or bonds, *S*'s current account deficit is matched by a simultaneous and equivalent surplus in his sale of financial assets.

The conclusion we have just reached seems to prove definitively the lack of analytical foundations of the dichotomy between expenditure-flow relationships and asset-stock adjustments. Yet, some scepticism is still justifiable. After all, this negative conclusion could somehow have been predetermined by the choice of our example. In a different context it would perhaps be possible to verify the dichotomy and take advantage of the theoretical distinction between flow and stock variables and between their equilibrating processes. In particular, we should try to apply this distinction to the analysis of inter-regional and international exchanges in order to see if it holds true and if it can help us to find new solutions to the crucial problem of the debt.

2. Analysis of inter-regional exchanges in terms of the dichotomy between stocks and flows

Taking up the traditional line of arguments based on the dichotomy between stocks and flows, Goodhart (1975) sets out to show that inter-regional current-account deficits are often easily settled because of the high degree of substitution of financial claims issued in different regions of the same currency area. What distinguishes the problems relative to inter-regional debt and the problems arising from an international trade deficit would therefore be, according to Goodhart, the much higher degree of substitution of regionally issued claims. Now, besides the obvious observation that financial claims issued in different countries have a lower degree of substitution than the financial asset issued in different regions (and considered within the same country), what we should try to determine is whether or not it is correct to distinguish the formation of inter-regional imbalances from the financing of these deficits. In fact, were the dichotomy to be confirmed, the degree of substitution between financial assets would then be a privileged key to the understanding of the debt problem; were it not, we would have to find another way of dealing with it. What we suggest here is not to reject the analysis of how current-account deficits are financed, but to first establish if this analysis can be kept separate from the mechanism associated with the formation of the current-account imbalances or, on the contrary, if the two events form a unity which, under the actual system of international payments, can lead to a 'pathological' indebtedness that cannot be accounted for by the commercial deficit alone.

Let us start by considering two regions, *A* and *B*, within the same currency area. Suppose region *A* runs a trade deficit with region *B*. This obviously means that economic agents of *A* have been purchasing more goods (and services) from *B* than economic agents of *B* have been purchasing from *A*. Hence, if agents of region *A* are net purchasers of goods, agents of *B* must necessarily be net purchasers of financial assets (shares or bonds) issued by *A*'s economic agents. In other words, for agents of *A* to be net purchasers of goods and services from *B* it is necessary that agents of *B* invest their savings in region *A*. If no saving were available in *B*, residents of region *A* would not dispose of the capital (income) necessary to finance their net expenditures and would therefore not be able to purchase goods in excess of their sales. It is tautological to say that expenditures are positive only if they define the effective expenditure of a sum of money income. Thus, the financing of *A*'s net purchases are an essential condition for *A*'s net purchases to be positive.

From what we have just been arguing it follows that the problem of regional current-account deficits cannot be dissociated from the problem of its financing. The commercial deficit of region *A* can be a reality only if the net expenditures of *A*'s residents (all the economic agents of *A*, public sector included) can be financed through their net sale of financial assets. Hence, it is logically impossible to consider the formation of the deficit as a phase separate from the search of its monetary backing. As Goodhart admits: 'the portfolio adjustments required *to finance* a current-account surplus/deficit can be much more smoothly and easily arranged in inter-regional transactions, indeed so simply facilitated that they may pass virtually unnoticed' (Goodhart 1975: 264).

Now, the reason for these portfolio adjustments passing virtually unnoticed is found in the absence of any dichotomy between expenditure-flow relationships and asset-stock adjustments at a regional level. Let us be clear. This does not mean that any desired level of regional net purchases will necessarily find its financial counterpart. Obviously, what matters is not the desired (or virtual) level of expenditures, but their effective (real) level, and what the absence of the dichotomy implies is simply that portfolio adjustments have to be real in order to have any net expenditure. If residents of region *A* were to buy goods at term from region *B* this, of course, would not define any real expenditure till maturity of the credit granted by the residents of *B*. And it is only at that moment — if *A*'s expenditures were not matched by an equivalent sale of goods but by a sale of financial claims — that we could speak of a current-account deficit (expenditure-flow relationship) for the residents of region *A*.

3. Debt and trade deficit

3.1. *No region as a whole is ever indebted*

What mainly distinguishes regions from countries is the use of a common currency. Within a given country or a given currency area there is no problem of monetary substitution and this is certainly one of the reasons why financial-asset adjustments can take place more easily inter-regionally than between countries. But the uniqueness of money is not only of consequence for the degree of substitution between regional financial assets. An extremely important effect of the use of a unique monetary standard is the impossibility for a region to be in a debt position relative to the other regions of the same country. This is not true of its economic agents, of course, who can be net creditors or debtors of any regional bank. But, even if all the economic agents (public sector included) of a given region were indebted towards the bank of another region, this would not define the indebtedness of the region itself.

When Goodhart says that 'The concern in each individual country over the adequacy of its stock of international reserves simply has no counterpart in inter-regional transactions' (Goodhart 1975: 268), he implicitly admits that, as opposed to what happens to nations,[3] regions do not need to hold any reserve to face the financial engagements of their residents. If regions themselves were liable to become indebted because of the trade deficits of their residents, they would have to build up some financial reserves in order to be able to honour their debt. Economists would thus have to deal with the same problems which arise at the international level. In particular they would have to explain how the debt of a resident can entail the debt of an entity (the region or the nation) which cannot be identified with the sum of the residents.

The fact that regions as such are not indebted with respect to one another is, therefore, highly positive, not only because it relieves the burden which hangs over the economist, but also, and foremost, because it tells us that the debt problem does not arise within a single currency area.

Surprising as it may appear, the previous result is perfectly consistent with theory and observation. Trade deficits being paid, from *A* to *B*, in the same currency used in both regions, it is clear that, as the result of this payment, region *A* cannot be found indebted towards region *B*. Moreover, it is also evident that if *A*'s residents did not pay for their net purchases of goods and services from region *B*, their net expenditure would pertain to the imaginary world. Let us present the argument once again. To say that *A*'s residents have a trade deficit is equivalent to saying that they spend more than they earn, which is possible only if they find on the financial market the sum of money income necessary to the financing of their net purchase of goods and services. Thus, if the current-account deficit of the economic agents of *A* implies, as it effectively does, the payment of *B*'s residents in one and the same money, it would be vain to look for the indebtedness of *A*.

But, if *A* cannot be indebted, what is the meaning of the expression 'inter-regional debt'? The answer is not as straightforward as it may appear. The fact that the debt cannot be ascribed to the region itself restricts the possibility of indebtedness to the residents alone. Yet, it would be wrong to conclude that the inter-regional debt is a measure of the resident's trade deficit. It is perfectly possible, in fact, for a given economic agent to run a commercial deficit without increasing his liabilities at all. The simplest example, of course, is the purchase of goods and services financed through the sale of shares. When a firm sells shares on the financial market it obtains money income without incurring any debt, so that its net commercial expenditures are financed by an operation which is perfectly neutral from the debt-credit point of view. Therefore, it is only when the residents of one region finance their current-account deficit by borrowing money from the residents of another region that their debt can be taken to define an inter-regional debt. It is obvious, however, that this is not the meaning usually conveyed by that expression. Now, the inter-regional debt of, say, region *A* is not only conceived as the debt of the region as a whole, but it is also thought of as the unavoidable, negative, result of a prolonged situation of trade deficit. Let us spend a few words on this commonplace.

3.2. *Even a region's protracted commercial deficit cannot lead to its indebtedness*

We should have already proven that the inter-regional debt can never be defined for any region considered as a whole. Transactions take place between residents, and if they are carried on in a common currency they can, at most, entail the debt of some residents and not of the region itself, which does not even exist as a proper economic entity. Economically, countries can have a separate (though interrelated) existence relative to their residents, since each country has its own national currency as guarantor of its sovereignty. And, as we shall see, under a particular system of international payments the use of national currencies can lead to the indebtedness of the countries themselves. At the regional level, however, no monetary distinction is possible. The use of a single currency makes the inter-regional debt problem completely different from the international one. Because of the lack of monetary sovereignty, regions cannot share the same economic status of countries, and that makes it impossible to define the inter-regional debt proper. If, for example, a payment is made from region *A* to region *B*, nothing allows us to conclude that *A* has now a debt towards *B* or *B* towards *A*. On the contrary, from the obvious observation that the payment can only be made by a resident, it immediately follows that, even if this payment is financed by a loan, *A* cannot be charged with the financial engagements of its residents. The conclusion would be different only if, after the payment, *B* had a claim directly on *A*. Yet, since *A* and *B* act within the same currency area, the money paid by the residents of *A* is not different from the money used in *B* and, therefore, it cannot be said to define the debt of *A* more than it defines the debt of *B*.

If by inter-regional debt it is meant the debt accumulated by the public sector the analogy remains exactly the same. Indeed, the public sector is a regional resident as are firms and householders, and its debt does *not* define the debt of the region itself. Moreover, just as firms can run a commercial deficit without incurring a debt, the public sector can finance its net expenditures through a sale of financial assets which do not define a loan to the public sector but the net investment of the buyer. Economic agents of region *B* can freely invest their savings buying shares issued by firms of region *A*. If they do so, firms in *A* can increase their expenditures on the commodity market without getting indebted. Likewise, the public sector of *A* can get hold of the money income necessary to finance its net expenditures by a sale of financial assets which do not define its debt. Thus, and *a fortiori*, it would be wrong to relate the concept of inter-regional debt to the commercial deficit of the whole set of economic agents operating in a given region. As both theory and facts tell us, a commercial deficit does not necessarily entail an equivalent debt of the economic agent running it. And, if this is true for every single agent, it is also true for their aggregate. Finally, it should be clear by now that the very concept of inter-regional debt is at stake. Goodhart is right when he states that 'by definition, the local authorities in a single region are not in a position to use *monetary policy* to counter any reduction in incomes, employment and wealth, arising from falling inter-regional competitiveness, that may occur in their locality' (Goodhart 1975: 266-7). What he does not seem to see, however, is that the same reason that makes the inter-regional use of monetary policies impossible — the existence of a unique currency — also denies any specific meaning to the concept of inter-regional debt.[4]

3.3. *International versus inter-regional debt*

In economic theory, international and inter-regional debts are often considered as similar in kind. According to Goodhart, for example, current-account imbalances can be settled either by variations in the exchange rates (in the case of a multiplicity of currency areas) or by fiscal measures (in the case of a single currency area). Imbalances, both international and inter-regional, are therefore seen as a negative aspect which has to be tackled as rationally as possible in order to avoid major disturbances for the whole system. Hence, the choice between a unique currency area and a series of different national currency areas is, *ceteris paribus*, a matter of costs minimization. From a strict economic point of view, then, if the costs linked to fiscal policies were less than those relative to exchange rates policies, it would be rational to put the entire system under the same monetary sovereignty. Obviously, this kind of solution would face all kinds of socio-political difficulties, and could easily be taken for a utopian dream; yet this is not the point here. The important aspect of the whole argument is, in fact, that a choice can be made (at least theoretically) between the two systems on the basis of a comparative costs principle. This means, of course, that inter-regional imbalances are considered perfectly possible, and that international debts could be transformed into inter-regional debts by switching from a multi-currency to a single-currency world and vice versa.

However, as we have seen, on closer examination international and inter-regional debts appear to be very different, so much so that no relationship of any sort can be established between them. As is confirmed by factual observation the debt of a region is a linguistic, if not a poetic, licence which has no effective counterpart in the real world, whereas international debt is a sad reality which characterizes our international monetary system more and more. The distinction could not be greater, which means that we cannot take advantage of the analysis of inter-regional debt to reach a better understanding of international debt. Since true inter-regional debt cannot be accounted for, the analysis of what happens at the international level has to be started afresh. Yet, the lack of analogy between the two kinds of debts has some positive aspects for the economist inquiring into their nature. In particular, it puts the emphasis on the fact that the international debt problem arises from the specific kind of relationship between national currencies that characterizes the actual monetary system of international payments. It is the existence of a multi-currency world that creates the problem, and it is within this context that a solution has to be found.

Chapter Two

Specificity of the International Debt Problem

1. The two-sided nature of international debt

1.1. *A country's external debt is the sum of the debts of its residents*

This first proposition is almost self-evident, and perfectly in line with the analysis relative to the debt of each element of the set of residents. If residents of country *A* were to borrow more from residents of country *B* than residents of *B* borrow from them, it would be extremely easy to infer that the sum of residents of country *A* is a net borrower. Hence, if *A*'s residents borrowing implies their getting indebted, it immediately follows that the country is indebted as a result of the indebtedness of its residents. Of course, this does not mean that the debt of the country adds up to the debt of its residents. Let us take a very simple example to illustrate this last point. Suppose the country to be made up of only two elements *a* and *b*. Suppose further that *a* borrows from a non-resident, say *c*, and is therefore indebted towards his bank. The debt of *a* is obviously independent of *b*'s situation, which could be that of a perfect financial equilibrium. In this case, it could equally well be said that resident *a* has a debt towards non-resident *c* or that its country has a debt towards *c* (debt contracted by its element *a*), but it would clearly be wrong to claim that both *a and its country* are indebted. The debt of *a* cannot entail an additional debt of the country of which *a* is a resident.

Let us suppose the existence of a trade deficit of the residents of country *A*. We already know that the financing of this imbalance does not necessarily entail the debt of the residents. It is only if their net purchases are financed by an equivalent sale of bonds (and not of shares) that the trade deficit ends up with a financial debt. Now, the loan granted by the non-residents does not have the double effect of making both the residents and their country indebted. What the residents owe the non-residents is not also owed by the country itself, whose borrowing is in no way distinguishable from that of its residents. Once we have taken into account the net debts of all residents, we have a complete picture of the debt situation of the country itself. This is so obvious that there is hardly any need to insist upon it. If we do insist, then, it is not because the conclusion is not so obvious as may first appear, but because the actual system of international payments does not respect it. More precisely, it is possible to show that the debt of the country is added to the debt of its residents, and that it is this double effect which characterizes the international debt problem.

1.2. *The distinction between a nation and the sum of its residents*

If it is true that the sum of residents has no proper existence relative to the residents themselves, it is not also true that a nation can be reduced to the sum of its residents. In other words, the nation has a kind of autonomous existence, not only from a political or a sociological point of view, but also from an economic standpoint. Why is this so? How can a country be considered as an economic agent distinct from all the economic agents defined as its residents?

The state itself being a resident, the question seems almost paradoxical. Yet, it is certain that nations exist as economic agents if only because their debts are an evident reality of the international monetary system. The question is, therefore, whether these debts are the mere double of the residents' financial deficit or an additional claim on the countries themselves. Apparently, the answer is straightforward. Is it not evident, in fact, that, were we to cancel out all the net external debts of residents of country *A*, it would no longer be possible to speak of *A*'s international debt? And is this not proof that the debt of the nation is only the duplicate of the debt of its residents? However, a cross-examination is needed, since factual observation shows that indebted countries are very rarely successful in paying off their international debt. Indeed, the external debt of the major indebted countries is getting greater and greater, which could well be a symptom of the effective existence of a debt peculiar to the nations, and which adds up to the debt of their residents.

Let us start the analysis by considering the debt contracted by a given economic agent of country *A* in order to finance his net external purchases of goods and services. To pay off his debt, the resident of *A* has simply to find the necessary amount of money income. Supposing he is able to save the amount required, he will then ask his bank to credit his economic correspondent, and, by doing this, he will recover the financial bonds he had previously sold and cancel out his debtor position. But the analysis of the operation is not finished yet. We still have to consider what happens to the national currency spent by the resident of *A* in order to honour his debt. The bank of the economic correspondent of our resident (let us call the two agents *c* and *a* respectively) will now own a deposit labelled in the national currency of country *A*. And, since every national currency defines the spontaneous debt incurred by the banking system which issues it,[1] it immediately follows that country *A* is itself indebted towards *c*'s bank by the exact amount of *a*'s payment. The result of the payment made by *a* is, thus, asymmetrical: on one side *a* has effectively cancelled out his debt to *c* while, on the other side, country *A* finds itself indebted because of this very payment.

Between different regions of the same country, transactions are settled by means of a common currency that does not define the debt of any of them. The pounds issued in Cornwall and deposited in the London banking system are no more the evidence of the debt of Cornwall towards the London area than the pounds issued in London and deposited in Cornwall define the debt of London towards Cornwall. Between different countries, on the contrary, payments imply the transfer of national currencies which, outside national boundaries, define the debt of the country through whose banking system they were issued. Hence, the pounds issued in London and earned by the United States define an equivalent debt of Great Britain in the same way as the dollars owned by British banks define a debt of the USA. It thus follows that, whereas the inter-regional payment of the debt incurred by a resident has no consequences for the financial situation of the regions themselves, the payment of an international debt by a resident ends up with the indebtedness of his own country.

The fact is that, because of the international use of national currencies, international debts have to be paid twice, a first time by the residents who have initially contracted them, and a second time by their countries. According to logic, international debts should be paid only once, as are inter-regional debts. If facts do not conform to logic, this means that there is something wrong in the actual international system of monetary payments. Yet, on first approach, things do not seem to be so dramatic. Indeed, is it not true that most countries are effectively not allowed to pay their external debt in their national currency? In this case, how could they get indebted following the payment of their residents? The situation would therefore be critical only for those few countries whose national currency is accepted world-wide as a means of international payments. But, even then there would be no reason to worry too much, since these countries would never be asked to honour their debt (their currency being necessary to the rest of the world for the settlement of international transactions), and, if they were, they would do so simply by sending abroad another, equivalent, amount of their own money (which, being accepted as an international standard, is the best monetary form of payment available in the system).

A first criticism of this kind of argument is that it supposes that things can be put right not by modifying the system in order to make it conform to logic, but by generalizing a practice founded on the illogical use of national currencies. A second criticism is that, even if few national currencies are used as international money, countries whose money is not internationally accepted cannot avoid getting indebted when their residents pay off their debts. Let us consider again the case of resident *a* paying non-resident *c*. Whether or not the national currency of country *A* is accepted by country *C*, it is certain that for *a* to be able to pay his debt it is enough to get hold of the required sum of money income. Having found this sum, *a* can ask his bank to credit *c*, an operation which the bank can either carry out in terms of the money of country *A* or in terms of any other national currency. If *c*'s bank is credited in money *A*, country *A* will find itself indebted towards country *C*, whereas if the payment is made in another currency, say the US dollar, *a*'s bank has to find the necessary amount of dollars on the financial market. Now, things change according to whether or not *A*'s banking system already disposes of this sum. If no dollars are available within the country's banking system, then *A* has to acquire them through foreign lending, which obviously entails the increase of *A*'s external debt. If, on the contrary, dollars have already been earned through net commercial exports, external debt servicing can take place without incurring another debt with the rest of the world. Yet, *A*'s banks do not offer their dollar deposits gratuitously which, in fact, have to be bought on the exchange market by the bank of the indebted resident. The compulsory purchase of dollars by country *A* defines a net demand for dollars in terms of money *A* which, according to the law of supply and demand, provokes an increase in the relative price of the dollar. In other words, when the banking system of a country whose national currency is considered too 'weak' to be internationally accepted has to buy dollars in order to service the country's external debt, its money suffers from a devaluating pressure relative to the dollar. As we shall see in the following chapters, and particularly in the second part of the book, the net demand for dollars entails a loss of the indebted country's external gain, so that it can positively service its foreign creditors only by getting into a new, equivalent debt. Thus, in both cases *a*'s payment has a negative effect for his country which cannot carry out its external debt payments without getting newly indebted. This argument being central to our analysis, we shall develop it at length, starting from Keynes's analytical treatment of the problem of external debt payment.

2. The international debt problem as analysed by Keynes, Ohlin and Rueff in their debate about the budgetary and transfer problems

The controversy originating with the German transfer problem is still of great theoretical interest not only because the arguments debated by Keynes, Ohlin and Rueff are as relevant as ever, but also because their analysis is of great importance for the understanding of the difficulties related to external debt servicing. As testified by the contributions offered by several well-known economists such as Pigou (1932), Viner (1937), Johnson (1956), Machlup (1964b) and Samuelson (1952, 1954, 1971), the debate about the possible consequences of transfer payments over the terms of trade occupies a relevant place in the history of economic thought, and remains an essential step in the search for a satisfactory solution to the debt problem (Reisen and van Trotsenburg 1988). Hence, if we re-examine some aspects of that controversy here it is not to look at it from an historical point of view, but to try to put forward the analytical elements which can help us in this search.

2.1. *Budgetary and transfer problems*

In a famous paper published in the March issue of the *Economic Journal*, Keynes (1929a) analysed the debt problem faced by Germany after World War I by focusing on its twofold aspect. To be able to pay its debt, he argued, Germany had to find the necessary amount of both internal saving and international currency. The so-called budgetary problem was therefore that of 'extracting the necessary sums of money out of the pockets of the German people' (Keynes 1929a: 1), while the transfer problem was that of 'converting the German money so received into foreign currency' (p. 1). Several economists, and among them Ohlin and Rueff, did not consider the transfer problem of great importance, and it was against their views that Keynes developed his arguments. According to him, the increase in German exports necessary to provide Germany with the required amount of foreign currency could not simply follow from a 'relative increase in German industrial efficiency' (Keynes 1929b: 179), and from 'the reduction in consumption directly caused by reparation taxes' (p. 179). On the contrary, as clearly follows from the next quotation, the solution of the transfer problem is not implied in the solution of the budgetary problem and requires a particular set of measures which do not ensue from the payment of reparation taxes.

The expenditure of the German people must be reduced, *not only* by the amount of the reparation-taxes which they must pay out of their earnings, but also by a reduction in their gold-rate of earnings below what they would otherwise be. That is to say, there are two problems, and not — as those maintain who belittle the difficulties of transfer — one problem. Indeed, a short way of putting the case is this. The *Transfer* Problem consists in reducing the gold-rate of efficiency-earnings of the German factors of production sufficiently to enable them to increase their export to an adequate aggregate total; the *Budgetary* Problem consists in extracting out of these reduced money-earnings a sufficient amount of reparation-taxes.

(Keynes 1929a: 4)

Apart from the paradoxical significance of the measure proposed by Keynes, it is important to analyse the theoretical aspects of the controversy between the English economist and his critics. By stressing the importance of distinguishing the transfer from the budgetary problem, he recognized the double nature of the international debt problem in a way which seems to have been totally missed by his opponents. In fact, that distinction finds its *raison d'être* in the impossibility of identifying international and inter-regional debt problems. To pay its debt it was not enough for Germany to find a given amount of its national income through the payment of reparation-taxes by its residents. International debts have to be paid in the currency used as international standard, and when a country has not the privilege of issuing it, it must find a way of converting its money into foreign currency. This was precisely the case of Germany after World War I, and Keynes was perfectly aware that the payment of the residents had to be followed by the payment of the country itself.

Now, Ohlin and Rueff did not share Keynes's point of view though they agreed with him about the necessity of increasing Germany's exports in order to allow for the effective payment of its external debt. Both authors, in fact, shared the belief that Germany was not really faced with a transfer problem.

Let us consider Ohlin's standpoint first. His argument against the importance of the transfer problem is centred around the idea that, given the high level of German borrowing, a reduction in this level would have brought about a reduction in imports and an increase in the marketing of export goods. Ohlin, in fact, was convinced that German borrowing could only end up with an equivalent increase in the imports of Germany and, reciprocally, in the exports of the rest of the world. In order to increase German exports it was therefore necessary to reduce its imports, which required a drastic reduction in its external borrowing. Against this line of argument, Keynes maintained that, if Germany borrowed less it would simply have paid less in reparations, and 'if Reparation payments are diminished to the same extent that foreign borrowing is diminished, the world is exactly as it was before' (Keynes 1929b: 180). Ohlin reasoned that as the amount of borrowing was fixed, so a decrease in German borrowing would necessarily have led to an equivalent increase in the borrowing of some other country. Keynes refuted this implicit assumption, and claimed that other changes were needed in order to increase German exports, namely 'a reduction in the rates of gold-wages of German factors of production relative to rates elsewhere' (p.179).

So far the analysis does not show a radical disagreement between Ohlin and Keynes. They both wanted Germany to export more, and their divergence seems to be limited to the choice of measures which could have brought about this result. And in this respect even Rueff's contribution to the debate was not in opposition to that of his colleagues. Putting the emphasis on the hypothetical working of a classical equilibrating mechanism, Rueff claimed that an alteration in the level of exports could have been caused 'arbitrarily' and 'deliberately' by a sudden change in the financial movements of the country. To support his thesis, Rueff put forth the case of France in the early twenties, when its commercial balance was greatly modified by a sudden drop in the financial credits previously granted by Great Britain and the United States (the commercial deficit of France fell from 23 milliard francs to 2.5 milliard). This same balance passed then from a deficit of 2.5 milliard francs to a surplus of 1.5 milliard francs as soon as France witnessed 'the beginning of the great period of the exportation of capital' (Rueff 1929: 393). From this and from other, similar, empirical observations Rueff inferred that the change in the commercial balance was always brought about by a change in the balance of capital. He thus concluded that every modification (whether arbitrary or not) of the balance of capital would necessarily provoke an opposite equilibrating variation of the commercial balance. Equilibrium would, therefore, be granted by a mechanism where the balance of trade adjusted itself to changes in the financial balance.

Following Ohlin and Rueff, then, a case could be made for the necessity of linking the payment of the debt to capital movements. In order to decide whether to endorse their views or not we must therefore establish whether or not capital movements bring about changes in the trade balance of the capital exporting country. In other words, we should answer the following question. Is there a transfer of buying power between countries and, if there is, does it have any repercussions on their trade movements?

2.2. *Transfers of buying power*

One argument in Keynes's rejoinder to Ohlin's comment on the reparation problem is of particular interest. Let us suppose that Germany succeeded in paying a great amount of its reparation by increasing its domestic savings and by sending abroad part of its purchasing power. Would this have caused an increase in the 'buying power' detained by other countries and, therefore, a whole series of adjustments which would have finally profited Germany? Keynes answer is straightforward: 'The increased "buying power", due to the fact of Germany paying something with less assistance than before from borrowing, will have been *already* used up in buying the exports, the sale of which has made the Reparation payments possible' (Keynes 1929b: 181). According to Keynes, the income earned by the Allies through the German payments of war reparations was thus the very income which the Allies had spent for the purchase of Germany export surplus. In this example, the transfer of buying power from the importing to the exporting country would have been totally absorbed by the debt payment, and could have had no repercussions on the future commercial sales of either country.

As clearly appears, the divergences between Keynes's line of thought and the analysis followed by Ohlin and Rueff were not a matter of detail. On one side Keynes claimed that in order to service its foreign debt Germany had first to increase its exports, on the other Ohlin and Rueff maintained that it had first to increase its financial flows. In fact, they argued, the outflow of German capital would necessarily have increased its exports of domestic goods by increasing the foreign demand for these goods. The key of their argument is the assumption that through monetary movements, such as the German payment of war reparations, buying power could be shifted from one country to another, thus affecting the distribution of the demand for international goods. As Ohlin put it: 'A and B are two countries with normal employment for their factors of production. A borrows a large sum of money from B this year and the same sum during each of the following years. This transfer of buying power directly increases A's demand for foreign goods while it reduces B's. Thus, A's imports grow and its exports fall off' (Ohlin 1929a: 174). Whether this transfer of buying power was to be brought about by a reduction of German external borrowings or through an increase in the reparation payments is obviously not essential to Ohlin's argument. In both situations the financial outflows would have been positive and would have not only decreased 'the buying power in Germany and thus its importation of foreign goods' (p.173) but also increased 'the buying power in the lending countries and, thus, their importation of German goods' (p.173).

Ohlin reasoned here that the international capital movements between Germany and the rest of the world were analogous to the capital movements occurring within a single currency area. As long as he was assuming that international financial flows took place in the form of gold, the analogy would have held good. 'The only essential difference between this case [A and B being separate countries with different currency systems] and the last case [of capital movements between two districts with the same currency system] is that no transfer of monetary buying power in a literal sense can take place, except in the form of gold' (Ohlin 1929b: 401). Yet a problem arose when he shifted his analysis from gold to foreign bills expressed in terms of a key currency. Claiming that, through the transfer of foreign bills, credit expanded in *A* (the debt receiving country) and was restricted in *B* (the country servicing the debt), Ohlin was postulating both that Germany would have been able to obtain foreign bills without first increasing its exports of real goods, and that bills could have replaced gold as a vehicle for international transactions. But how would it have been possible for Germany to earn foreign bills if not by selling abroad a greater amount of its domestic output? Certainly not by exporting gold, otherwise it would have been able to pay its creditors directly in gold. Buying it in its own national currency then? Again no, since Germany was precisely in a situation where its currency was not accepted by foreign central banks, and, had it been accepted, Germany would have used it directly to service its debt. Likewise, it could not have borrowed it, for, by doing so, it would have increased its debt in order to decrease it. Were there other possibilities for Germany to get hold of the amount of foreign bills or foreign currency necessary to the payment of its creditors?

In his reply to Ohlin's comment, Keynes denied any such occurrence, maintaining that Germany could find the necessary financial resources only through a net surplus of its balance of commercial trade:

> Of course if *B* (Germany) can pay *A* (the reparation-receiving countries) in foreign bills expressed in the currency of a third country, there is no difficulty. But this is begging the whole question. The problem arises precisely because, on our hypothesis, Germany has no such foreign bills. Germany can only acquire such bills if she has already sold the necessary exports; so that these bills cannot be part of the mechanisms which is to establish the situation which will permit her to sell the exports
>
> (Keynes 1929c: 407-8)

Both Keynes's and Ohlin's positions are clearly argued, and the crucial role in their debate appears to be played by the concept of purchasing power transfer. If we were to accept that buying power can be transferred from one country to another, then it would become possible to maintain, as Ohlin, that financial flows are the prime mover of the whole process of re-equilibrium between an indebted country and its foreign creditors. On the contrary, if purchasing power cannot be exported, it is Keynes's line of argument which applies, and commercial exports have to be seen as the necessary (but not sufficient) condition for the positive servicing of external debt.

Let us momentarily put aside the case of international transactions being financed through the transfer of gold. The point which has to be settled is whether or not international monetary transactions can convey positive flows of purchasing power. Now, the choice appears to be restricted to only two logical alternatives. Either it can be established that, outside its original banking system, every national currency defines a positive buying power, or it has to be concluded that no purchasing power can be exported through the outflow of national money. If domestic currencies had the faculty to transfer purchasing power abroad, then Ohlin's thesis could be made even more rigorous, since it could easily be argued that, for Germany to pay its war reparations, it would have been enough to send abroad an equivalent amount of its domestic currency. Yet, Ohlin himself was well aware of the impossibility of such a solution. All his arguments were based on some real flows of gold, and even the transfer of foreign bills was supposed to be working through their sales and purchases in terms of gold. Neither Keynes nor Ohlin, then, were prepared to argue for a transfer of purchasing power brought about by flows of national currencies. They both agreed, on the contrary, that international payments had to be made in kind, for they both maintained that, in order to pay its debt, Germany had to export more in terms of domestic output.

The problem of money's purchasing power is of a great importance, in national as well as international money, and we shall resume it in a later part of this work. For the time being, let us simply stress the fact that neither of our authors believed in the possibility of exporting national purchasing power, if not in the form of gold (which, in fact, is a real good so that payments in gold can indeed be equated to payments in kind). Of the two authors, Keynes was certainly the one who developed the more rigorous and updated analysis. His claim that, in order to pay reparations, Germany had first to earn a positive amount of foreign currency was perfectly in line with both empirical evidence and theoretical inquiry. German currency was not accepted as an international standard, and it would have been wrong, factually and theoretically, to claim that, being a *national* vehicle of purchasing power, it should indeed have been considered a good means of external payments. 'If Germany was in a position to export large quantities of gold or if foreign balances in Germany were acceptable to foreign Central Banks as a substitute for gold in their reserves, then it would be a different matter' (Keynes 1929c: 407).

In reality, national currencies do not carry any purchasing power outside their monetary systems, so that international payments become effective only if they are carried out in kind. Currencies are simply an intermediary. Hence, monetary flows should never be an end in themselves. This is however not what happens in our international monetary system, where currencies are bought and sold as if they were real goods. We are thus confronted with a system characterized both by the use of a few national currencies as international standards, and by the existence of an exchange market where currencies are traded. Keynes's analysis is based on this double characteristic. Having clearly understood that international transactions cannot be reduced to inter-regional flows, he coherently maintained that commercial exports are the prerequisite for the payment of external debts. But this is only half the story. Following the arguments he developed in his second rejoinder to Ohlin's comment on his first paper, the analysis can indeed be pushed further. Not only is it wrong to claim that, in the case of debt payments, capital movements can have repercussions on the trade balance, but it is also possible to show that the payment of international debts poses a particular problem of which neither Ohlin nor Rueff were fully aware.

2.3. *The self-defeating process of debt payment*

As we have seen, Keynes rightly observed that a necessary condition for Germany to be able to pay its war reparations was the earning of foreign currency.[2] Although Ohlin and Rueff did not fully agree with Keynes on this point, they would have certainly acknowledged that, in order to earn foreign monetary assets, Germany had to export part of its domestic output. Yet, only Keynes realized that the need to pay the debt in a foreign currency could not be satisfied even by the earning of the necessary sum through a net commercial surplus.

The passage from inter-regional to international transactions is marked by the transition from a one-currency reality to a multi-currency world in which not every national money can play the same role. In particular, a country like Germany after World War I could not claim for its currency the status of a world monetary standard. Accordingly, Germany had to pay its foreign creditors in their own money, which it would not have been able to do had it not increased its external sales of domestic goods. An inflow of foreign currency, however, was not sufficient to guarantee the payment of a country's external debt. As Keynes had clearly pointed out, this payment had first to be made by German debtors in their own national currency. This is, in fact, the meaning of the budgetary constraint: through taxation the German government had to collect the national income necessary to the financing of its external debt. 'The *Budgetary* Problem of extracting the necessary sums of money out of the pockets of the German people and paying them to the account of the Agent-General' (Keynes 1929a: 1). The very existence of the budgetary problem and its general acceptance show that the foreign currency earned through commercial exports *has still to be bought by domestic debtors*. Whether this purchase is made by private economic agents or by the government does not make any substantial difference. In both cases a sum of domestic income is spent on the purchase of the foreign currency which flows into the country. The foreign monetary asset is thus identified with a real asset, and not with a pure means of circulation (like Smith's famous 'wheel of circulation') which, as such, would neither be sold nor bought by national currencies. But, if money is taken to be similar to a real asset, then its 'price' will be submitted to the same laws governing the prices of goods. In our example, the foreign currencies will be submitted to an excess demand exercised by the German government, excess demand which will provoke an increase in their price relative to the German currency. In other words, the payment of war reparations or, more generally, of any kind of external debts by a country whose money is not accepted as a world standard entails, necessarily, a depreciating pressure on the country's national currency relative to the money used as an international means of payment, a downward pressure which has the effect of nullifying the external gain realized by the country through its net commercial exports and which can be 'neutralized' only through a new external loan which leaves the country as much indebted as before the payment of its foreign creditors.[3]

The conclusion we have just reached can easily be derived from a thorough analysis of Keynes's theoretical treatment of the German reparations problem. As we have already pointed out, his distinction between the problem of drawing 'the necessary sums of money out of the pockets of the German people' (Keynes 1929a: 1) — known as the 'budgetary problem' — and that 'of converting the German money so received into foreign currency' (p.1) — the so- called 'transfer problem' — does not leave any doubt about the dichotomous nature of external debt servicing. And that the necessary purchase of foreign currency has a depreciating effect on the value of the debt servicing country results unequivocably from the following quotation:

> For I hold that the process of paying the debt has the effect of causing the money in which the debt is expressed to be worth a larger quantity of German-produced goods than it was before or would have been apart from the payment of the debt; so that the population of the debtor State suffers a loss of purchasing power greater than the original equivalent of the amount of the debt.
>
> (Keynes 1929c: 405)

The devaluation of the German domestic money pointed out by Keynes is the first clear symptom of the asymmetry characterizing the external debt servicing in a system centred around the use of a key currency as international means of payment. As we shall repeatedly claim, analysis shows that the strain on the indebted country's domestic currency is neutralized only through a net new borrowing, which becomes the necessary condition for the country's positive servicing of its foreign debt. In the light of this analysis, we can therefore maintain that German economic agents were not only losing a part of their income equivalent to the amount of the external debt servicing, but twice as much, since their country had to contract a new debt in the exact proportion of its external debt payment. This is the dramatic effect of what Keynes called the transfer problem. On one hand, German debtors had to find a sum of national income out of their savings (a sum that was collected by the state through taxation), and, on the other hand, they were suffering an additional loss of purchasing power due to the asymmetrical pressure exerted on their national currency.

Now, if by servicing its debt Germany was necessarily submitting its national money to an asymmetrical pressure, it appears that the payment of its foreign creditors had, in fact, a self-contradictory effect. Indeed, the decrease of Germany's external debt was totally absorbed by the loss suffered on the exchange market. Hence, the international gain obtained by Germany through its trade surplus was compensated by this loss, and the country could service its external debt only by getting into a new debt.

The presence of the transfer problem is a clear symptom of the difficulties characterizing the international system of payments. As long as we refer to a single currency area, the problem does not arise. The settlement of inter-regional debts takes place without there being any need to convert the domestic money into any foreign currency. Capital can be easily transferred from one region to another since it is immediately made homogeneous by being expressed in one and the same monetary standard. Yet, as soon as more than one country is concerned, it is no longer possible to speak of a monetarily homogeneous world. Rates of exchange are established between the different currencies, and one (or a few) of them is (are) chosen as international standard. When it is carried out by a country whose money is not accepted as international currency, external debt servicing cannot be confined to the payment made by the debtors in their national money. A further step is needed, namely the purchase of the foreign currency to be sent to the external creditors. The settlement of international debts requires, therefore, a double payment, the first being the expenditure made by the indebted agents (budgetary problem) and the second the purchase of foreign currency made by the central bank (transfer problem). But, then, the second payment is the source of a net excess demand of foreign currency which has the annoying consequence of nullifying an equivalent part of the gain realized by the country through its commercial surplus.

In his analysis of the German transfer problem, Keynes pointed his finger at a serious anomaly of the international system of monetary payments. The passage from a single currency to a multi-currency world is not as smooth as some economists would like it to be, and Keynes was the first theorist to point this out clearly and rigorously. The problems faced by Germany after World War I are substantially the same as those which nowadays hamper the development of most indebted countries. The rules of the dollar-exchange standard are such that external debt servicing is made logically impossible; a matter of fact which does not fail to have serious consequences for both the debtor and the creditor countries.

3. The payment of external debt in the dollar-exchange standard as a cause of major disturbances between nations

Despite the rigour of the analysis first propounded by Keynes in his contribution to the debate about the transfer problem, the reader could still be reluctant to accept it entirely. It is true, he could argue, that the purchase of dollars puts a downward pressure on the price of the domestic currency, but it is also true that, at the moment these same dollars were earned, an equivalent yet opposed pressure was exerted on the currency of the indebted country so that, on the whole, the two asymmetries compensate and no unilateral devaluation can finally be verified. To answer this objection we have to inquiry into what effectively happens in the banking system of the country credited in dollars.

Let us call *A* the country earning dollars. *A* can either be the indebted country when it earns the dollars that it will later send to foreign creditors, or the creditor country when it gets paid by its debtors. The payment of *A* is made by *B* via a bank, and is recorded as an increase in the assets held by *A*'s banking system in the form of a claim over the deposits in dollars of bank *B* (whether the dollars are entered in the accounts of the Central Bank or of a commercial bank the following argument remains substantially unchanged, as the reader can easily verify by disaggregating the banking system into its two fundamental components) (See Table 2.1).

Now, the payment made by bank *B* does not have bank *A* as its final beneficiary. On the contrary, the national banking system acts here as a simple intermediary, and must transfer the payment to the residents to whom it is actually addressed. Bank *A*, however, does not send dollars to its client, but an equivalent amount of domestic currency. Thus, the

Table 2.1

Bank *A*	
Liabilities	Assets
	Bank *B* $x

crucial point is to determine from where bank *A* gets this sum of money *a*. And, since both theory and empirical evidence lead to the same result, no doubt can be allowed in this matter. In fact, bank *A* gives its client an amount of domestic money which it *creates* on the basis of the claim over the deposit in dollars recorded on the asset side of its balance sheet. As is confirmed by Rueff, the foreign claims earned through the export of real goods and services give rise to an equivalent emission of national currency carried out by the banking system of the receiving country. 'The claims transferred for the settlement of the deficit are bought against the creation of money, by the banking system of the creditor country' (Rueff 1963: 323).

When dollars enter the country (under the form of claims on American deposits), an equivalent sum of domestic currency is created to the benefit of the residents effectively paid by the rest of the world. In our example, dollars are changed into money *a*, but money *a* is created in this same operation. According to economic theory, this means that the supply of currency *a* is infinitely elastic, and, therefore, that the relative exchange between dollars and *A*'s domestic currency will not modify their relative price (exchange rate). If money *a* were not created in the operation, then its price would rise in terms of the American currency, and this upward movement would counterbalance the following fall caused by the forced purchase of dollars. Yet, things work quite differently. The price of currency *a* does not rise when it is created against dollars, whereas the price of dollars rises when they are unilaterally demanded by money *a*. The excess demand for dollars is not matched by an equivalent excess demand for currency *a*, and this can only lead to a devaluating pressure on *a* relative to the dollar.

But the disequilibrating working of the actual system of international payments does not prove unfavourable only to the debt servicing countries. In fact, creation of domestic currency against dollars will take place in the creditor country every time that it is paid for its foreign sales. Apart from the USA, where the inflow of dollars has an inflationary effect since it implies the 'internalization' of the duplicate previously sent abroad (see pages 50-51 and 60-61 of this book), the countries which benefit from an external payment carried out in dollars verify an equivalent, nominal, emission of their national currencies. And, since this creation is not linked to an increase in current output, it necessarily defines the beginning of an inflationary process which will negatively affect the entire system.

What makes the situation worse is that the inflation caused by the creation of domestic currency is not compensated by an equivalent destruction which would occur at the moment dollars were to be spent abroad, for the purchase of foreign goods and services. Unless such expenditures were made by the same economic agent beneficiary of the domestic currency creation (and at the same instant of the creation), they would not fill the inflationary gap, which would therefore be cumulative in time. Let us illustrate our argument with reference to the book entries of the banking system of the creditor country *C*. The first entry defines the creation of domestic currency *c* against the claim in dollars entered on the asset side of the balance sheet (See Table 2.2).The second entry is the expenditure of an equivalent amount of national currency by, for example, the importing industries of country *C* to purchase foreign goods (See Table 2.3). If we put the two entries together, we can easily see that the second operation does not diminish the sum of domestic currency available in *C* (See Table 2.4). It is only if national creditors and importing industries are one and the same agent selling and buying the same (foreign) output that the two sides of the balance sheet will cancel out. In this case inflation would exert its negative effect only in the interval of time between the first two entries. In all other cases, however, inflation cannot be neutralized and will continue to upset the relationship between national money and domestic current output.

Table 2.2

Bank *C*

Liabilities	Assets
Exporting agents equivalent of $x in money *c*	Bank *A* $x

Finally, the payment of external debt is a source of devaluation for all the debtor countries whose currency is not given the status of international standard, whereas the use of a national money as international means of payment is a source of inflation for all exporting countries. Perfectly consistent with the analysis propounded by Keynes and with the lucid insights of Rueff, this conclusion has to be

Table 2.3

Bank *C*

Liabilities	Assets
Bank *A* $x	Importing agents equivalent of $x in money *c*

Table 2.4.

Bank *C*

Liabilities	Assets
Exporting agents equivalent of $x in money *c*	Bank *A* $x
Bank *A* $x	Importing agents equivalent of $x in money *c*
Exporting agents equivalent of $x in money *c*	Importing agents equivalent of $x in money *c*

tested against facts, and particularly against the various theoretical and empirical attempts worked out to solve the international monetary problems.

It is in order to test these attempts, therefore, that we shall investigate the possibility of avoiding the double payment of the external debt within the gold standard, the gold-exchange standard and the dollar-exchange standard respectively.

Chapter Three

The Gold Standard, the Gold-Exchange Standard and the Dollar-Exchange Standard Offer No Solution to the Problem of International Monetary Disorder

1. From the gold standard to the gold-exchange standard

1.1. *The theoretical advantages of the gold standard*

Ricardo was undeniably one of the greatest theorists of the gold standard. In a period when banknotes were already a reality of growing importance, he maintained that international transactions had to be carried out in gold to guarantee their effective payment.[1] Though at a national level gold could have been advantageously replaced by paper money, internationally, payments required the direct use of the precious metal. Even in the form advocated by Ricardo (the gold bullion standard), the system implied the automatic settlement in gold of every commercial deficit. And it is relative to the rigorous appliance of this particular measure that the gold standard system has to be assessed.

From a theoretical point of view, even a superficial analysis of the international economic reality reveals that it pertains to an economy of trade. No true international production ever existed, and it would be hopeless to look for an output which were not already accounted for by the production taking place in the different elements of the set of the world national economies. Now, the classical economists soon realized that the simplest way to allow for the settlement of international transactions was to transform every monetary payment in a payment in kind. This is, in fact, the fundamental role played by the system of the gold standard. Paying the deficit of its balance of trade, country *A* was indeed sending abroad a commodity, gold, and not a pure monetary item. Nobody would deny that gold is a real good even when it is used as international currency. The exchange between imported goods and gold pertains, therefore, to the category of exchanges in kind. Under the strict gold standard, the exporting country, *B*, would thus obtain a real asset in exchange for part of its exported domestic output.

In general, the Ricardian system was such that every country was bound to pay its imports of goods and services with the simultaneous and automatic sale of its own goods and services. Every commercial deficit being immediately covered by an equivalent flow of gold, the equilibrium was always automatically guaranteed in a perfectly symmetrical way. No asymmetrical purchase of currencies was needed, and the problems relating to the external debt payment were totally alien to the system.

The theoretical advantages of the gold standard scheme are clearly evident, particularly if we refer to the inextricable mess which seems to qualify the actual system of international payments. Yet, Ricardo's teaching, according to which international transactions have to be settled in real terms (as opposed to monetary terms), was only partially followed. Indeed, very few economists, among whom Rueff played a distinctive role, recognized the true importance of this principle, which was almost never fully applied in practice.

1.2. *The impossibility of reverting to gold*

The theoretical soundness of the Ricardian system notwithstanding, it is a fact that the gold standard was propounded by a country, Great Britain, whose currency was generally preferred to gold. Hence, English external transactions were mostly paid in pounds rather than in gold (for example, in 1911 the gold reserves of the Bank of England represented only 3 per cent of the annual amount of its international trade).

> It is because the Pound was considered by the rest of the world as an essential means of payment that it was sought after, and that it nourished a wide monetary market. In this sense, it is possible to say that, in that period, the system of the Gold Standard was a Sterling Standard System, since the two standards were in fact confounded.
>
> (Byé 1965: 567, our translation)

Another argument which has been put forth to explain why, during the ninenteenth century, the world monetary economy was based on a system, the gold standard, which did not need to be effectively implemented was worked out by Triffin. Following Taussig's line of thought, he maintained that even persistent current account deficits did not require the intervention of the corrective mechanism postulated by the Classics, since the deficits of the balance of trade were compensated by equivalent superavits of the balance of capitals. The capital movements were such that countries which were net importers of goods and services were net exporters of private capitals, and could, therefore, easily equilibrate their overall balance of payments.

> Large, persistent and often growing disequilibria showed no sign of, or need for, correction over several decades, or even over the whole century

separating the Napoleonic wars from the first world war. The net capital inflow into the United States, for instance, is estimated to have averaged $50 million a year or more throughout the period from 1850 to 1914, while the net outflow of capital from the United Kingdom rose from about $30 million a year in the first half of the century to approximately $250 million in the second half, and close to $900 million in the last years (1906-1913) before the first world war.

(Triffin 1961: 26-7)

Trade and capital movements did not always perfectly equilibrate, of course. But even when residual commercial deficits would have required the use of gold, the transfer of the key currency of the times was often preferred to that of the precious metal. Finally, as suggested by Triffin, another factor played an important role in the passive preservation of the gold standard, namely 'the fact that the emergence of *major* imbalance was *prevented ex ante* by the institutional monetary and banking framework of the times, rather than *corrected ex post* by large price and income adjustments' (Triffin 1961: 27).

Apart from the fact that the mechanism based on the gold standard was never fully applied, convertibility broke down after the World War I, and the uncertainty following this event gave rise to an animated debate about the future of the international monetary system.

The point at issue was whether to return to a pseudo-gold system, and if so, at what parity for the pound. In Great Britain both the British Treasury and the Bank of England were in favour of a return to the gold standard, as was the Cunliffe Committee, which was set up to assess the virtues and defects of the equilibrating mechanism propounded by the Classics. Against this point of view Keynes, in his *Tract on Monetary Reform* (1923), claimed that the stability of prices and the stability of exchange were two requirements which were often opposed, and also that, giving priority to the maintenance of the external value of the pound (as implied by convertibility) would have forced Great Britain to sacrifice the level of employment and the standard of living of its residents.

Exchange rates and prices are the two key variables, and *a priori* they can both fluctuate. Under the gold standard, however, only one kind of fluctuation occurs. If the classical system is generally adopted, exchange rates are stable, and variations can only take place in domestic prices.

In pre-war days, when almost the whole world was on a gold standard, we had all plumped for stability of exchange as against stability of prices, and we were ready to submit to the social consequences of a change of price level for causes quite ouside our control, connected, for example, with the discovery of new gold mines in foreign countries or a change of banking policy abroad.

(Keynes 1972: 170-1)

Now, according to Keynes, the instability of internal prices would not have been the only disadvantage of the return to convertibility. Unemployment and a decrease of real income would have been the unavoidable consequence of the restoration of the gold standard. In a critical comment to Churchill's decision to resume the gold parity system, Keynes wrote:

> Money wages, the cost of living, and the prices which we are asking for our exports have not adjusted themselves to the improvements in the exchange, which the expectation of your restoring the gold standard, in accordance with your repeated declarations, has already brought about. They are about 10 per cent too high. If, therefore, you fix the exchange at this gold parity, you must either gamble on a rise in gold prices abroad, which will induce foreigners to pay a higher gold price for our exports, or you are committing yourself to a policy of forcing down money wages and the cost of living to the necessary extent.
>
> (Keynes 1972: 214)

Despite Keynes's intervention, Britain and most European nations went on to restore the pre-war system, which in fact did not resemble the theoretical scheme advocated by Ricardo any more than its predecessor. The Great Depression of the thirties effectively sanctioned the end of a system which never really worked in accordance with the Ricardian laws. 'One country after another left the gold standard during the deepening depression of the 1930s. By 1936, France and a few other countries constituting the gold bloc were forced to abandon gold. The international financial system collapsed. Countries resorted to direct controls over the use of foreign exchange, to trade restrictions, and to multiple exchange rates' (Meier 1982: 28).

After a period of great instability and competitive depreciations, let alone the tragic experience of World War II, 44 member countries of the United Nations met at Bretton Woods to work out a new system of international payments, which resulted in the establishment of the International Monetary Fund, and in the adoption of the gold-exchange standard.

1.3. *The gold-exchange standard: a political solution that has proved fallacious*

The nations that met at Bretton Woods were looking for a system which would have allowed them to pursue their domestic policies without suffering from external shocks due to international monetary problems. Their decision to shift from the gold standard to the gold-exchange standard was perfectly in line with the development of the way transactions were practically carried out, and with the increasing economic and political weight of the United States. As we have seen, the pound was already playing a role of key currency long before the end of the gold standard. The Bretton Woods Conference mainly sanctioned this state of affairs, and officially granted the same status of key currency to the United States dollar. The currencies of the two most developed countries were, therefore, to be used as world reserves and as an international means of payment. Theoretically, the key currencies were convertible with gold. In practice, they never were converted since they were considered as good as gold itself. Now, even if they had been converted for the settlement of trade imbalances, the system based on their general use would have been totally different from the one proposed by Ricardo, and would have posed the same problems which characterized the gold-exchange standard as it was effectively applied.

Let us analyse the difficulties of the working of the exchange standard in the following chapter, and concentrate here on the attempt to prove that the gold payment of trade deficits (or, more generally, of external debts) can only work under very strict conditions, which are not fulfilled under the traditional gold-exchange standard.

Ricardo's principle is clear. Debt payments must automatically take place in gold if we want to grant the payment in kind of every international transaction. Now, if the currency of a given country were given the particular status of key currency, would it still be possible to implement this kind of automatic mechanism? Let us take the example of the dollar. As key currency, the dollar would be, and actually is, used by the United States to monetize all its external transactions, and would have to be converted into gold only in order to allow for the settlement of the American trade deficit. Yet, precisely because it is made to play the role of key currency, the dollar would also be used by other countries in their external transactions. Thus, the country whose balance of trade is positive relative to the USA will not require the gold payment of its surplus but, instead, use the dollars to pay for its imports from other countries. Hence, the countries finally holding the amount of dollars defining the US trade deficit would not be the same as those which realized a trade surplus in their commercial transactions with the American nation. According to our assumptions, the conversion of these dollars into gold would still be possible, of course, but what would be its meaning?

The respect of the principle advocated by Ricardo requires the immediate payment in gold of every trade deficit. It is only if the conversion of the key currency into gold takes place automatically as soon as the deficit is ascertained that international transactions can be transformed into payments in kind. In the system following the rules of the gold-exchange standard, neither the automaticity nor the simultaneity are guaranteed. The dollars are used as if they were gold, so that they never need to be truly converted. Under the Bretton Woods system it was generally accepted that the dollar came to fulfil the function of world money more efficiently than gold, and its convertibility was not only theoretically limited (to maintain the international value of the dollar it was made inconvertible with gold through transactions with official foreign authorities; dollars held by monetary authorities of countries member of the IMF were convertible into gold), but practically useless. Now, in this system the dollar is considered as a real asset, and not as a pure intermediary allowing for the settlement *in kind* of all international transactions.

Apparently reflecting the strength of the US internal economy, the American currency was so praised that it soon became the primary world reserve asset. Yet, like every other domestic currency, outside its national boundaries the dollar cannot be identified with a real good. For a country it is not the same thing to be paid in dollars as in gold since dollars are a mere IOU issued by the American banking system whereas gold is a true real asset. The classical economists were perfectly aware of this fundamental distinction, and this explains why Ricardo so firmly propounded his principle of the real payment of every transaction taking place between nations. The international use of bank money is not fundamentally opposed to the Ricardian principle. However, the rules of monetary payments must be compatible with the requirements of final, real exchanges. One solution is that proposed by the strict gold standard, where commercial imbalances are settled by the automatic conversion of the key currency into gold. If the dollar were used as international currency under the condition of its immediate and automatic conversion into gold whenever the balance of trade required it, then there would be no theoretical reasons to oppose the gold-exchange standard. The rigidity of a system like that, however, would make it neither particularly interesting nor very efficient. A better solution would be to find a system which, though entirely based on the use of bank money, would make real payments possible without there being any need to resort to convertibility. The central feature of this solution would be the perfect circularity of the world currency which, being confined to the role of pure intermediary, would never be detained in any official or unofficial reserve.

The system elaborated at the Bretton Woods Conference certainly did not conform to this functional definition of international money. As key currency, the dollar was supposed to share the same value of the gold to which it was said to be legally associated. The fact that the dollar was issued by the American banking system almost without cost was apparently not considered of great importance, except by few sceptical economists,[2] and the American money was thought to be as good internationally as it was within its national boundaries. But, if it is certain that inside America the dollar acquires the value of the current output that it carries, is it likewise safe to maintain that outside the national borders the dollar still holds a positive value? If we look at the very nature of bank money it becomes difficult to answer this question affirmatively. Every currency is issued as a spontaneous acknowledgment of debt[3] of the banking system, and there is no reason to believe that this definition changes when the currency leaves its original country. Now, as long as a currency is kept within the banking system that issued it, there are no major difficulties in explaining that it maintains a positive value over the nationally produced goods and services. Yet, when the currency is sent abroad things change radically. No international output is available, in fact, to account for an original value of the international money. And when it is further considered that the monetary payments from country *A* to country *B* do not decrease the deposits of money *a* available within *A* (the ownership of part of the deposits changes, this is certainly true, but not the place where the deposits are held, which necessarily remains the bank of emission), it becomes clear that current national output cannot account for both the internal and the external value of the currency chosen as world money. The money deposited within the national monetary system of *A* has the value of the domestic output, the money 'held' by the rest of the world as the counterpart of its net exports has none; it is an acknowledgment of debt issued by *A*'s banking system in favour of *B* and, as everybody knows, an acknowledgment of debt is a simple promise to pay at term. Hence, by giving to its creditor its own money, country *A* is not paying its net commercial imports, and it is only because it erroneously identifies currency *a* with a real asset that *B* accepts an IOU as final payment of its domestic goods.

The gold-exchange standard was not revolutionary enough to solve the international monetary problems according to the true nature of bank money, and it was too modern to apply the strict rules of the Ricardian system. This ambiguity was to cause its final abandonment in August 1971. Under the period of its enforcement, the Bretton Woods system created, in fact, a whole series of difficulties to the member countries of the IMF. The dollar itself entered a serious crisis because of the rules of the gold-exchange standard. In particular, it can be recalled that the United States maintained the parity of its currency by 'freely buying and selling gold against dollars offered by foreign monetary authorities at a fixed price of $35 per ounce. The United States was the only government committed to selling gold at a fixed price. Because other countries used the dollar as a unit of account and an intervention currency, US monetary authorities were technically unable to change the relationship between the dollar and other major currencies. It was the *other* currency that had to be devalued or revalued — or maintained within the set margins of parity — vis-à-vis the dollar. Other countries had to change the price at which *they* bought and sold dollars to bring about a change in the exchange rate of the dollar' (Meier 1982: 77-8). The great commercial deficit that the United States was accumulating was a constant source of worry, and the lack of confidence in the dollar was rapidly growing among government officials, central bankers and several academic economists.[4] When, during the latter part of 1970, capital outflows began to put additional pressure on the dollar, it became evident that something radical had to be done in order to allow for the free adjustment of the dollar exchange rate. Moreover, the mechanism of the gold payment of deficits never worked, and the disproportion between the dollar liabilities and the gold reserves was so evident that it was difficult to find any theoretical or empirical reason to stick to the formal rules of a system which had already moved towards what was to be known as the dollar-exchange standard.

> Clearly the gold exchange portion of the Bretton Woods system is by sheer numbers no longer working. The dollar liabilities outstanding greatly exceed our gold supply and the idea of a gold exchange standard is no longer workable. Likewise, the exchange rate mechanism of adjustable pegs envisioned in the Bretton Woods system is under serious doubt both from the action of member countries and from academic arguments.
>
> (Willett 1971: 409)

Before analysing the dollar-exchange standard, let us spend a few words on the payment of external debts under the hypothetical working of the gold-exchange standard.

1.4. *External debt servicing and the gold-exchange standard*

If the gold-exchange standard strictly followed the Ricardian principle, the problems usually related to the payment of external debts would not even be raised. In fact, in order to get indebted, a country should find on the international market a loan, in gold, of the amount necessary for the payment of its current account deficit. This clearly means that the indebted country will later have to find an equivalent sum of gold to be able to pay back its creditors. The two operations would be perfectly symmetrical and no disequilibrating pressure would be exerted on the domestic currency of the debtor country. The use of gold for the settlement of trade deficits would make it impossible for any country to pay in terms of a purely nominal money, were it the key currency or not. Hence, the external debt servicing would be reduced to a payment in gold made by the debtor country in favour of its creditors. The sole problem would be the earning of a sufficient amount of gold. But this is in no way surprising, since every debtor, whether national or international, has the possibility of spending today more than he earns precisely because he is prepared to spend less than what he earns tomorrow. Within the same currency area, debts are honoured through the transfer of a positive purchasing power from the indebted resident to the creditors; internationally, debts will be serviced by the transfer to the creditor country of a positive amount of the world's most appreciated real asset: gold. In both cases the payment would be real (money's national purchasing power defining a claim over current output, it is fundamentally the same as being paid in kind or in buying power), and, leaving aside momentarily the payment of interest, the debtor country would have to pay its debt only once.

As we have repeatedly said, however, the gold-exchange standard never worked in accordance with the strict rules propounded by Ricardo. On the contrary, deficits were, and still are, settled in monetary terms, and the United States dollar was chosen as the privileged means of international settlements. This state of affairs was to create a major asymmetry between two categories of countries, namely those who could settle their current account deficits by a simple stroke of a pen, and those who had to purchase the key currency in order to pay their external debt. The United States and, to a lesser extent, Great Britain were the main beneficiaries of this unfair system, their national currencies being considered as world standards and being therefore accepted as final payment. Since national currencies are the acknowledgment of debt of the monetary system which issues them, the gold-exchange was effectively so structured as to allow these countries to pay their net purchases of goods and services by the simple transfer of an IOU.

> It has been said that by financing its deficit through its own creation of international money, the United States obtains a kind of 'free' command over real resources, which can be used to enlarge its purchases of foreign goods, services, and assets (including interest-paying reserves) ... By running a cumulative deficit in its balance of payments, the United States can create internationally held dollars in a costless fashion and gain an increase in real national expenditure relative to national income.
>
> (Meier 1982: 79)

As Meier so lucidly observes, the United States still benefits from the great advantage of obtaining real resources in exchange for a promise (its acknowledgment of debt) which it will never be asked to maintain, since the dollar is indeed the means internationally chosen for the settlement of every transaction (American engagements included). Now, if it is clearly preposterous to expect that payment of debts and acknowledgment of debts are equivalent, it is even more absurd to ask countries to buy these acknowledgments of debt and use them to honour their external engagements. The nations whose money is not a key currency are, in fact, obliged to purchase foreign IOUs, and this forced purchase is the mark of a serious anomaly which does not fail to cause them, through a depreciating pressure on their domestic currencies, a positive and final loss of international income. Indebted countries who cannot pay their creditors by using their own currencies are therefore heavily penalized by the system propounded by the Bretton Woods Conference. As we have seen analysing the problem of German war payments, Keynes had already warned against the danger deriving from the 'transfer problem'. Unfortunately his arguments were not fully understood, and the world entered a period of increasing international disorder of which it is still difficult to perceive the end. The following analysis of the system which was to take over from the gold-exchange standard will confirm this negative result.

2. Debt servicing problems inherent in the gold-exchange standard are not removed by the dollar-exchange standard

2.1. *The inconvertibility of the dollar and the international liquidity problem*

In the sixties an important theoretical debate developed about the use of a national currency as an international standard and a means of payment. At the origin of the dispute were the arguments put forth by Triffin relative to the international liquidity problem. The starting point for Triffin's analysis was the gold-exchange standard, and the impossibility of conciliating the rule of convertibility with the increasing need for international liquidity. The rapidily increasing volume of world trade required, in fact, an ever greater disponibility of key currencies which, however, could not be supplied without endangering their stability. Under the gold-exchange standard, their value was linked to their legal definition in gold, and to their proclaimed convertibility into the precious metal. And, if the gap between gold reserves and monetary liabilities of the key currency countries was to grow too big, it would have become extremely difficult for people to believe in their external value. 'The basic absurdity of the gold-exchange standard is that it makes the *international* monetary system highly dependent on individual countries' decisions about the continued use of one or a few *national* currencies as monetary reserves' (Triffin 1961: 67).

Triffin saw a 'vicious circle' in the working of the gold-exchange standard system, since the use of one (or few) national currency (ies) as world reserve inevitably weakens the reserve position of the country whose currency is chosen as international standard. A worsening of the liquidity problem would then be the unavoidable, paradoxical, result of a system worked out to solve this very problem.

Let us consider the case of the American dollar. It is a fact that the increase in the world disponibility of dollars is the result of a growing American deficit, and that the foreign holding of US monetary liabilities puts the whole of the American monetary system under pressure. Now, this pressure was even more dangerous when the dollar was pegged to gold and formally convertible at a fixed rate. As Bernstein wrote 'The continuation of the deficit has, however, caused a greater depletion of US gold reserves than is desirable. Furthermore, the large foreign holdings of short-term liquid dollar assets expose the United States to the danger of massive conversion of dollars into gold in the future' (Bernstein 1963: 187).

Apart from very few economists, among whom are the authors of the already quoted paper 'The Dollar and World Liquidity: A Minority View' (1966),[5] theorists generally agreed that world liquidity could no longer be fed through US deficits, since the foreign accumulation of dollars had grown so much as to undermine confidence in the American currency. Hence, under the Bretton Woods system the situation was seen as characterized by the simultaneous presence of two opposed requirements: the necessity of increasing international liquidity, thus accepting the correlated US deficit, and the necessity of granting the convertibility of the dollar in order to maintain confidence in its external value. In the words of Johnson 'The gold exchange standard is a precarious system of international monetary organization. Two main problems are inherent in it. The first is associated with the reliance of the system on the use of national currencies to provide international reserves ... The second major problem is associated with the system's reliance on increases in monetary gold stocks and increases in reserve currency holdings to provide the increase in international reserves needed to support the expansion of international trade and commercial transactions' (Johnson 1963: 371-2).

Following the line of arguments proposed by Triffin, the gold-exchange standard was put under critical examination, and the conclusion was reached that it was a highly unstable system which had to be rapidly and drastically modified in order to favour the development of the world economy.

The indictment of the present, unorganized gold exchange, or key-currencies, standard is that it can only operate — and has indeed operated for nearly half a century — in an utterly haphazard fashion, creating far too little liquidity at times, and at other times far too much, but then only through generalized currency devaluations or through a persistent piling up of sterling or dollar I.O.U.'s.

(Triffin 1963: 427)

After the decision, taken by US President Nixon on 15 August 1971, to suspend convertibility of the dollar into gold, the danger of seriously putting the American monetary system under strain was apparently removed. The dollar was left free to find its new parity against other currencies, and the problem was posed whether to adopt free floating exchange rates or an adjustable (managed) floating system. Yet, the world liquidity problem was far from having been solved. In particular it remained true that even under the dollar-exchange standard the key currency country had to incur ever larger monetary liabilities to foreigners in order to expand the international reserves of other countries. Under these circumstances, it is evident that the pressure on the dollar would not have decreased, and that the system would still have been caught between the same horns of the dilemma: to guarantee the necessary amount of world liquidity or the stability of the dollar? It seems possible to maintain, therefore, that in the dollar standard system, as well as under the gold-exchange standard 'long-run balance-of- payments deficits of key-currency countries are both necessary yet alarming' (Yeager 1963: 161).

According to Wallich, for example, American deficits were a necessary condition for the building up of other countries' international reserves. 'If we no longer have deficits, the rest of the world will no longer have surpluses. It will have no source from which to increase its international reserves' (Wallich 1963: 284). From this assumption and from the observation that pressures on the dollar grew with the growing of the amount of the American liquid liabilities held by foreigners, he then explained the dilemma faced by the international monetary system as follows: '*The dollar, which is the basis of the world payments mechanism, is no longer invulnerable. To reduce its vulnerability, the United States must balance its international accounts. If the United States succeeds in doing that, however, it may be laying the groundwork for a world financial crisis at some future time*' (Wallich 1963: 284). The foreign holding of dollars is essentially linked to the US capacity of buying any kind of asset by sending abroad its own currency. Even the purchase of other national currencies can lead to this result, so that we can easily conclude that the American deficit, which is said to be necessarily associated to the growth of world liquidity, has to be understood as the amount of claims over the US banking system held by the rest of the world. 'By liquidity I understand the supply of credit in national currencies as needed to finance and provide the means of payment for trade and production. As far as international trade is concerned, the availability of credits in the currencies of the major industrial countries is of paramount importance — and the world liquidity problems will therefore be mostly a question of the capacity and readiness of those countries to provide credits and sustain the volume of means of payment' (Jacobson 1963: 227).

On the basis of what has just been said, it is possible to infer that, under the dollar-exchange standard, what has to be faced 'is not primarily a balance-of-payments problem. More fundamentally, the problem is the basic inadequacy of the international monetary mechanism in relation to requirements of the Free World' (Grubel 1963: 407). The US currency is under strain because it has been made to play the role of international standard and means of payment. Being the main world reserve currency, the dollar is accumulated throughout the world, and the United States is effectively acting as bank of the world, providing credits and increasing the volume of international liquidity. Let us analyse the international function carried out by the American monetary system.

2.2. *The USA as bank of the world*

The dollar being the main key currency, international transactions are settled by means of the claims issued by the US banking system. Thus, the national banking system of the USA is also made to play the role of international bank, with the precise task of providing the rest of the world with the necessary amount of international money.

> If the dollar is a world money, the United States is a bank and not a firm as other countries are. The difference between a firm and a bank, of course, is that the liabilities of the former are expected to be paid off at regular intervals, while those of the latter are passed from hand to hand as money, and tend to be permanent in fact, despite being 'demand' in form.
>
> (Kindleberger and Shonfield 1971: xiii-xiv)

Yet, the dollar is a national currency, and United States banks are not a supranational institution. National and international monetary functions are thus mixed up, and this confusion is bound to create serious difficulties for the dollar-exchange standard. The first is related to the use of the dollar as international unit of payment. In fact, if the American currency is certainly a perfect means of payment within the USA, things change radically when the dollar is used outside its domestic boundaries. Issued by the American banking system, the dollar is a claim over this very system. Hence, if an American agent *A* pays a fellow citizen *B* in dollars, the payment is perfectly valid since *A* gives *B* the acknowledgment of debt of a bank, and not its own IOU. *A* does not merely promise to pay *B*, he effectively pays him. When the

USA pays the rest of the world, on the contrary, it sends abroad a simple promise since, outside its national economic system, the dollar defines the acknowledgment of debt of the whole American nation. We reach, thus, the same conclusion as in our previous chapter, namely that the United States is given the absurd privilege of importing foreign resources by giving in exchange an IOU which it will never be required to honour.

Rueff was one of the economists who denounced this state of affairs with the greatest lucidity. Analysing the gold-exchange standard, which relative to the use of key currencies as a means to settle international transactions is not fundamentally different from the dollar-exchange standard, the French economist maintained that key currency countries can get foreign resources without ever paying for them.

> This is how the gold exchange standard brought about an immense revolution and produced the secret of a deficit without tears, to the countries in possession of a currency benefiting from international prestige allowing them to give without taking, to lend without borrowing, and to get without paying.
> (Rueff 1963: 322)

Now, it could be argued that the use of the dollar at the international level is not really free of cost for the United States. Moreover, since by getting dollars the rest of the world also gets a purchasing power over the American current output, it is difficult to see why dollars should not be as good outside the American economy as they are inside. Based on a superficial observation of facts, this argument is fallacious, for it does not take into account the duplication to which the American currency is submitted as soon as it is used to settle international transactions. When an American resident asks his commercial bank to pay his foreign creditor, the operation is not carried out by sending abroad part of the US domestic currency. Indeed, the foreign bank is credited by the US bank, which remains the monetary institution where the dollars paid are still deposited. In other words, the bank of the creditor obtains a claim over a deposit in dollars which will always be defined as a US deposit. In the balance sheets of the two banks this payment will be synthetically recorded in the following way (See Table 3.1.). The rules of double accounting are such that US payments are made without decreasing the amount of deposits of the American banking system. The United States do not lose the amount of dollars earned by the rest of the world, and it is hard to see how it could still be possible to claim for the validity of US international payments. Again, it is Rueff who brought out the problem in the clearest way. Examining the international use of key currencies, he stated that 'everything happens as if these currencies had never been exported in the first place.

Entering the credit system of the creditor country, but remaining in the debtor country, the claims representing the deficit are thus doubled' (Rueff 1963: 324).

Table 3.1.

USA Bank		Foreign Bank	
Liabilities	Assets	Liabilities	Assets
Foreign bank $x	Imp. $x	Exp. equivalent in national currency of $x	USA bank $x

The anomaly resulting from the use of an IOU issued by the debtor country as means of payment is thus confirmed by the maintenance of the deposits held within the country's banking system. In the case of US external payments, this means that America can get hold of foreign assets without losing a fraction of its purchasing power over domestic output. In exchange for its current resources, the rest of the world obtains an empty, nominal, money which could be transformed into American real and financial assets only if the United States's balance of payments were to define a substantial and stable surplus for many years to come. How far we are from a situation like this is clear to everybody, and even if it were possible to reach an overall American surplus, the world would still be faced with the problem of providing the economy with the necessary amount of international liquidity. As it is, the USA and the whole system faces a dilemma:

> On the one hand, US balance-of-payments deficits make the rest of the world increasingly reluctant to go on accumulating liquid dollar claims, and they hamper pursuit by the United States of vital domestic and international objectives. On the other hand, large and sustained surpluses may not be attainable; even if attained, they would not be desirable since they might not free the United States from undesirable constraints and they would impose constraints on other Free World countries.
>
> (Grubel 1963: 407)

Both alternatives would bring us to an impasse, and must therefore be rejected. The dilemma in which we are apparently caught is in reality the product of a system resulting from a wrong understanding of the nature of bank money. However, if we are to work out the elements of a reform of the actual structure of world payments we have to investigate its mechanisms further, and, particularly, the process distinctive of external debt servicing.

Chapter Four

The Monetary Approach to the Balance of Payments: an Unsuccessful Attempt to Associate National and International Monetary Analyses

1. The monetarist model rests on a *'petitio principii'*

The central feature of the monetary approach to the balance of payment theory is that balance of payment deficits or surpluses reflect stock disequilibria between demand for and supply of money. As stated by Mundell (1968, 1971), the author who contributed most to the development of the modern version of this approach,[1] the flow of money between countries has a direct impact on the internal relationship between the two stock variables: the money supply and the demand for money. Thus, monetary inflows or outflows, associated with surpluses or deficits, influence the domestic money supply, which is supposed to be a stock variable, and modify its relationship to the demand for money, which is likewise assumed to be a stock. The aim of the theory, therefore, is to obtain flow equilibria on the basis of stock adjustments in the domestic money market.

> The basic assumption on which this system of balance-of-payments analysis rests, and which forms the point of departure of the new 'monetary' approach to balance-of-payments theory, is that the monetary consequences of balance-of-payments surpluses or deficits can be and are absorbed (sterilised) by the monetary authorities so that a surplus or deficit can be treated as a flow equilibrium. The new approach assumes — in some cases, asserts — that these monetary inflows or outflows associated with surplus or deficits are not sterilised — or cannot be, within a period relevant to policy analysis — but instead influence the domestic money supply. And, since the demand for money is a demand for a stock and not a flow, variation of the supply of money relative to the demand for it associated with deficit or surplus must work towards an equilibrium between money demand and money supply with a corresponding equilibration of the balance of payments.
>
> (Johnson 1974: 152-3)

In the monetary approach, the balance of payments is also defined as the difference between aggregate receipts and aggregate payments by residents, and the international monetary problem is reduced to a problem of an available quantity of money. The sum of national currency and international reserves is the limit within which transactions can expand, and the policy followed by the monetary authorities becomes decisive for the expansion or the reduction of this limit. For example, if foreign purchases reduced the cash balances of residents, a process of readjustment could take place through a rise in interest rates, tighter credit conditions, a reduction of aggregate expenditures etc., provided the amount of international reserves was large enough to allow the self-correcting process to run its course. In this case, the role of the national monetary authorities is to grant a large amount of international reserves in relation to the domestic supply of money. On the other hand, if the cash balances of residents were being replenished by the monetary authority (through open market purchases of securities) in order to maintain the supply of domestic money, the self-readjustment problem would not even present itself, unless the decrease of the reserves of international assets required some corrective change of policy.

The monetary approach to the balance of payments is often worked out in terms of income-expenditure relationships. Hence, when only current account deposits are considered, the balance of payments is defined as 'the difference between the value of the country's output (its national income) and its total expenditure i.e. $B = Y - E$' (Johnson 1974: 55). According to this definition, then, exports increase the amount of the overall income available, whereas imports decrease it.

$$(1)\ Y = C' + I' + (\text{Exp.} - \text{Imp.})$$

In a single currency world, the validity of equation (1) could easily be maintained, since it would always be true that the income available in a given country can be increased or decreased through foreign transactions in the same way as any individual can increase or decrease the income of which he disposes through borrowing or lending. Every country would be a region of the same monetary nation, and the transfer of money from one country to another would be identical to a transfer of income. Within a single country, firms of a given region can increase their capital by selling shares or bonds inter-regionally. Likewise they can increase their profits through the purchase of the residents of other regions, and do this without modifying the relationship between national currency and domestic output. The new distribution of income between the different regions does not alter its global amount, and current output maintains its rigorous monetary definition.

The approach followed by the Monetarists rests on the implicit assumption that international transactions are essentially similar to inter-regional exchanges, an assumption which could partly be maintained under the strict gold standard system, but which is clearly far-fetched under the present world system. Each country has its own national currency, and its national income is defined by the association between money and domestic output. Hence, the heterogeneity which can be found between national currencies can also be verified relative to national incomes. Unless we were able to homogenize the space of international transactions, we could not even compare these different incomes which the monetary theory unhesitatingly mingles. What we have to determine, therefore, is whether it is possible to remove the monetary heterogeneity and, were it possible, whether the solution is consistent with the international migration of national incomes.

Let us start with the attempt to solve the problem on the basis of the establishment of exchange rates. In the absence of any link between currencies and gold how could exchange rates be maintained if not arbitrarily? Of course, a case could be made for the choice of those rates which allow for purchasing power parity or for those which are compatible with the equilibrium of the balance of payments. But, the point is not whether a level of exchange rates can be justified better than others or not. The choice of exchange rates is a matter of international agreement and, in this sense, it will always be partially arbitrary. The crucial point is whether, once determined, the exchange rates would remain constant or would be submitted to disequilibrating pressures due to factors totally alien to the processes of integration taking place within every single country between national money and current output. Now, as is implicitly recognized by Goodhart, far from being neutral the actual system of international payments has a disruptive effect on exchange rates, and is the main cause of their instability.

> The authorities charged with running the international monetary system, as set up at Bretton Woods, have heretofore kept their eye fixed on the wrong measure. They have usually been concerned with parity *levels* and controlling, pegging, or adjusting these levels. But they do not, and cannot, know what levels are correct; their attempts to maintain such levels lead to the imposition of distortions on the world economy (e.g. via direct controls); and the occasional large-scale jumps in exchange rates to rectify an impossible situation are disruptive.
>
> (Goodhart 1975: 309)

The reasons of this precarious state of affairs are again to be found in the rules of international payments worked out since the Conference of Genoa of 1922. In particular it is the use of national currencies as international standards and means of payment which appears to be the major cause of disturbances. In fact, in a system where international transactions can be settled in terms of money, currencies are made to play the role of exchangeable goods and are, therefore, bought and sold on the market as if they were final assets. Not all currencies share the same socio-economic status though; only reserve currencies are effectively compared to final goods. Hence, two asymmetries can be pointed out: the first being that between the nature of money and its international use, and the second that between reserve and non-reserve currencies.

As for the first asymmetry, its importance is revealed through a simple comparative analysis between what happens at the national and at the international levels. Within every country money circulates domestic output, and it is only in so far as it defines this very output that it can be used as a means of payment. Thus, money is not a final asset in itself. Whereas goods and services are purchased through the expenditure of money, money is not itself purchased. To claim the opposite is to maintain that output can be spent, which is equivalent to saying that money is essentially a commodity. Theory [2] and facts have so clearly established the falsity of this assumption that there is no need to insist upon it. The double accounting nature of bank money is a reality to which every monetary analysis has to conform. Hence, according to its definition, money is simply a vehicle whose value is given by the real output it is made to circulate. What can be bought at the national level is the 'charge' of money and not the 'vehicle' which is always a mere intermediary. Now, things should not radically change when we go on to consider world transactions. The lack of international output makes it impossible to determine any international income, it is true, but this simply means that the vehicular function of international money is complementary to that of national currencies. The same output which is circulated inside a country by national money is moved from one country to another by means of an international vehicle which has no more intrinsic value than its national equivalent. There is, therefore, no reason to believe that, leaving their original countries, currencies are transformed from simple intermediaries into final assets. If it is wrong to assert that national moneys are bought and sold within their own country, it is even worse to claim that the international trade of currencies is perfectly in line with the requirements of a correct system of monetary payments.

Now, according to the rules of the dollar-exchange standard the international purchase of national currencies is not only possible but necessary for the settlement of external transactions. Except for the key currency countries, all nations are bound to purchase foreign currencies in order to pay for their imports or to service their external debts. National currencies are constantly traded on the international market, and this obviously causes a permanent pressure on their relative prices.

The variation of exchange rates is made worse by the second asymmetry characterizing the dollar-exchange standard. The different economic status granted to national currencies leads, in fact, to the forced purchase of key currencies by the countries whose money is not recognized as reserve currency. The ensuing excess demand for key currencies relative to external debt servicing brings about a devaluation of the LDCs currencies and, therefore, an equivalent loss of external income which cannot be justified except by the anomalous working of the system of international payments.

Finally, if we also take into account the variations of exchange rates due to the investments of international speculative capital, we can uncompromisingly conclude that, within the gold-exchange standard, national currencies remain fundamentally heterogeneous. The monetarist definition of the balance of payments rests therefore on the a-prioristic assumption that national currencies can easily be made homogeneous through exchange rates. In a way, the advocates of this theory reason as if, from the monetary point of view, the world itself was a homogeneous economic space. Reality is both less perfect and more rigorous. Nations are not only distinct politically, but also economically, and their sovereignty is strictly related to their monetary autonomy. Output is defined in terms of the currency to which it is associated, and it is through this relationship that it can be said to pertain to a given national space. Unless humanity is able to create a world-wide nation, currencies will be independently issued by a number of national banking systems. This means that, under the present structure of international payments, inter-regional and international monetary transactions cannot be made equivalent by implicitly assuming a homogeneity which could only be achieved if the world were reduced to a single currency area. In fact, countries will continue to issue their own currencies and, in order to solve the problem of heterogeneity, we would have to find a system whose working would not modify the key necessary to translate one currency into another. Unfortunately today's system is far from granting this neutrality, and under these circumstances it is obviously difficult to keep claiming the validity of equation (1). Yet, it could still be argued that, even if it cannot be exactly quantified, the impact of exports and imports over national income is nevertheless certain, since no monetary payment can occur without modifying the supply of money. The impossiblity of establishing a rigorous relationship between national currencies would thus be only a minor difficulty which would not preclude the acceptance of the monetarist approach to the balance of payments. This objection being of importance, let us deal with it at some length.

2. National income and international expenditures

As we have seen, in the monetarist approach to the balance of payments monetary disturbances are said to be caused by variations in the demand for money. Thus, given the quantity of money, a disequilibrium between this amount and the demand for money requires the intervention of the monetary authority which, either through an expansion of domestic credit or a combination between income-expenditure divergences and balance of payments surplus or deficit, is called upon to match the supply of and the demand for money. The basic idea of this model is that the domestic money supply is modified by changes in the exports-imports relationship. For example, if the income holders of a given country were to reduce their expenditures and increase their cash balances the exports of the country would grow and the inflow of foreign currency would inflate its money supply. Symmetrically, an increase in the income holders' expenditure and a reduction in their cash balances would lead to a growth in the country's imports and to a fall in its money supply. Let us analyse these two cases separately.

2.1. *The balance of payments deficit*

A deficit of the balance of payments implies, so we are told, an excess of payments over receipts. In this case, and before the intervention of the monetary authority, 'the cash balances of residents are running down, as domestic money is transferred to the foreign exchange authority' (Johnson 1974: 49). Now, given the peculiar characteristic of the dollar-exchange standard, we have to distinguish between two possible trains of events, according to whether the currency of the country which runs the deficit is accepted as an international means of payment or not.

Starting with the deficit of non-key currency countries, we have to work out what the consequences of the deficit over their domestic money supply are. Independently of whether the deficit is due to stock or flow decisions (i.e. to the desire to shift out of domestic money into securities or to increase the purchase of foreign goods), these countries have to back the foreign expenditures of their residents by a forced purchase of dollars (the key currency). Since the domestic currency of these countries is not given the privilege of setting international transactions, the payments made by the countries' residents are not final. The money sent abroad flows back and in exchange for it the debtors' countries have to buy dollars on behalf of their foreign creditors. Now, this forced purchase of dollars is supposed to imply a transfer of domestic money in exchange for foreign currency, and from this transfer it is inferred that deficits entail a negative variation of the money supply. 'The excess of payments by residents over receipts by residents inherent in a balance-of-payments deficit necessarily implies ... that cash balances of residents are running down, as domestic money is transferred to the foreign exchange authority' (Johnson 1974: 49). But, if the purchase of dollars simply implied the transfer of domestic money, it would be wrong to assume a decrease in the money supply. Issued by the banking system of a given country, domestic money remains deposited in this same system even if its ownership is transferred abroad. The amount of available (and, therefore, deposited) domestic money is not altered when it is entered on the asset side of some foreign bank balance sheet. What is transferred is simply the right to the deposit and not the deposit itself, so that the payment of the deficit would not entail, in this case, the decrease in the supply of domestic money.

A closer analysis reveals that facts are rather different from what is claimed in the monetarist approach. The overall deficit of the balance of payments itself is a *petitio principii* which is not confirmed by reality. Precisely because of the nature of bank money, in fact, the net purchases made by a key currency country define an equivalent sale of monetary deposits to the rest of the world so that the net imports of goods, services and non-monetary financial assets are always balanced by an equivalent export of monetary financial assets (the bank deposits of the 'deficit' country). As for the non-key currency countries, the balance of payments equilibrium is the unexpected consequence of the asymmetrical working of the actual system of international payments. Indeed, under the dollar-exchange standard when they run a trade deficit they have to run also a financial deficit. The commercial deficit of any such a country, for example, can only be financed through an external sale of financial assets so that, on the whole, its balance of payments is perfectly equilibrated. Things would be different only if the country could pay for its international purchases in its own domestic currency, which is obviously not the case here. Having to find, on the financial market, the amount of reserve currency necessary to cover its trade deficit, the country realizes a surplus in its exports of non-monetary financial assets. The payment of the commercial deficit is thus carried out by means of the key currency invested in the country by the rest of the world, and not by means of the country's domestic money. The payment of the trade deficit by 'weak' currency countries can therefore not be identified with a transfer of domestic money. On the contrary, the domestic money which is paid by national debtors flows back immmediately and has to be replaced by an equivalent amount of dollars acquired on the financial market. The synthetical representation of the book entries of the country's banking system is the following (See Table 4.1).

Entry 1 defines the internal situation before imports. Given a national production equal to x units of domestic money, the banking system is indebted towards the income holders for this very amount and has the current output on the asset side of its balance sheet. Liabilities and assets are perfectly balanced, and the money supply is equivalent to the amount of available income. Entry 2 relates to the payment of imports made by the residents in their national

Table 4.1.

Banking system

	Liabilities		Assets	
1.	Income holders	DM x	Output	DM x
2.	Foreign bank	DM y	Income holders	DM y
3.	Foreign bank	$ z	Foreign bank	DM y
4.	Income holders	DM y	Eurobank	$ z
5.	Income holders	DM x	Output	DM x

currency. The credit of the income holders towards the banking system is reduced by the amount of their external payment and is transferred to the bank of the foreign exporter. However, since the money of this country is not a key currency, the foreign bank immediately sends back its new deposit and asks for payment in dollars (entry 3). The liability of the banking system towards the foreign bank in domestic money is thus cancelled out and replaced by a liability in dollars. This implies either a reduction in the country's international reserves (which is but the result of previous external sales of real assets) or the sale of non-monetary financial assets, which is entered by the bank as an increase of its assets in dollars and an equivalent debt in domestic money towards the residents selling the financial assets (entry 4). Finally, the banking system we are considering owes z dollars to the foreign bank and x units of domestic money to national income holders. The amount of available domestic money and of current output thus remains equal to x (entry 5).

We therefore reach the conclusion that the deficit of the balance of current account does not effectively reduce the money supply of those countries whose currency is not an international means of payment. What we have still to examine, however, is what happens to the domestic supply of money when the deficit has to be ascribed to a key currency country. In the system derived from the decision taken at the conferences of Genoa (1922) and Bretton Woods (1944), these countries benefit from what Rueff (1963) called 'deficits without tears'. The USA, for example, pays for its foreign purchases in dollars, i.e. in a currency which is issued by its banking system (almost free of cost) and which defines the acknowledgment of debt of this very system. Now, US external payments are the source of another important anomaly, namely the doubling of the American currency, which can simultaneously be found within the country, as a liability (deposit) of the US banking system, and abroad, as a sum of eurodollars. As stated by Rueff, 'everything happens as if these currencies had never been exported in the first place. Entering the credit system of the creditor country, but remaining in the debtor country, the claims representing the deficit are thus doubled' (Rueff 1963: 324).

It is in the nature of bank money to define a deposit, and, once created, this deposit can never leave its place of birth. It can be used as a means of payment, of course, but the settlement of national or international transactions does not imply its actual transfer. US dollars, for example, remain deposited in American banks and foreign creditors receive a claim on this deposit and not the deposit itself. Hence, it is clear that the payment of key currency countries deficits does not entail a decrease in their money supply. The fact that the domestic currency available in the US is not diminished by the American balance of payments deficit proves, therefore, that the income-expenditure relationship postulated in the monetarist approach is far from being a well established principle of political economy.

Let us now analyse what happens in the countries that benefit from a surplus of their balance of payments.

2.2. *The balance of payments surplus*

Here again we can consider separately the case of the USA and that of the non-key currency countries. As for a hypothetic American surplus, the payment of the rest of the world could either be made in dollars or in another reserve currency. In the second case, the American banks would record the foreign currency on the asset side of their balance sheet and, as its counterpart, an equivalent amount of dollars on the liabilities side. The foreign payment would provoke, therefore, an equivalent emission of dollars automatically carried out by the banks on the basis of the claim to foreign deposits transferred to them by the rest of the world. 'The claims transferred for the settlement of the deficit are bought against the creation of money, by the banking system of the creditor country' (Rueff 1963: 323). American creditors would be paid by means of newly created dollars, and it can certainly not be denied that this operation would modify the original relationship between domestic money and current output or, in other words, that the domestic money supply would grow relative to the amount of money initially required for the purchase of national output.

Despite appearances to the contrary, if US creditors were to be paid in dollars by their foreign debtors the result would fundamentally be the same. In fact, the American banking system would record a positive amount of eurodollars on its asset side and an equivalent amount of dollars, to the benefit of the American creditors, on its liability side. Instead of taking place on the basis of a foreign reserve currency, the creation of domestic American money would therefore occur on the basis of a sum of eurodollars, yet this would not alter the fact that the foreign payment of the American surplus is a source of internal disequilibrium. The synthetical representation of the balance sheet of the US banks will show this clearly (See Table 4.2). Entries 1 and 2 refer, respectively, to the national production and the net imports of the period preceeding the balance of payments surplus. Entry 3 defines the production of current output whereas entry 4 refers to the payment, in dollars, made by the rest of the world and addressed to the American creditors via the US banking system. The dollars created by the American banks are not compensated by the extinction of the foreign bank liability so that, finally, the national creditors who benefit from the foreign payment do not take the place of the income holders who had initially purchased goods, services or financial assets from abroad. As we have seen in the previous chapter, the payment of American exports would not be a source of internal inflation only if exports were carried out by the same agent who carried out the American imports and if these two transactions had the same (external) output as their object. In all other cases the creation of dollars relative to the positive entry of eurodollars on the asset side of the American banking system alters the domestic relationship between output and US currency. It is true that, if American exports reduce the amount of domestic output, the payment to the exporting agents reduces the amount of domestic income, yet the currency issued as domestic counterpart of the eurodollars has no real content and is definitively inflationary.

Table 4.2.

US banking system

	Liabilities		Assets	
1.	Income holders	\$x	Output	\$x
2.	Foreign bank	\$y	Importing agents	\$y
	Income holders	\$x-y	Output	\$x
	Foreign bank	\$y		
3.	Income holders	\$x	Output	\$x
4.	Exporting agents	\$y	Foreign bank	\$y
	Income holders	\$2x	Output	\$2x-y
			Importing agents	\$y

In the case in which the surplus were realized by a country whose money is not granted the status of reserve currency, we would again be faced with the inflationary growth of the money supply. Since these countries cannot pay their deficits with their national currencies, the corrective mechanism applying in some particular cases to the US surplus does not work here. We have to remember, in fact, that these countries' commercial deficit is matched by an equivalent sale of non-monetary financial bonds. Thus the net imports previous to the current surplus and the surplus itself would be recorded as follows in the balance sheet of country *A* (See Table 4.3) Entry 1 describes the domestic production of period p^{o}, while entries 2, 3 and 4 define the operations relative to the payment of the net commercial imports of the same period. In particular, entry 3 defines the sale of non-monetary financial assets by *A*'s residents. The dollars earned through this sale are recorded on the assets side of *A*'s balance sheet while the residents are paid by the creation of domestic money. In the following period, p^{1}, a new domestic output is produced (entry 5) and the country's net exports bring \$y to *A*'s banking system which, on the basis of this monetary asset, creates an equivalent amount of domestic money to the benefit of the exporters (entry 6). On the whole, the national production of periods 0 and 1 amounts to 2x units of domestic money whereas the income totally available in the country is equal to 2x + y. The inflationary gap relative to the payment of *A*'s surplus is thus not compensated when it is referred to *A*'s previous deficits, and the growth of the domestic money supply is definitively confirmed.

Table 4.3

A's banking system

	Liabilities		Assets	
1.	Income holders	DMx	Output	DMx
p^{0} 2.	Foreign bank	DMy	Income holders	DMy
3.	Income holders	DMy	Foreign bank	\$y
4.	Foreign bank	\$y	Foreign bank	DMy
5.	Income holders	DMx	Output	DMx
p^{1} 6.	Income holders	DMy	External bank	\$y
7.	Income holders	DM2x + y	Output	DM2x
			Foreign bank	\$y

The mechanical working of the model proposed by the monetary approach derives from the irrealistic assumption of the fundamental equivalence between inter-regional and international monetary transactions. In a one-currency world, the problems related to the use of the dollar would no longer be of an international order, and the anomalies associated with the distinction between key currency and non-key currency countries would be totally absent. Now, the homogeneity implied by the monetarist assumption also accounts for another important principle taken over by the monetary approach: purchasing power parity.

2.3. *The purchasing power parity postulate*

Let us start this section by quoting Frenkel and Johnson.

> One of the major cornerstones of the classical and the neo-classical schools that is adopted by the monetary approach is the conception of a system of world markets. Profit maximisation implies that when there is free and frictionless trade in both securities and goods, rates of return on identical domestic and foreign securities must be equalised, as must the money prices of goods in terms of either currency'.
>
> (Frenkel and Johnson 1974: 33)

The basic idea of the principle postulating the purchasing power parity is that the entire economy can be seen as a unity, which is made up of nations and characterized by the presence of 'a single world market and a single world price' (Hawtrey 1932: 144). Behind the classical postulate of PPP was the assumption that gold was the overall currency, and that prices, world-wide, were expressed in terms of gold. Whether we consider the works of Ricardo (1811), Mill (1893), Laughlin (1903) or Hawtrey (1932) we always find that the mechanism allowing for the PPP is an international flow of gold obeying the rules of arbitrage and competition. Yet, Wicksell's claim that 'there could not possibly exist different prices of the same commodity on both sides of the frontier' (Wicksell 1918: 405) is said to hold even when the restrictive conditions of a single currency world are removed. The actual system of international payments works both under a fixed exchange rate and under a floating exchange rate regime. In both cases the PPP principle is supposed to hold and to determine either the national price level (when exchange rates are fixed) or the foreign exchange rate (in the case of floating exchange rates).

Now, whereas it is easy to understand how the PPP can be advocated in a world made homogeneous through the use of a common monetary standard such as gold, it is very difficult to maintain that under the gold-exchange standard equilibrating forces tend towards a world-wide price uniformity. Empirical facts are constantly disproving this claim, and theorists often cast doubts on the validity of PPP as both a short and long-run equilibrium condition. 'On the basis of our empirical findings, hence, we can question the soundness of models embodying the PPP hypothesis, even if only as long run benchmark' (Giovannetti 1987: 504). Moreover, modern monetary analysis shows that the international use of the dollar provokes disruptive variations in the exchange market which can certainly not be attributed to the attempt to implement PPP.

A situation in which prices are uniformly determined throughout the world can be aimed at only if the international monetary system is not a source of continuous disturbances altering the relationship between national currencies. The forced purchase of dollars on one side and the privilege of purchasing without paying on the other, provoke important variations in the exchange rates, and so does the erratic migration of international speculative capital. The consistent periods of devaluation and re-evaluation of the American currency cannot be ascribed to the working of PPP, and McKinnon's (1988) suggestion to adopt a system of fixed exchange rates and an articulated control over domestic money supply in order to make PPP a monetary standard is just one example of the underestimating of the anomalies characterizing the present monetary system.

The existence of a world market is not simply a matter of free circulation of goods and capital. The monetary framework where this circulation has to be carried on is also of the utmost importance. If the world could be economically assimilated into a unique confederation of States, things would be quite different, of course. In the system postulated by the Classics, gold was the common denominator of national currencies and the ultimate means of international payments. World prices were therefore expressed in terms of gold, and PPP was the obvious consequence of monetary homogeneity and free circulation. Another postulate of the classic approach to international monetary analysis is, in fact, that of the natural distribution of money among countries. According to Mill, for example, 'A newly acquired stock of money would diffuse itself over all countries until money has diffused itself so equally that prices had risen in the same ratio in all countries, so that the alteration of price would be for all practical purposes ineffective' (Mill 1893: 194-5). The uniqueness of money and its neutral distribution are assumptions which lead directly to the principle of PPP and to the claim that a balance of payments deficit is linked to an excess supply of money and not to a variation of international relative prices. This is also the central claim of the monetary approach to the balance of payments. As repeatedly asserted by its advocates, the balance of payments should be viewed as a monetary phenomenon dependent on the income-expenditure relationship and not on the composition of expenditures. 'The accumulation or decumulation of assets depends on the aggregate relationship between domestic expenditure and income and does *not* depend on the composition of expenditure' (Frenkel and Johnson 1974: 23).

The link between the classical and the new monetary approach is not as evident as is openly claimed by the supporters of the modern analysis generated with the works of Meade. The unsuccessful attempts to explain balance of payments phenomena in terms of the elasticity approach to devaluation have contributed partially to strengthening the monetary point of view, and to implementing a monetary policy consistent with this particular approach. However, the question of whether the balance of payments deficit can be better accounted for through a relative prices analysis or through considerations relative to the quantity of money cannot be settled by assuming the existence of a single currency world where money is essentially neutral. Indeed the realization of an international monetary unit is still far away, and we live in a world where every country has its own national currency and where international payments have to comply with the rules of the gold-exchange standard. In this context, the strict analogy between international and inter-regional transactions postulated by many economists is but wishful thinking. Exchange rates vary according to the anomalous working of the system, and even a superficial analysis shows that balance of payments deficits cannot be explained by the simple mechanism propounded by the monetary approach.

2.4. *External debt servicing and the monetary approach to the balance of payments*

The regime of the gold-exchange standard requires the indebted countries to earn dollars in order to service their external debt. According to the monetary approach, the surplus needed by these countries can only be obtained if other countries run an equivalent deficit. And, since a balance of payments deficit is compatible only with a growth of the domestic money supply (corresponding either to a dishoarding or to a money or credit creation), the payment of the external debt would be linked to the decisions of monetary policy taken by the creditor countries as well as to the availability of foreign reserves. However, since the deficit would be compensated by the payment of the debt, there seems to be no reason to believe that the mechanism would not work satisfactorily.

The disturbing element of this analysis is the mechanical correspondence between deficit and surplus implicit in the monetary approach. The monetary homogeneity which is supposed to exist at the international level is associated with the principle according to which one agent's expenditures are another agent's receipts, and it is thus inferred that a country cannot realize a surplus unless another country realizes a deficit. In other words, it is supposed that, for a country to pay its external debt, it is enough to increase its exports relative to its imports. The surplus thus realized could be sent to the creditor countries, and the debt problem solved without any difficulty due to the monetary system itself. How far this analysis is from reality is clearly evident. The dollar deposits earned by the income holders of the debtor country have, in fact, to be bought by the indebted residents, and this purchase is certainly not neutral from the point of view of exchange rates. Now, the ensuing devaluation of domestic currency is the symptom of a problem which is simply ignored by the monetary approach. Not only is the income-expenditure principle based on the gratuitous assumption of a perfect monetary homogeneity, but it also fails to account for the logical distinction between a nation and the sum of its residents. Likewise, the existence of a unique world market, a corollary of the homogeneity postulate, is a state of affairs clearly inconsistent with a reality where private international transactions cannot occur without modifying the countries' external 'debtor' position. As the international payments of the residents are made by means of national currencies, and national currencies are acknowledgments of debts of the countries' banking systems, it appears that what is a positive payment for the residents is not necessarily so for the countries themselves. Indeed, it is only when the domestic currency is the world key currency that the external debt servicing has no direct negative repercussions for the debtor country. Being allowed to pay with its own acknowledgment of debt, the key currency country finds itself only nominally indebted when some of its residents service their debt. On the contrary, the debt is real for all the other countries whose money is not internationally accepted. Although residents do effectively pay their debt, their country has to pay it once again, and it can only do so through the purchase of an equivalent sum of dollars, which entails a loss of national resources to the benefit of the rest of the world.

The difficulties relative to the working of the actual system of international payments notwithstanding, to reason in terms of complementarity disequilibria is dangerously misleading for two reasons. First, because it does away with the problem of national currencies heterogeneity in a rather a-prioristic way and, second, because it does not account for the possibility of running a trade deficit without getting indebted. By this we do not mean, of course, that countries should be given the chance to import goods and services without paying. If the USA were not to be allowed to finance their foreign purchases by a simple stroke of a pen, no other country should be endowed with this unjustified privilege in its place. Yet, the payment of the commercial deficit should not entail a debt for the country itself. The sale of bonds necessary to finance the trade deficit is carried out by the country's residents, and there is no reason why the country should find itself additionally indebted. From the country's point of view, the commercial deficit is perfectly matched by a financial surplus (the sale of non-monetary financial assets) and no external debt results from this balance.

Even from the restricted point of view of the country's residents the net purchase of foreign goods and services does not necessarily entail their indebtedness. In fact, the trade deficit could well be financed through the sale of shares, in which case the operation would be perfectly neutral. To claim that a country's residents can be net purchasers of foreign resources only in so far as they get indebted (or, which is basically equivalent, in so far as they decrease their foreign deposits) is to limit international transactions to barter. Now, one of the advantages of money is precisely that of widening the narrow boundaries of traditional barter by allowing for unilateral investment. The sale of shares by a given country defines a positive foreign investment, and it is thanks to this investment that the residents' net real purchases can be neutral with respect to their external debt situation. Analogously, through foreign investment a country can finance its external debt servicing irrespective of whether its balance of trade is positive or negative.

Finally, the monetary approach to the balance of payments is shown to be founded on a series of assumptions which are corroborated neither by empirical observation nor by theoretical analysis. Monetary homogeneity, market uniformity and purchasing power parity are inconsistent with the rules of the gold-exchange standard, and there is no reason to believe that, were this system to be replaced, they would be verified under another theoretical setting. As appears in the case of external debt servicing, the surplus-deficit relationship has not to be viewed in too mechanical a way. The same can be said relative to PPP. Why should we maintain, in fact, that PPP is a necessary condition for long-run equilibrium if current account equilibrium is no longer a prerequisite for economic development and price stability?

This does not mean, however, that the monetarist claim that 'balance of payments problems are essentially monetary' (Johnson 1974: 51) is fundamentally wrong, and that the monetary approach has to be replaced by a structural approach where only 'real' factors are taken into account to explain problems of international economic order. Theory shows, in fact, that the deterioration of the real terms of trade is a reality which is made worse by the actual system of international payments. Were this system to be radically modified, the gap between rich and poor countries could narrow through an increase of foreign investment in the LDCs, and the terms of trade of these countries would eventually tend to improve. What matters, anyway, is that problems of structural order would no longer be mixed up with problems pertaining to the monetary working of the system. The main objective of a rigorous analysis of international transactions is, therefore, to work out a system where money would play an essential, though *neutral* role. Albeit postulated by the monetary approach, the neutrality of money has never really worked. This principle, in fact, is totally alien to the system of international payments based on the use of a key currency, and its implementation requires a fundamental reform of the gold-exchange standard.

Chapter Five

The Dollar-Exchange Standard as Primary Source of International Speculative Capital

'One country's overall surplus is another country's overall deficit.' This is the best known principle of traditional international economic theory. In order to earn a positive income at the international level it is necessary to have an overall surplus — so we are told — and, since for each surplus there corresponds an equivalent deficit of some other country, it is evident that not all countries can simultaneously earn an international income. The analogy with what happens at a microeconomic level within a common currency area is evident. In fact, agent *a* can obtain a positive income only if another agent loses it. One agent's gain is another agent's loss, this is the simple and straightforward message of everyday economics, and if reality is more benevolent it is only because production allows for the simultaneous earning of all individuals. Internationally, however, things work quite differently. The international economy is only based on exchange, and in such a context it seems perfectly justifiable to apply the principle of reciprocity characteristic of the whole theory of relative exchange. A surplus of the balance of payments, therefore, would be the necessary and sufficient condition both for a country to gain and for another to lose an equivalent sum of international reserves. On the whole, surplus and deficit would balance and the global international situation would show a perfect equilibrium.

Yet, once again, facts are much more prosaic and have repeatedly shown that the symmetry between deficit and surplus is a mere figment of the imagination. The external debt of less developed countries has not stopped increasing and has recently (1988) reached 1.300 milliard dollars, while the USA has been maintaining a substantial balance of payments deficit for the last twenty years. This situation raises two questions: who are the creditors of the LDCs' debt and what are the consequences of the huge international deficit accumulated by the USA?

1. US balance of payments deficit and the growth of 'pathological' capital

The adoption of the dollar-exchange standard has caused the appearance of a phenomenon of ever-growing importance whose presence is, alone, sufficient to testify to its pathological nature: the large and ever-expanding pool of time deposits denominated in dollars and held offshore. Known as eurodollars, these deposits are totally free to be traded on the euromarket and represent a speculative capital whose erratic movements are always capable of creating disruptive pressures on any national currency.

'When the United States ran large deficits in its balance of payments, foreign banks and companies accumulated short-term dollar deposits that became the basis for the development of the Eurodollar market' (Meier 1982: 175). The process of eurodollar creation is strictly related to the use of the dollar as key currency and to the American external deficit. Every time the USA pays for its imports a foreign bank is credited, and the amount of dollars recorded on the asset side of its balance sheet defines a sum of eurodollars. Now, since a eurodollar deposit is a deposit in dollars with a foreign bank, it is evident that the eurodollar market expands as the US deficit increases. In fact, the existence of the American deficit is reflected in the positive offshore dollar deposits.

When the USA pays the rest of the world it does it by means of its own currency, which signifies that it sends abroad its own acknowledgment of debt. Recorded as an asset by offshore banks, the American currency is nevertheless still deposited within its original banking system. The fact is — we already know this — that the settlement of US international transactions implies a duplication of the American currency which, while remaining within the American banking system is entered in the accounts of foreign banks as a deposit in its own right. The dollars available on the eurocurrency market are not distinct from the dollars available within the USA, so that every variation of the exchange rate due to interventions on the international market is automatically reflected in the domestic currency. Eurodollars, however, are not under the control of American monetary authorities. Their movements follow the changing rules of speculation, irrespective of the consequences they could have on the working of the world economic system. The duplication of dollars, as well as of any other national money used as key currency, gives rise, therefore, to a mass of speculative capital whose pathological nature is constantly verified through the disequilibrating effects it bears on the monetary markets. 'The rapid growth has had significant effects on the international monetary system — through the sizeable amount of Eurodollar deposits held in official reserves and through the enormous amount of public sector borrowing in the Eurodollar market by government entities in both developed and less developed countries' (Meier 1982: 175).

A foreign held deposit of dollars appears every time that an American resident pays his external correspondent, but it is only the deposits defining the American deficit, of course, which increase the mass of eurodollars. Hence, this same mass could be reduced only if the US overall balance of payments became positive over a consistent period of time. Now, even if this unlikely result could be attained some day, things would not radically change since other national currencies are already contributing to the increase of international 'speculative' capital, and they would inevitably take over the role of key currency eventually abandoned by the dollar. But what about stopping the possibility of the growth of speculative capital under the actual international monetary system?

A solution would seem to be the perfect equilibrium of all balance of payments. If every country were to balance its international transactions, how could dollars or other key currencies increase the amount of deposits held offshore? In particular if the US dollars spent abroad were to be exactly equivalent to the amount spent in America by the rest of the world, the mass of eurodollars would not be inflated and the disruptive effects of speculative capital would somehow be delimited. Yet, things do not follow this path. Every country, in fact, tries to get the most out of its foreign transactions, and it is not at all evident why it should restrain from increasing its exports of goods and capital. Maybe to preserve world monetary stability? But, if the USA were to stop its net supply of dollars this stability would be constantly shaken by the need for international liquidity. The exchange standard system is so conceived as to require the use of a key currency, and as soon as a national money is made to play this role the mechanism of eurocurrency creation is set at work and can only be dismantled by a radical change in the entire structure of monetary payments.

2. The influence of external debt servicing over the process of speculative capital accumulation

Even from a brief analysis it should be evident that an orderly system should favour imports by the LDCs and exports from the most developed national economies. No one doubts that poor countries should be able to import much more than they actually do if they are to be given a chance to develop. Likewise it is certain that rich countries would find a great benefit from increasing their exports. The interests of these two categories of countries are therefore complementary, and the structure of international monetary payments should not represent an obstacle to their fulfilment. Under the actual system, however, the growth of speculative capital seems the unavoidable consequence of the foreign purchase of currency necessary for the LDCs to be able to increase their imports. Since these countries can purchase foreign goods only in dollars (or in some other key currency, which we shall ignore for the sake of clarity), they must find a way of getting hold of the required amount of American currency. Two possibilities are offered them; either they can earn dollars through a sale of financial assets, or they can borrow dollars on the eurocurrency market. In the second case LDCs would increase their commercial imports only at the price of getting indebted. The advantage of disposing of a greater amount of foreign resources would be more than matched by the disadvantage of increasing their external debt and the whole operation would put these countries in an even worse position than the initial one. The first possibility seems far better. Dollars would be invested by foreign residents and, thus, earned by LDCs thanks to a surplus of their financial balance. However, if the financial assets were bought by US residents, their purchase would be financed, like any other US purchase, by an increase in deposits of dollars held offshore. The consequences are well known: the mass of eurodollars would increase and the speculative capital available offshore would grow bigger. It is true that part of this pathological capital would be reabsorbed if LDCs were to increase drastically their imports from the USA. Yet, it is likewise true that part of the dollars invested in these countries would be spent elsewhere, and in this case the amount of eurodollars created by the American purchase of foreign shares would not be decreased. Thus, in the present system of international payments it is hard to see how it would be possible to conciliate the complementary needs of rich and poor countries with the necessity of fighting against the tumoral growth of speculative capital.

Let us analyse a last possibility. It is a fact that the eurocurrency market has grown so much that it would be possible to keep the whole international system going by making use of the eurodollars accumulated so far. In such a context, it would also be conceivable to have all the investments in LDCs made with eurodollars. If this were the case, the international 'pathological' capital would not be inflated and LDCs could perhaps increase their imports without increasing their external debt. National currencies would still be created as counterparts of eurodollar deposits, of course, and the system would still be far from being neutral. But, at least, the growth of speculative capital would be stopped and LDCs would be given the chance of improving their standard of living and developing their economies at a lower cost than nowadays. A solution similar to this and known as consolidation of foreign exchange reserve was effectively proposed as a possible remedy against the exorbitant privilege of the countries whose national currency is used for the settlement of international transactions. As stated by Cooper, the arguments in favour of its enforcement were '(1) that it will reduce an important source of instability in the system, (2) that it will eliminate the special privileges arising from the ability of the reserve currency countries, in effect, to print international money, and (3) that it will permit these countries to deal with imbalances in payments more readily through changes in exchange rates, without being concerned, as they now must be, with a whole range of inhibiting factors not present for other countries' (Cooper 1972: 326). However, the advocates of foreign exchange reserve consolidation accepted both the principle of private markets for multilateral clearing and the possibility of open market operations dealing in national currencies. 'In particular, reliance continues to be placed on private exchange markets for multilateral clearing of international payments, and on maintenance of official exchange rate obligations by intervention in that market by central banks as buyers and sellers of their own currency against a single foreign currency, usually the US dollar' (Cooper 1972: 326). Cooper was, therefore, able to show that the claim for reserve consolidation is inconsistent with the use of a system which was still essentially derived from the currency-exchange standard. In order effectively to consolidate the sum of eurodollars it would be necessary to implement a totally new system of international payments. Till then it would be wrong to believe that the USA, or any other key currency country, would not go on printing international money for the settlement of international transactions, and it would be naïve to think that the solution to the problem rests on the goodwill of the surplus countries who should encourage domestic demand in order to reduce their external surplus and, by the same token, the deficit of their international partners. Not only, as is shown by the existence of speculative offshore capital, is it not true that surpluses and deficits are complementary, but it is also absurd to claim that an orderly world requires LDCs to limit their imports and rich countries to reduce their exports.

Now, the strain that the actual system puts on the LDCs and the impact it has on the growth of speculative capital is increased by another important anomaly, namely the double payment of external debt.

The mechanism is familiar; having to serve their external debts by means of a foreign currency, the LDCs have to exert a forced demand for dollars, thus submitting their domestic currency to a devaluating pressure which is neutralized only through a new external loan. Paid once by the residents who contracted it, the foreign debt is paid a second time by the country itself, and it is this second payment which characterizes the actual regime of international payments. As a result of external debt servicing within the dollar-exchange standard, the indebted countries find themselves in the paradoxical situation of being as much indebted after as before their external payment. Under the present system, the price which LDCs have to pay in order to service their debt is so high that it is becoming common to speak of their 'eternal' debt. While this expression is usually justified either by resorting to structural considerations or by evoking internal policy reasons, modern analysis provides a new 'logical' argument to prove its dramatic validity. Poor countries cannot pay their debt, whatever the products they export and independently of the national monetary policy they follow. The impossibility is not contingent but logical. Unless the system of international payments is substantially modified, the external debt of LDCs cannot be paid under any circumstance, and this is precisely because it is the system of payment itself which causes this state of affairs.

The double payment of the external debt has also a negative consequence over the amount of accumulated eurocurrencies. In fact, by increasing the international demand for dollars, the external debt servicing of LDCs provokes an equivalent increase in the mass or in the density of eurodollars, either through their new emission (if the dollars come from the American banking system) or through the pyramiding of eurobanks' lending (if the loan to LDCs is subscribed by eurobanks). This growth in the mass or in the density of the deposits of dollars held offshore increases the importance of the international speculative capital, and shows that it is precisely this pathological capital which is the beneficiary of the double external debt servicing.

Nations are not the only elements of the world system. Offshore capital is a reality derived directly from the working of the dollar-exchange standard, and as long as this system is implemented countries will be faced with the disruptive effects of that capital. Thus, while speculative capital increases because of debt payments, the consequences of this increase are not only felt by the debt servicing countries. To the traditional causes of the rise in the value of US domestic currency (which is often seen as a major cause of the American balance of payments deficit) have to be added the disturbing effects which the erratic movements of speculative capital necessarily have on exchange rates. The uncontrolled periods of rise and fall of the dollar which we have all witnessed in recent years are but an example of these effects, and it could hardly be denied that it is impossible to find any serious or durable conciliation between monetary stability and speculative interests.

The origin and growth of speculative international capital is therefore linked to the offshore deposits of the national money used as key currency, as well as to the double payment of external debt. In both cases a process of duplication can be pointed out. The US balance of payments deficit defines, in fact, the duplication of dollars (which can be simultaneously found in the American banking system and in the eurobanks), while the rise in the mass or in the density of eurodollars is the mark of the second, redundant, payment relative to external debt servicing. If international transactions did not have this duplicative effect, no pathological capital could ever be found, and since the duplication is linked to the regime of the gold-exchange standard (dollar-exchange standard) its final defeat will only be possible through a radical reform of the actual system of international payments.

Chapter Six

Empirical and Pragmatic Attempts to Solve the International Liquidity Problem

1. The international liquidity problem under convertibility

By 'international liquidity' we generally mean the aggregate stock of assets available for the settlement of international transactions. Gold is a relatively small part of this stock which, following the decisions taken at Bretton Woods, was and still is essentially made up of official holdings of reserve currencies. Until 1971 international liquidity consisted mainly of convertible dollars, and its amount was directly related to the American balance of payments deficit. World liquidity problems, therefore, were mostly thought of as being related to the capacity and readiness of the USA 'to provide credits and sustain the volume of means of payment' (Jacobson 1963: 227). Now, since the US government was committed to selling gold at a fixed price against dollars offered by foreign monetary authorities, some economists were starting to worry about 'the vulnerability of a world monetary system whose operation becomes increasingly dependent on one or a few *national* currencies as major components of *international* monetary reserves' (Triffin 1961: 19). According to Triffin, the increasing US deficit necessary to the growth of international liquidity would have made it practically impossible for the American monetary authorities to respect convertibility and, by the same token, would have led to a generalized lack of confidence in the dollar and, finally, to a major crisis of the international monetary system.

> The gold exchange standard *may*, but *does not necessarily*, help in relieving a shortage of world monetary reserves. It does so only to the extent that the key currency countries are willing to let their net reserve position decline through increases in their short-term monetary liabilities unmatched by corresponding increases in their own gross reserves. If they allow this to happen, however, and to continue indefinitely, they tend to bring about a collapse of the system itself through the gradual weakening of foreigners' confidence in the key currencies.
>
> (Triffin 1961: 67)

The use of the American exchange imbalances as a remedy to world illiquidity would have weakened, in the opinion of Triffin, the reserve position of the USA. The ensuing crisis of confidence in the American currency would thus have worsened the very problem which the adoption of the gold-exchange standard was supposed to solve. Yet, not only was Triffin's pessimistic point of view not shared by the majority of economists, but some of them went as far as to claim that the US deficit related to the increase of the world liquidity was not to be considered as a disequilibrium. On the contrary, they claimed that this particular deficit was caused by the fact that the USA was called upon to play the role of international financial intermediary, and that financial intermediation can perfectly well give rise to a deficit compatible with a fundamental economic equilibrium. 'While the United States has provided the world with liquid dollar assets in the postwar period by capital outflow and aid exceeding its current account surplus, in most years this excess has not reflected a deficit in a sense representing disequilibrium' (Salant 1972: 608).

The idea followed by Despres, Kindleberger and Salant was founded on the observation that no equivalent surplus of the major foreign countries corresponded to the US balance of payments deficit. To have a disequilibrating impact, a deficit must put a strain on the economy, but as long as the US dollar is accepted as key currency world-wide, the American deficit cannot be viewed as a symptom of a dangerous pathology. 'The U.S. balance-of-payments "problem" has never been a direct function of our own balance-of-payments deficits. A real "problem" has occurred for the United States only when surpluses accrued to countries unwilling to hold their reserve increments in dollar form' (Bergsten, in Meier 1982: 103).

The outstanding dollar liabilities greatly exceeding the American gold supply, convertibility was seen as a possible danger even by these economists, but the remedy which they advocated was the suppression of the official link between dollar and gold and not the abolition of the US deficit. 'The crucial flaw in existing arrangements is not really the use of key-currency reserves, as such, but the use as international liquidity of key currencies *precariously pegged to gold on a fractional-reserve basis*. With no official gold reserve whose shrinkage could sap confidence and with no possibility of one-way-option speculation on a possible devaluation of the dollar against gold, the precariousness of today's system would be gone' (Yeager 1963: 175). As Yeager recognized, the abolition of official gold reserves and convertibility would, however, have been insufficient to cure the system if more than one key currency were used as international standard and means of payment. Thus, according to this analysis, the correct solution to world liquidity problems would have required the use of only one key currency: the American dollar. 'Mutual recognition of the role of the dollar holdings would provide the most desirable solution' (Salant 1972: 658).

This radical defence of the US currency as international liquidity can be more clearly understood if we consider that for many years after

Bretton Woods the American balance of current account was mainly positive. During this period, the USA was exporting more goods and services than it was importing, and the growth of foreign-held dollar deposits was due to a repeated deficit of the balance of capital. The net exports of capital, under the form of loans and gifts, were a source of international liquidity particularly needed by a world economy which had to recover from the injuries of World War II. No wonder, therefore, that some economists did not see the US deficit as a threat to equilibrated economic growth, but as a necessary and sound generator of world liquidity.

After the decision officially taken by President Nixon on 15 August 1971 to suspend convertibility of the dollar into gold, the situation rapidily deteriorated. The US balance of trade became negative and the balance of current account decreased almost constantly. The dollar reserves accumulation by foreign official institutions (including Central Banks) and by commercial banks rose from 50 billion at the end of 1970 to 772 billion at the end of 1986, and there are no consistent signs that the process will stop in the near future. Analysing this situation, Triffin reiterated his warnings about the use of the dollar as international currency and claimed, for example in a 1986 paper, that 'if last year's purchase of dollars had decreased by one third this would have led to a 62 billion increase in the official interventions necessary to limit to 20 per cent the depreciation of the dollar relative to the deutsche mark, the yen and the pound' (Triffin 1987: 310, our translation).

Now, a rigorous analysis of facts shows that the use of the dollar for the settlement of international transactions does not depend on the state of the American current account balance. Whether the USA is running a commercial deficit or a surplus, things do not radically change. In both cases, in fact, an IOU of the American banking system is used as international means of payment. An acknowledgment of debt which will never be called upon for redemption is thus given in exchange for real resources. Whether the purchased assets are goods, services or bonds does not matter fundamentally. In each case the USA is given the chance to obtain something for nothing, to purchase without paying, and once it has taken advantage of this opportunity the rest of the world disposes of American IOUs as international liquidity. The following international purchases financed through the use of these acknowledgments of debts will therefore share the same status of 'empty' payments which characterizes foreign American expenditures. A dangerous anomaly is thus introduced in the system of world payments as soon as a country's domestic currency is transformed into an international monetary asset. So, the crucial point is not whether the key currency increases world liquidity through purchases of goods and services or bonds, or through mere gifts. The US would profit more from the purchase of real assets, of course, but the entire world would suffer equally even if dollars were gratuitously offered by the USA In fact, external dollar deposits are identified with real assets, and as soon as they are transferred as final payment of real transactions their entry on the asset side of the exporting country's balance sheet entails an inflationary creation of domestic money, whatever the reasons for the initial American payment. Analogously, the use by LDCs of dollar deposits for their external debt servicing provokes a proportional devaluation of their national currency irrespective of the origin of the deposits.

Finally, the US deficit has a negative overall consequence not simply because it could undermine the general confidence in the dollar but, more fundamentally, because the American currency is given the status of international money. In itself a deficit, either a current account or a financial deficit, is not a sign of disequilibrium. In a sound system of international payments, in fact, money would be perfectly neutral, and deficits of the balance of trade would therefore necessarily be matched by equivalent surpluses in the flows of non-monetary financial bonds of the same country and vice versa. It is only in the actual 'pathological' system that this symmetry is not always respected and that a deficit can be seen as a source of disequilibrium. Yet, the American deficit is an exception precisely because, according to the rules settled at Genoa and Bretton Woods, the USA will never be asked to honour its external debt, so that America can easily finance its deficits by a simple remittance of its own IOUs. Under these circumstances it is not clear why, from the American point of view, the dollar should be made convertible into gold. The effect of convertibility is to put strain on the US monetary authorities, and it is not difficult to understand the reasons which pushed the US government to abandon its commitment to selling gold at a fixed price.

2. A further attempt to increase world liquidity: the creation of Special Drawing Rights

The final decision to abandon convertibility was not taken until August 1971, maybe for fear that it would undermine the psychological confidence in the American currency. In the meantime, as the private demand for gold was increasing and the gold holdings of national monetary authorities declining, several countries started to worry about a possible shortage of international liquidity which would have led to trade restrictions. To face this eventuality a decision was taken at the 1967 IMF meeting in Rio de Janeiro to provide the world economy with a facility based on special drawing rights in the Fund (SDRs). As explained by P-P. Schweitzer, the Managing Director of the Fund, 'These special drawing rights, created, as it were, by a stroke of the pen, will be essentially entries in the books of the Fund' (Schweitzer, in Meier 1982: 90).

The economists' reaction to the decision taken at Rio de Janeiro, and which became effective in January 1970, was not unanimous. Some regarded the creation of SDRs as a revolutionary event in monetary history, others called attention to the opportunity cost related to 1967 agreements, which did not effectively improve the international adjustment mechanism. Even on the analytical definition of SDRs there was no general agreement, though nobody doubted that the SDRs were a new international reserve asset to be ranged along with gold and the US dollar. 'Some people like to think of them as money, others as a form of credit ... The material point is not how they are named but what can be done with them. Their value will derive essentially from the fact that participants will be obliged to accept them when properly transferred and to provide in exchange convertible currency or gold' (Schweitzer, in Meier 1982: 90).

In practice, the new drawing facilities were allocated to the Fund members at specific intervals and according to each country's quota in the IMF. As is clear from point 1, article V, of the Agreement signed at Rio and relative to the right to use SDRs, 'A participant will be entitled, in accordance with the provisions of V, to use special drawing rights to acquire an equivalent amount of a currency convertible in fact. A participant which thus provides currency will receive an equivalent amount of special drawing rights'. Participants were expected to use their SDRs only for balance of payments needs, and not to change the compositions of their reserves, and they had to reconstitute their position in accordance with the amount and the duration of the facilities.

Although it was often claimed that gold had been superseded by the creation of SDRs, at the end of the sixties it was still not clear whether the dollar would be gradually substituted by the new IMF asset or not. 'As matters now stand, the SDR is headed nowhere in particular ... The system is on dead center, waiting for some evolutionary changes to give content to the new directions it is going to take' (Kindleberger 1981: 297). A few years later a major objective of the Fund was declared to be to make the SDR the principal reserve asset of the international monetary system. In 1978 the second Amendment of the Fund's Articles of Agreement introduced some important changes in the use of the SDRs. In particular it was agreed that IMF members would be allowed to use all of their SDR holdings and that they would not be obliged to reacquire them according to any fixed schedule. This change was mainly introduced to stress the reserve asset aspect of the SDRs and to enable countries to increase their use of SDRs as well as to maintain lower levels of their day-to-day SDR holdings. Moreover, to face the large and violent fluctuations occurring under floating exchange rates, mainly 'due to the widespread use of the dollar as a unit of account for international trade, to its large share in the Eurocurrency and other offshore money markets, as well as to its preeminence as a transaction and reserve currency' (Habermeier 1979: 11), it was made possible to settle financial obligations using SDRs which did not have to be first changed into currencies, 'to lend SDRs and to pledge them as security for a loan by another central bank or government' (p.12). The credit mechanism of the Fund, denominated in SDRs and guaranteed by Fund members in SDRs was also substantially expanded and the international reserve assets held as SDR positions rapidily increased.

Now, apart from the practical difficulties relative to the implementation of the amended articles of agreement, it is worth analysing, in purely theoretical terms, if the scheme based on the generalized use of the SDRs is suitable to prevent the asymmetries characterizing the actual system of international payments.

A first, important, feature of the Rio agreements is the belief that world liquidity problems would have to be solved through the creation of a new *reserve asset*. Like US dollars, SDRs were therefore thought to be issued with a positive value irrespective of their being used at the international level and, thus, irrespective of their link with real output. While dollars are issued by the American banking system, however, SDRs are created by an international organism, and this seemed enough to avoid the injustice of letting a country purchase foreign resources by the simple remittance of its own IOUs. Indeed if some countries are still not entirely satisfied with this solution, it is merely because the SDRs are allocated on the basis of quotas, which makes it practically impossible for most LDCs to obtain them without increasing their external debt. If SDRs were really to be used as international money, it should be generally agreed that conversion into national (key) currencies will no longer be required. What is actually a right to draw on national currencies should be transformed into a right on the SDRs account of the Fund which would be used as international means of payment by its simple transfer to the creditor country. Even then, the problem of allocation would not be easily solved. If the traditional drawing rights shared the value of national currencies and could be allocated according to each member's quota, the new international money would possess its own value and there would be no clear cut criteria to determine its distribution among countries. As a matter of fact, it would also not be at all clear why an international institution should be allowed to issue net monetary assets. Of course, having identified the need for world liquidity with the need to increase the amount of internationally available assets, it is not surprising that a solution to the world monetary problems has long been sought on the side of assets creation. Yet, it is astonishing that international monetary authorities so easily accepted the principle according to which one or more countries can purchase foreign riches without incurring any real costs. This is indeed the case of the USA paying in dollars, but also of every country which could pay its net purchases by means of newly created SDRs. In the *IMF Survey* of September 1979, under the point *Wider Uses of SDRs* we can read the following:

A further provision of the amended Articles enables the Fund to 'prescribe' (permit) operations in which participants may use SDRs by agreement without exchanging them directly for currency. During the past year, the Executive Board has taken a number of decisions which permit the use of SDRs as follows:

To settle financial obligations.

To make loans of SDRs, at interest rates and maturities agreed between the parties. Repayment of loans and payment of interest may be made with SDRs.

From this quotation it appears that the 1978 amendments to the Rio Agreements were appropriate to transform the dollar-exchange standard into an SDRs standard. The possibility of settling financial obligations by means of SDRs is a substantial step towards the generalized use of the Fund's facility as international currency. If a country pays for its purchases of foreign resources by means of a loan and if it is allowed to repay the loan with SDRs, it is clear that it could equally well be allowed to use SDRs directly for the settlement of its commercial transactions. Hence, consistently with the new SDRs system, the Fund should create international assets, distribute them among member countries and let these countries use them at their will, as a means of international payments and as an international store of value.

Again, it is difficult to understand why, instead of paying for their foreign purchases through the sale of goods, services and bonds, countries should be allowed to dispose of international monetary assets freely. And, even if this difficulty were ignored, it can hardly be seen how countries could agree on the sum of assets to be created by the Fund and on the way these assets should be allocated among them. Indeed, as facts have shown, the incapacity of the leading industrial countries to agree on the emission of SDRs by the IMF has constantly decreased the use of this international facility and postponed *sine die* the replacement of the US dollar by the SDR.

The refusal of the major industrial countries to agree to issue SDRs is therefore not only a violation of the Articles of Agreement which require all member countries to cooperate with the Fund in making the SDR 'the principal reserve asset in the international monetary system' (Article XXII). It also creates a serious imbalance between those countries that are able to

borrow reserves and those that are compelled to earn their reserve holdings through additional curtailment of imports at a time when the Fund and the World Bank are in full agreement that the most important constraint on the heavily indebted developing countries is a shortage of imported goods.
(Dell 1988: 12-13)

Dell is certainly right in stressing the difficulties faced by the heavily indebted countries in finding the liquidity necessary for the servicing of their external debt. Under the present regime of international payments these countries, whose development requires a substantial growth of their imports, must, on the contrary, expand their exports, and even when this austerity policy is successful they suffer a loss of internal resources because of the double payment mechanism (described in Chapter 4). However, to let countries pay their debts by means of a monetary asset issued by the IMF is no solution. As the Classics clearly pointed out, to be effective the payment of the deficit must be real, and this condition can obviously not be satisfied by a simple entry in a new account of the Fund. In reality, the use of SDRs as *final payment* is not essentially different from the use of dollars made by the USA: in both cases a book-entry of no real value is given in exchange for a positive amount of national resources.

Now, even if it were granted the possibility to create SDRs as positive net assets, the system could not avoid the trap of double debt servicing. In fact, although according to the Rio Agreement and to its successive amendments SDRs are distributed and used only in official transactions, in a generalized SDRs system they would have to be purchased by the banking system of the indebted countries. In the same way as dollar deposits have to be bought even when they have been positively earned through net exports, the use of SDRs as international money would imply their purchase and would therefore be the cause of a loss of the indebted countries' external earnings (and, therefore, of their domestic resources). It is true that under an SDRs standard not only LDCs would be submitted to this disequilibrating purchase. But the fact that even the US dollar would suffer from the same asymmetry relative to the new international currency is not a good enough reason to support the implementation of the Amended Articles of Agreement. A satisfactory solution requires the abolition of the double payment mechanism and not its generalization. The system of international payments must allow every country to pay its external debts only once, independently of whether its currency is thought to be 'weak' or 'strong'. Unfortunately, neither the use of the dollar nor that of the SDRs can fulfil this task.

Let us briefly reconsider the case of a country's external debt servicing under the SDRs standard. The debt being first accumulated by the country's residents (including the state), its repayment implies an expenditure of domestic money by these same residents. Yet, since in our example international payments can only be made using SDRs, this initial expenditure has to be taken over by the official remittance of SDRs to the creditor nations. Supposing that our country were allocated the necessary amount of international currency by the Fund, is there any reason why it should give up what is thought to be a net asset without obtaining an equivalent counterpart? If SDRs were not issued as net assets and if they were used among nations only in their vehicular function, then there would be no reason to buy and sell them. But this is not the case here. Being issued with a positive value *ex hypothesis*, the SDRs are a final means of payment and, as such, they would be sold to the indebted residents, and not simply put at their disposal. The outflow of SDRs from the indebted country takes place because it is assumed that international payments can only be carried out in SDRs. This means that the indebted residents spend part of their domestic income on purchasing the right to use (at the official level) the international asset issued by the Fund. Hence, as happens under the dollar-exchange standard, the SDRs are submitted to a net demand which provokes the loss of the country's foreign earnings and defines the second payment of the external debt; a second payment which could well entail the growth of speculative capital were the SDRs to be allowed to circulate outside the official circuit of Central Banks.

As far as SDRs inflow is concerned, things would also be very similar to what happens under the actual dollar standard. Apart from the initial endowment, SDRs would be earned by countries through surpluses of their balance of payments. In order to obtain the amount of SDRs necessary for the servicing of its external debt a country would have, for example, to increase its commercial exports relative to its imports. The following inflow of SDRs, however, would not define a net demand of the country's domestic currency. Exporters, in fact, would not be paid with part of the national available income, but with an equivalent amount of newly created domestic money. And this would be because the SDRs officially earned would be considered as a net asset and recorded as such in the Central Bank balance sheet. Issued to counterbalance this asset, the new national money would not be bought (and, therefore, also not demanded) in the operation. If we still wanted to express this in terms of supply and demand we would have to say that, the supply of domestic currency being infinitely elastic, no net demand can ever be verified relative to the inflow of SDRs.

The preceding conclusion being also true, *a fortiori* if the SDRs were to be directly obtained from the Fund as initial endowment, it thus follows that the net demand for SDRs characterizing their outflow would not be compensated by a net demand for domestic money when they flowed in. The asymmetry is evident and so is its consequence: the double payment of external debt. As for the inflationary growth of domestic money determined by the use of a net asset as international means of circulation, it is certain that it would occur every time that SDRs were earned through international transactions, as well as in the hypothetical case they were gratuitously allocated by the Fund. In this second case, in fact, it is on the asset side of the Central Bank balance sheet that the SDRs would be recorded and, since this entry would benefit the country, the Central Bank would credit the state by an equivalent amount of domestic money. This book-entry creation of the Central Bank would have an international net asset as its counterpart, not a domestic output, and would therefore define an inflationary increase in the national quantity of money.

Despite our negative conclusions, however, the attempt to transform the dollar standard into an SDRs standard was an important and positive step towards the reform of a system which had proved to be a source of substantial disequilibria. The idea that a true international currency had to be issued by an international institution was certainly sound, and the confinement of this unit to the official level was more than a simple precautionary measure. Yet, even the partial realization of the SDRs project required changes which some of the leading countries were not prepared to endorse. The 79 proposals for the creation of a Substitution Account administered by the Fund which would have accepted 'deposits of foreign exchange from members on a voluntary basis in exchange for an equivalent amount of SDR-denominated claims' (Meier 1982: 248) were never put into practice, and the interest of the USA and of their nine colleagues of the Group of Ten in an internationally issued and administered reserve asset lessened as the international monetary system moved towards a multi-currency reserve system. As results from the *IMF Survey* supplement of July 1985 show, for the countries of the Group of Ten 'the expansion of international financial markets has provided a feasible and efficient source of reserve for many countries, and the emerging multi-currency reserve system has reduced dependence on a single currency in international settlements and reserve holdings' (1985: paras 71-2). The amended articles of the Rio Agreement were, thus, put aside and so was the purpose of placing the SDR at the centre of the international monetary system as the main reserve asset.

3. Floating exchange rates and the international debt problem

After the mid-1960s, fixed exchange rates were increasingly put under pressure and, despite the growing volume of official interventions, the major currencies entered a crisis which was to bring about substantial devaluations and, eventually, the end of the par-value system adopted at Bretton Woods. By March 1973 there was world-wide agreement on the necessity of switching to a system based on floating exchange rates. Yet, the attempt to reach a general agreement on the realignment of the world's major currencies and on the introduction of a margin of exchange rate fluctuation (2.25 per cent above and below the agreed rates) did not succeed, and this was to mark the beginning of a new era of managed floating. In the absence of a single system, countries chose to peg their currencies either against the dollar, the pound, the French franc, the SDR or some weighted basket of currencies. Different blocs appeared with different pegging rules (as, for example, the famous 'snake in the tunnel' characterizing the EEC exchange rate system). The management of floating rates was to be assumed by Central Banks and monetary authorities, which acted mainly through official purchases and sales of foreign currencies, while the academic debate between the advocates of free floating and the supporters of a more or less fixed exchange rates system (like the one based on the target zones principle) is still a source of controversy.

As Fellner recalls, in 1966, 27 economists signed a statement advocating a widening of the limits within which countries were bound to keep the gold value of their currencies, and the introduction of a shiftable parity system. According to these experts, it had 'proved impossible, under the present rules, for many countries to maintain stable prices and high employment levels and at the same time to avoid the imposition of more and more controls on international payments. To achieve these domestic economic goals simultaneously with equilibrium in external payments requires more leeway for variations in exchange rates than exists now' (Fellner *et al.* 1966: 112-13). This point of view was to gain great acceptance among economists, who also claimed that the maintenance of fixed exchange rates would, practically, imply the abandonment of independent control over the domestic money supply. Despite the advantages of the par-value system, it was recognized that 'even when confidence in the permanence of the fixed-rate system allows imbalances to be *financed* with the minimum of fuss and difficulty, inability to induce an equilibrating move in relative costs and prices can allow marked disparities in incomes and wealth to develop, and lead to significant differences in regional unemployment rates and/or large-scale "forced" migration' (Goodhart 1975: 301).

Verified by facts, the impracticability of the fixed exchange rates system seems also to be definitely confirmed by modern monetary analysis. Indeed, Rueff's duplication principle explains the formation of the speculative capital held offshore whose unpredictable movements are bound to exert a strong pressure on exchange rates, a pressure which cannot evidently be neutralized by artificially maintaining fixed the rates of exchange between currencies. On the other hand, the double payment of external debts to which non-key currency countries are constrained by the actual system of international payments manifests itself through a devaluating pressure which, again, cannot be avoided simply by the official adoption of fixed exchange rates. On the contrary, the downward pressure would accumulate and the barrier would sooner or later break down letting the exchange rate collapse at once by as great an amount as the one which would have been gradually observed if exchange rates had been left free to float. 'Can one claim that a longer retention of a fixed parity, *vis-à-vis* other currencies, a less frequent occurrence of parity changes imparts a net benefit to the community? It would seem doubtful. The less frequent are the parity changes, the larger they are likely to be' (Goodhart 1975: 308).

The choice between floating and fixed exchange rates is, in reality, only apparent under the present non-system. Even if constrained to vary within narrow limits or even not to vary at all, exchange rates are so strictly linked with the entire network of international transactions that they cannot be maintained fixed without provoking some equivalent disequilibrium elsewhere. Like a stream of water which, although momentarily stopped by a dam is not in the least neutralized, international expenditures never cease to exert their disruptive action. Hence, under the actual state of affairs, exchange rates are constantly submitted to disequilibrating forces which make them essentially unstable. By choosing to maintain fixed their exchange rate, a country is therefore simply switching from one disequilibrium to another (such as the one existing between official and black market prices) which is but another form of uncontrolled floating.

In the light of our analysis the decision to install a new exchange rate system based on managed floating can hardly be seen as a step towards the solution of the problems posed by international payments. The case of external debt servicing is symptomatic. The double payment to which, say Mexico, is constrained is neither disposed of by maintaining the exchange rate of the peso officially fixed nor by letting it float. In both cases, in fact, Mexico's external debt payments are subjected to an asymmetry which inevitably leads to the country's partial loss of internal resources and to its subsequently incurring a new debt. Were the peso to be held fixed despite increasing devaluation pressures, Mexico would either have to borrow the foreign currencies needed for the servicing of its debt on the exchange market, an operation which would obviously increase its external debt, or sell its domestic resources at an increasingly discounted price suffering, thus, an ever greater loss of internal saving which defines, in real terms, a growth of its foreign debt. Hence, far from being a viable alternative, letting the peso float against the dollar is simply to recognize that Mexico can pay its external debt only by weakening its capacity for economic development. Having serviced its debt, Mexico will still be as much indebted in terms of pesos (because of the devaluation of the peso against the dollar) and, therefore, will have to find the same amount of internal resources as before just to keep its debt (interest included) constant. Finally, free or managed floating systems are no solution to the debt crisis which, by preventing development and growth of the LDCs also hampers growth in the developed countries and threatens the functioning of the entire world economy.

Though the external debt of developing countries has never ceased to increase, it would be wrong to credit the floating exchange rates system for this dramatic situation. The debt crisis is not the effect of exchange rates instability, but part of its own definition. In other words, the debt crisis manifests itself through fluctuations in the exchange rates. Were the system of international payments compatible with the neutral servicing of external debts (as well as with the neutral working of international money), exchange rates would remain stable, without there being any need for the official re-equilibrating intervention of the monetary authorities. Unfortunately this is not so. The international use of the dollar is in no way 'neutral' and its net asset definition makes it an object of exchange whose price varies according to the law of supply and demand. This confusion between money and assets leads to the non-payment of American foreign purchases, and to the forced purchase of dollars by indebted countries. And it is this evident asymmetry which is the fundamental source of the serious threat to the viability of the international banking system constituted by the actual debt crisis.

If it is true, as it is, that 'this situation encompasses all countries and pervades all sectors and aspects of the world economy' and that 'it is potentially disruptive to the world economy' (Bernal 1987: 155), a means has to be found to dispose of this asymmetry definitively. To speak of a more effective control over monetary fluctuations is simply not enough. To avoid depreciation, the intervention of monetary authorities is required, but this means first that countries should have huge amounts of international reserve assets at their disposal (which LDCs certainly do not have) and, second, that they should be prepared to lose all their foreign reserves simply in order to defend an exchange rate which will continue to undergo devaluating pressures. The managing of exchange rates is, thus, an illusory alternative for LDCs, and so is the adoption of target zones, which are but a revised version of the Bretton Woods system (when zones are narrow and adjustment difficult) or an incentive for private speculators (when they are too broad and adjustment too easy).

As is stressed by Sprinkel 'For target zones to be meaningful, they must imply some commitment to adjust domestic economic policies in order to keep exchange rates within the zones. However, if domestic policies are sufficiently compatible and external shocks sufficiently restrained, there should be little need for a target zone system' (Sprinkel 1986: 71). This clearly means that exchange rate fluctuations are seen as the result of divergent economic policies and strong external shocks. Consistent with this point of view, indebted countries are being asked to conform their economic policies to the strict rules worked out by the IMF experts in the attempt to control their domestic money supply (via deficit spending) and to increase their exports. As it is, however, even if these countries were able to increase their exports relative to their imports, they would still be bound to purchase the foreign currencies necessary to their debt servicing and, whatever the level of their domestic money supply, this purchase would have a negative impact on the exchange rate of their national currencies. Depreciating pressures, therefore, are not simply the effect of some monetary mismanagement, but of the way international transactions have to be carried out under the dollar (or the key currency) standard. Free floating, target zones, managed floating and fixed parity are but empirical attempts to solve a problem which is not conjunctural and does not depend on behavioural variables. External debts are paid twice irrespective of the agents' behaviour, and it is thus vain to look at the microeconomic level for a solution to the debt crisis.

A last argument requires some further considerations. Balance of payments disequilibria are generally considered to be the main pathology of our international monetary system. Cooperation between countries is therefore often seen as an essential instrument to cure the world monetary system, and in this context the compatibility between monetary and fiscal national policies is regarded as one of the essential goals of international economics. Of course, adjustment obligations of surplus and deficit countries cannot be expected to be symmetrical, their own situation often being rather different if not altogether opposed. Thus, the set of remedies would have to be worked out very carefully, taking into account as much as possible the particular needs of each country. 'The group of countries needs to reach a realistic consensus on the above points, that is, rough targets for employment, growth, and the rate of price increase for the group as a whole. If such a consensus could be reached, it might be possible to define the adjustment obligations of deficit and surplus countries by relation to the rates of utilization and of price change in those countries' (Tobin 1966: 205). Objective differences and conflicting interests between economic partners notwithstanding, the question of international cooperation is given a central role in the search for monetary stability. Yet, the actual problems of world monetary order cannot be reduced to a matter of goodwill cooperation.

Once it has been clearly understood that the origin of the crisis lies within the system of international payments, the various solutions proposed in the last years appear to be mere palliatives with no real impact on the world monetary disorder. Limiting debt service, debt cancellation, rescheduling or restructuring pertain to this category of pragmatic attempts designed to cope with the most disturbing symptoms of the crisis but totally incapable of curing the disease. On the same level several other solutions have been put forth which do not imply a substantial reform of the system of international payments derived from the conferences of Genoa and Bretton Woods. Even the formal substitution of a multiple currency standard to the dollar standard, advocated by Lutz, Roosa, Posthuma and other bankers and economists, does not imply a radical change of the system, which would continue to suffer from the same shortcomings characterizing the actual non-system. It is not by allowing other countries besides the USA to pay for their foreign purchases by a mere stroke of the pen that the problems of international payments are bound to be solved. Likewise, it is not by decreasing their international transactions that countries are going to develop their economies and solve the debt crisis. New solutions are required, and a privileged way to get to them is to analyse critically the most important proposals of reform propounded since Bretton Woods.

However, before starting this critical investigation let us spend just a few words on clarifying the link existing between world liquidity and international capital.

4. International liquidity and offshore capital accumulation

In a pure dollar exchange system, world liquidities are increased through US external deficits, and the growth of the eurodollar market defines the rate of accumulation of international, speculative capital. Analogously, in a multiple currency standard system the increase of world liquidities is characterized by a multiplication of national liabilities consolidated as eurocurrencies. The link between offshore capital accumulation and international liquidity seems therefore to be of a very strict nature. And this impression is further confirmed by the observation that even the use of SDRs and other IMF facilities increases the available amount of speculative capital. The decisive argument is that what is used as international means of payment, be it dollar, mark, yen, SDR, CRU or ECU, is supposed to be a net asset. Thus, from a net asset point of view, SDRs and eurocurrencies are on the same level. They are both thought to define a positive value held internationally, and there are no reasons *a priori* why they should not both be used for speculative purposes. In fact, world reserves consist of SDRs as well as of eurocurrencies and gold, and the growth of these respective parts shows that the offshore accumulation of key currencies has never stopped increasing both in absolute terms and relative to the increase of other 'official' reserve assets.

As is shown by the enormous amount of euromonies accumulated abroad, one of the major problems of the actual monetary system is caused by the existence of this mass of pathological, speculative capital and not by the danger of it being insufficient for the financing of international transactions. The world liquidity problem is thus ill founded. Not only is it anachronistic to worry about a shortage of international liquidity, but it should also be evident that the main difficulties arise precisely from the fact that 'empty' liabilities are available for world wide speculation. If it is certain that world transactions require the use of an international 'wheel of circulation', it is not at all proven that this monetary 'vehicle' has to be assimilated to a net asset which can be positively earned and accumulated. The actual system of international payments is based on the assumption that currencies are essentially similar to real goods; yet there are no a priori reasons to believe in the axiomatic nature of this hypothesis, which we shall therefore rigorously test in the following pages.

Chapter Seven

Alternative Solutions to World Monetary Disorder and their Impact on the International Debt Problem

1. The Triffin plan: the rejection of the key currency system

Triffin is the economist who has most consistently denounced 'the vulnerability of a world monetary system whose operation becomes increasingly dependent on one or a few *national* currencies as major components of *international* monetary reserves' (Triffin 1961: 19). The Belgian economist sees a 'vicious circle' in the working of the gold-exchange standard since the use of one (or a few) national currency (ies) as world reserve inevitably weakens the reserve position of the country whose money is chosen as international standard. As we have already seen, a worsening of the liquidity problem would then be the unavoidable and paradoxical result of a system worked out in order to solve this very problem. To remove this difficulty, Triffin maintains that the use of national currencies as international reserves has to be replaced by the use of international credit money.

Since in its simplest form the gold-exchange standard is a system where key currencies are used instead of gold to settle international transactions, Triffin argues for its substantial reform. According to his plan, key currencies should be gradually substituted by IMF balances until, eventually, IMF deposits would become the unique international currency. Before reaching this final stage, Fund balances would have to be granted full convertibility into any currency, and Fund lending would have to be guaranteed through a sufficient accumulation of gold reserves. Yet these requirements are not essential to Triffin's plan but have been retained mainly for psychological reasons ('as a harmless example of cultural lag and as an inexpensive subsidy for the production of something that the world wants but does not need' (Altman 1963: 121), and can be omitted without modifying the core of his message.

It is true that several economists did not share this point of view, and maintained that the plan was too closely based on gold to be considered a true alternative to the gold-exchange standard. 'This is indeed the most fundamental objection to the Triffin plan: that it does not in fact remove the central weakness of the gold-exchange standard, which is inherent in the freedom of holders of reserve currency to demand conversion of their holdings into gold, but instead internationalizes the problem by transferring it to the International Monetary Fund'

(Johnson 1963: 388). However, as is clearly pointed out by Johnson himself, the Triffin plan can also be seen as a decisive step 'towards the gradual international demonetization of gold in favor of the use of Fund deposits as the ultimate international reserve money' (p.388). Though Triffin is not always clear-cut about the role which gold and key currencies should respectively play in his plan, we shall consider here only the new system in its logical extension to its most revolutionary final form. Leaving aside every practical difficulty relative to the implementation of the plan, we shall suppose that, through general agreement, countries have resolved to transfer their international reserve assets to the Fund. The IMF would thus be converted into an international Central Bank, and world transactions would be carried out by means of the new international money issued by the expanded Fund in the form of deposits. According to Triffin's plan, the creation of the new world currency by the XIMF would follow the same rules applying to the creation of domestic currency by national central banks. In particular, the XIMF would be allowed to expand world reserves through loans and open market purchases of securities. Now, both these operations are considered inflationary since, according to the traditional monetary approach, an increase in international liquidity when countries do not suffer a deflationary shortage of domestic liquidity entails a disequilibrating growth in the domestic money supply. It is thus inferred that the implementation of the Triffin plan would have wide inflationary effects, for its aim is to increase the trade capacity of deficit countries by lending them newly issued XIMF deposits. Being able to import more, these countries would provoke an equivalent surplus in other countries, which would therefore experience an inflationary increase in their national currencies. Yeager explains this process by underlining its 'three interrelated aspects: (1) net exports and thus withdrawal of real goods and services from the home economy; (2) expansionary operation of the "foreign-trade multiplier"; and (3) creation of new domestic money as the authorities absorb the local residents' surplus earnings of foreign exchange to keep exchange rates pegged' (Yeager 1963: 170).

The third aspect stressed by Yeager is particularly significant for our analysis. It clearly shows that Triffin's bancor is conceived as a net asset, issued by the XIMF in exchange for some other assets (gold, key currencies, securities or bonds), and whose purchasing power is essentially determined by the purchasing power of the national currencies to which it is tied. The earnings of bancor would thus be equivalent to the earnings of foreign exchange even if, under the new system, the settlement of international transactions were only made by the transfer of deposits at the XIMF. The central bank of the country whose residents are being paid would be credited by a deposit at the XIMF and, on the basis of this deposit it would create an equivalent amount of domestic money to the benefit of its customers (the residents to which the external payment is addressed). International and national monetary circuits would, thus, be as strictly connected as they are under the dollar-exchange standard.

Given this situation, the problems relative to the external debt servicing would either be reproduced or generalized but not solved by the Triffin plan. One of its features, in fact, is the possibility given to every member country to draw on its Fund deposit account in any currency whatsoever. 'Any loan granted by the Fund to a member would be credited to its Fund deposit account, and the member could draw on this account in any currency whatsoever without having to make any "representation" that it needs it to make payments in that particular currency' (Triffin 1961: 117). This means, for example, that an indebted country could choose to pay its external debt by drawing dollars on its Fund account. By doing so, however, the country would simultaneously reduce its external debt and its reserves with the Fund. The payment of the debt would be perfectly matched by the loss of international reserves and, globally, the operation would even be negative since this loss would have to be added to the loss of national income resulting from the payment made by the indebted residents. On the whole, no advantage would result from the reduction of the country's Fund deposits, and after the external debt servicing the entire nation would find itself in a much worse situation than beforehand precisely because of the reduction in the amount of domestic income available.

Now, another possibility is offered to the indebted country. Suppose international transactions were to be settled only by means of XIMF deposits. In this case the external debt would be serviced either by reducing the country's XIMF deposits, by the transfer of Fund deposits obtained through a new loan, or by the transfer of bancors earned through net exports. Obviously, it is in this last case that the payment of the debt seems to have the best chance of success. It is true that the country has to give away a certain amount of real resources (corresponding to its net commercial exports), but this is apparently the only sacrifice required in order to reduce its external debt. Yet, unfortunately this is not so. Indebted residents and countries, in fact, would both be asked to pay the debt previously contracted. Carried out in domestic currency, the first payment would be made by the owners of the debt, while the second would be borne by the whole country through a devaluating pressure on its currency. The reasons for this second payment are well known; let us, therefore, simply remind the reader that the XIMF deposits earned through the country's net external sales have to be bought if they are to be used for debt servicing purposes. When bancors enter a national banking system they do not exert any pressure on the country's domestic money (which, being immediately created on the basis of the XIMF deposits, shows here an infinite elasticity of supply); on the contrary, when they are bought to pay the external debt their net demand provokes a rise in their value relative to the value of domestic money.

If the Triffin plan were so implemented as to guarantee the gold value of the XIMF deposit liabilities and the gold value of its assets, the devaluation could maybe be stopped, but the price to be paid would be so high (a domestic loss of the gold reserves of the XIMF) that the entire system would collapse. Hence, the choice appears to be limited to two alternatives. Either the exchange rate between bancor and national currencies is maintained fixed, in which case the disequilibrating pressures due to the external debt servicing would be neutralized by the XIMF at the expense of all the state members, or the exchange rate is left free to float, in which case the indebted countries would be put in the same situation as under the actual system of international payments and would have to pay their external debt both in kind (through their exports) and monetarily (through the devaluation of their domestic currency).

The transformation of traditional world reserves into XIMF deposits is certainly an interesting attempt to avoid the ills of the dollar-exchange standard, yet the Triffin plan does not succeed in giving an entirely new answer to the problems which hamper the actual system. Following Johnson we can identify one of the reasons for this lack of success in the fact that it is 'something of a halfway house between the gold-exchange standard and the establishment of a genuine international credit currency entailing the demonetization of gold' (Johnson 1963: 388). Another reason is the net asset definition of the bancor which, instead of allowing for the establishment of a genuine international credit currency, creates a dangerous confusion between national currencies, real output and international money. Triffin's complaint about the serious flaws of the actual system of international payments still remains as does the necessity of finding a satisfactory remedy to a situation of generalized disease which has its most evident symptom in the debt crisis.

2. The Stamp plan

Propounded by Sir Maxwell Stamp, a former United Kingdom Director of the International Monetary Fund, this plan attempts 'to kill two birds with one stone' (Stamp 1963: 81), i.e. to aid underdeveloped countries while curing international liquidity shortage. In short, Stamp proposed the creation of Fund certificates which would have enabled their final holders to exchange them into the currency of any member country and which would have been used, particularly by underdeveloped countries, to finance international transactions. Issued by the Fund, these certificates would have been allocated, by an aid coordinating agency, to the countries most in need of external resources, either as gifts — as in the first version of the plan — or as loans ('the second modification to the original scheme might be that instead of being given away to the underdeveloped countries, the Fund certificates or Fund credit would be lent' (Stamp: 1963: 87)).

The Stamp plan was seriously criticized, mainly for its inflationary character and for its lack of precision about the convertibility of the Fund certificates by the Fund itself. On this last point, for instance, Johnson maintained that, had they not been made convertible, the countries would have soon abandoned them as reserve currency. 'In short, if the certificates are not intended to be convertible into gold at the Fund, their issue would amount to the creation of a special kind of international credit currency with restricted acceptability; if they are intended to be convertible, their issue would amount to disposal of part of the Fund's liquid assets' (Johnson 1963: 381). Yet, Stamp's propositions cannot be so easily dismissed. It is true that he considered the Fund certificates as a new net asset and identified their emission with the creation of extra purchasing power on an international scale. And it is correct, therefore, to claim that his plan was intrinsically inflationary. But it is also true that, by using his Fund certificates the automatic lending of the surplus to the deficit countries would have taken place. 'The certificates would end up with the countries which are in over-all surplus — which, therefore, would have automatically lent part of that surplus to the rest of the world' (Stamp 1963: 81). Under the scheme proposed by Stamp, foreign purchases by underdeveloped countries would not depend on the goodwill of their partners. Exporting real resources to the LDCs, in fact, the rest of the world would also provide them with the sum of international currency necessary for their payment.

The automatic lending realized through the plan is obviously different from the aid which could be provided by grants from the surplus countries, and it is of great interest to note that Stamp hoped to achieve this through the use of an international money which was neither issued by a sovereign State nor backed by gold. Answering his critics, he refuted, in fact, the point of view of 'those who are unable to imagine a money which is not issued by a sovereign state or "backed" in some mysterious way by gold or silver' (Stamp 1963: 86). Had he been extremely rigorous, he would have avoided any recourse to convertibility and tried to build a plan entirely based on the classical idea of a pure vehicular money. Unfortunately the world was not prepared to abandon the traditional conception of international money as reserve asset, and considered the non-convertible fund certificates as a fictitious kind of international reserve currency with no future.

Hence, in the revised version of his plan, Stamp introduced some radical changes which transformed the Fund certificates into international monetary assets. 'The country holding the certificates would have a real and valuable asset guaranteed by the Fund and not merely depending on the willingness of other countries to accept it' (Stamp 1963: 89). Issued as net assets, the Fund certificates would not fundamentally differ, however, from the domestic currencies with which they would be exchanged on request. As we have pointed out in our critical appraisal of the Triffin plan, compared to the actual situation where the great majority of countries cannot pay for their imports in their national currency, the use of Fund certificates (or bancor) seems indeed to be much more neutral. In reality, the solution advocated by Stamp shares the same theoretical shortcomings as the one endorsed by the Yale economist. In particular, the payment of the external debt would be possible only at the price of an equivalent loss of internal resources even if it were carried out through the automatic lending of surplus countries.

Let us investigate this last point.

Under the Stamp plan, Fund certificates would be lent to underdeveloped countries to finance their net purchases of foreign goods, and would end up increasing the international reserves of surplus countries, so that the LDCs' net imports would effectively be financed by the net exports of this last group of countries. Now, this train of events would essentially be the same if the LDCs were to use the Fund certificates to pay their external debt. In this case the rest of the world would be lending the financial resources necessary to the debt servicing, which is obviously not a self-defeating operation since the lending agents would not necessarily be the same as those whose credit is being paid. This is even more evident if we consider that, in our example, it can as well be said that the LDCs are paying their external debt with part of their exports and using the new loan to increase their commercial imports. In both cases, a debt is paid and the equality between exports and imports is maintained through an automatic loan by the surplus countries. What we have to analyse, therefore, is whether the use of Fund certificates would allow LDCs to pay their external debt without incurring the loss of internal resources characterizing the actual non-system of international payments.

The crucial point is relative to the nature of the Fund certificates. Would they be issued already endowed with positive purchasing power or not? Stamp's answer to this question is direct: the Fund would create credit and its certificates would therefore be issued as net assets. 'My original plan proposed to use the credit created by the Fund to provide additional purchasing power for the underdeveloped countries: they would spend the "credit" in the developed countries who would expand their exports to improve their balance of trade'

(Stamp 1963: 85). Now, the fact that Fund certificates would be given the same status which is nowadays attributed to the dollar would have important consequences for the countries receiving them as loans.

Let us consider any one of them, Mexico for example. The inflow of Fund certificates necessary for the servicing of the Mexican external debt would provoke, as a necessary consequence of the confusion between national and international monetary circuits, an equivalent creation of domestic currency. This new sum of national money would quite naturally be added to the money created as a counterpart of the current Mexican output, whose price would therefore be correspondingly increased. In particular, if Mexico were to borrow them up to an amount of say x millions in order to service its external debt without decreasing its imports, it would incur a new debt of twice as much, that is of 2x millions instead of the x millions corresponding to the initial loan. The reason for this further indebtedness is the devaluating pressure exerted on the exchange market by the forced purchase of the asset used as international vehicular money. The downward pressure on the peso, in fact, would nullify the external gain that Mexico would realize as counterpart of its debt, and push the country into borrowing a new amount of Fund certificates equivalent to that first borrowed by its residents. As this anomaly inherent in external debt servicing is being further analysed in the second part of the book, let us simply show here how it can be linked to the inflationary increase in internal prices.

Suppose current output to be equal to 10 million pesos, and let us put the exchange rate between pesos and Fund certificates at the level of 1 peso for 1 Fund certificate. If the Mexican external debt servicing amounted to 2 million pesos, the payment of the Mexican exports necessary for the servicing of its external debt would have to be equal to 2 million. Yet, this loan would cause the creation of an equivalent amount of national currency, which would inflate the domestic money supply and make the measure (in terms of prices) of current output grow from 10 to 12 million pesos. In the Mexican banking system we would have the following entries (See Table 7.1). The domestic currency created as a counterpart of the Fund certificates obtained through commercial exports would be the source of an inflationary growth of internal prices and of new, inflationary, profits. These profits, however, would be sent abroad through the external debt servicing. In fact, the payment of the external debt carried out by Mexican debtors would decrease the amount of domestic income available within Mexico, whose current output could no longer be totally purchased. In book entry terms the situation would be as follows (See Table 7.2). Given the insufficient level of domestic income, Mexico would thus have to contract a new loan in order to replace the income lost servicing its external debt (See Table 7.3). The new loan is the measure of the national resources lost by Mexico to the profit of the rest of the world. To state this in another way, analysis shows that by paying its external debts Mexico would send abroad part of its current income, and it is with this income that the rest of the world would partly finance its Mexican imports. In our example, where commercial imports are equal to exports, Mexico would get only x − 2 in exchange for its exports of x, which clearly shows that the payment of the external debt would be carried out both in money (2 million of Fund certificates) and in kind (the national output given for nothing to the rest of the world). Let us repeat this. In paying their external debt the indebted Mexican residents (including the state) would send abroad 2 million of Fund certificates and an equivalent amount of national income which the rest of the world would use for the purchase of Mexican output. Thus, the Mexican exports would be only partially paid by the rest of the world, the difference being covered by Mexico through its loss of internal savings.

Table 7.1

Mexican banking system

Liabilities	Assets
(creation) Income holders 2 pesos	Fund certificates \$2
Income holders 10 pesos	Current output 12 pesos

Table 7.2

Mexican banking system

Liabilities	Assets
Income holders 12 pesos	Current output 12 pesos
Fund certificates \$2	Income holders 2 pesos

Finally, the Mexican external debt servicing would have to be paid twice, which means that, having paid its debt, Mexico would find itself more indebted than before, its new, forced, indebtdness being the necessary consequence of the fact that the payment of the debt is nourished by the inflationary profit resulting from the creation of

Table 7.3

Mexican banking system	
Liabilities	Assets
Income holders 10 pesos	Current output 12 pesos
Income holders 2 pesos	New debt $2

domestic money against Fund certificates. Hence, under the Stamp plan the situation would not differ radically from the one which is the mark of the present dollar standard system.

Today indebted countries cannot avoid the double payment of their debt, which results in the loss of their external incomes and, consequently, in the incurring of a new debt. When exports equal imports, as in the case we have been analysing here, the payment of the debt takes place through an external loan of dollars and implies both an inflationary increase in domestic prices (caused by the creation of national money against dollars), and a loss of internal resources which has to be compensated by a new loan. Whether made by means of dollars or Fund certificates, the payment of the external debt leads, therefore, to the same paradoxical result: the logical impossibility of debt servicing. Yet, the observations relative to the Triffin plan apply equally well here. In particular, the attempt to replace the dollar with an international currency issued by the XIMF deserves our greatest attention. Opposing 'those who are unable to imagine a money which is not issued by a sovereign state or "backed" in some mysterious way by gold or silver' (Stamp 1963: 86), Stamp is, in fact, showing the way towards a new solution which, although still defective, could eventually prove suitable for dealing with the problems posed by international monetary transactions.

3. From the privatization of official reserves to the creation of an international currency

3.1. *Avoiding official reserves*

Following the publication of the Triffin plan several other alternative solutions to the world crisis were proposed. Among them, it is worth remembering one of the propositions advanced by Yeager, which consisted in 'relying exclusively on privately owned foreign exchange reserves' (Yeager 1963: 179). According to the American economist, the complete privatization of both the national and the international monetary systems would entail numerous advantages, like preventing the concentration in a few hands of sizeable percentages of particular currencies, allowing for the multiplicity of key currencies and lessening the impact of speculation over the international monetary system.

Now, like the majority of his fellow economists, Yeager considers money as being essentially analogous to goods. 'Foreign exchange even contrasts favorably with flour, paint, salt, and other ordinary commodities in that large amounts of it could, at a price, be "produced" quickly if necessary' (p.180). Being made equivalent to real assets, money would thus be purchased 'at some price, a price at which its total quantities supplied and demanded were equal' (p.180). Yet, what strikes one in Yeager's proposals is that, although endowed with a positive purchasing power, money can be freely issued to meet an increase in foreign demand, thus allowing for the cost free purchase of goods by the issuing country. 'The opportunity to create additional domestic money to meet the intensified foreign demand for balances of it would allow the country to acquire real goods and services on indefinite loan at zero or low interest from the foreign holders of its money or near-moneys' (p.181). Generally, in Yeager's plan countries would all be theoretically granted the possibility of paying for their real imports with their own money. These 'payments' would be made, therefore, by sending abroad a mere acknowledgment of debt, which would amount to giving countries the absurd privilege of paying by getting indebted. It is obvious that in such circumstances it would be extremely difficult (not to say impossible) to endorse a system in which every economic agent (country) can pay by creating money. What Yeager does not seem to have understood is that the fundamental problem is how to allow for the effective payment of international transactions, and not how to generalize a system of non-payments.

3.2. *The XIMF as international lender of last resort*

Another alternative proposal which was overtly supported by several economists was based on the creation of a new IMF operating as an international Central Bank. For example, in his contribution James Angell argued for the implementation of a system derived from the Triffin plan in which the IMF would have played a central role as international lender of last resort. The XIMF was, in fact, to issue its own deposit balances in favour of each member, and member countries were to agree to accept titles to IMF deposits as payment for their foreign sales. Created by the XIMF on the basis of each member quota, the new deposits would have been exchangeable against any national currency at a fixed (though adjustable) rate, and through their use the XIMF should have been able to provide substantial assistance to less advanced countries.

Let us note, first, that the main shortcoming of this attempt to solve the problems of international payments through the use of international credit is related, yet again, to the possibility of the XIMF creating a net monetary asset. Within a national monetary system it is already very problematical to accept the idea that banks can create net assets. Yet, money is not issued for the sake of it, but in order to be associated with current output. The purchasing power of national money can therefore be explained as soon as production is taken into account. On the international level, however, no international production can be invoked to justify the presence of positive purchasing power. How, then, could the XIMF issue money as a net asset? The only plausible answer seems to be that XIMF deposits are created in exchange for the members' international reserves with the Fund. The purchasing power of the new deposits would therefore be derived from the purchasing power of the assets with which they are exchanged. Unfortunately, this answer cannot be accepted, since it does not account for the fact, so clearly exposed by Rueff, that outside their own national monetary system national currencies exist only as duplicata of zero value. Hence, it is evident that, once abroad, national currencies cannot transfer to the XIMF deposits a purchasing power of which they are totally lacking.

None the less, following the traditional point of view, Angell defined the XIMF deposits as net assets exchangeable against any national currency of member states. Accordingly, international money and national currencies were perceived as being positive assets which could equally well constitute part of the central monetary reserves of every country. Now, the net asset definition of XIMF deposits was introduced by Angell within a context where no distinction is drawn, either theoretically or empirically, between national and international monetary circuits. The door was therefore opened on a whole series of difficulties which were only partly perceived by Angell. In fact, he mainly worried about the excessive holdings by the XIMF of a member's currency, and proposed a whole host of sanctions which should have given the Fund the means to deal with this disruptive situation. What he did not see, however, is that the confusion between the two circuits would lead to the inflationary creation of domestic money against XIMF deposits, and create the premises for the logical impossibility of external debt servicing.

Without repeating our previous analysis, let us simply note that even Angell's attempt to provide the underdeveloped countries with special provisions of XIMF deposits would not contribute to the solution of the crisis of international payments. The scheme propounded by Angell envisaged the lending, by developed countries (*A*) to less advanced countries (*B*) via the XIMF. The loan to *B* would have to be made in XIMF deposits, and not directly in *A*'s national currency (*a*), which would be lent by *A* to the XIMF. 'The principal importers A of member B's primary exports to the group A would make interest-free loans of their own currencies to the IMF (*not* to B) ... The IMF would then create an equivalent amount of its own deposit balances, and would lend them (also interest-free) to B against the security of B's own currency' (Angell 1963: 106). We could represent this scheme as in the Figure 7.1. At first sight, this seems to be an interesting model which, apparently, does not require the exchange between national currencies and XIMF deposits. And even the repayment of *A*'s loan seems not to imply any such exchange, since it would occur only in so far as *B* realized a surplus in XIMF deposits. 'Repayment of the IMF loans should, of course, be a first charge on any subsequent increase in B's export proceeds above some stated figure' (Angell 1963: 106). In reality, however, this scheme would generalize instead of solving the problems of external debt servicing. If every country is given the chance to change part of its domestic currency into XIMF deposits, they would all be allowed to share the privilege of paying with a mere IOU. Today only a few countries can pay their foreign purchases through the remittance of their acknowledgment of debt, tomorrow every country could do so through the intermediary of the XIMF. Moreover, as we have previously shown, the recording of XIMF deposits earned through commercial exports in the book entry of *B*'s central bank provokes the creation of an equivalent amount of domestic money and the subsequent appearance of an inflationary profit which, instead of being reabsorbed at the moment the country pays its external debt, defines the amount of internal resources lost by the country precisely because of its external debt servicing.

Figure 7.1

Despite the interesting attempt to create a correspondence between commercial imports and external loans, Angell's plan does not provide the theoretical framework required for the satisfactory solution of the world debt crisis. Is one of the alternatives mentioned by F. A. Lutz going to prove to be better equipped to deal with this serious problem?

3.3. *The automatic lending of surplus countries*

In a paper originally published as no. 41 of the *Essays in International Finance* (Princeton University 1963), Lutz rejected as excessively inflationary a solution which deserves some consideration. In his own words, this solution consisted of 'widening the foreign borrowing potential of countries by making provisions for countries with surpluses in their balances of payments to lend to those with deficits' (Lutz 1963: 240). The lending from surplus to deficit countries would have occurred automatically through the intermediation of an international institution which would have acted as the bank of central banks. 'Suppose an international institution were created similar to the defunct European Payments Union, but on a world-wide basis. All the surplus countries would "deposit" their surpluses with this institution, while all the deficit countries would run into debt with it to the extent of their deficits' (p.241). Suppose every international transaction were paid by means of an international currency (bancor) issued by the XIMF. Deficit countries would pay their external partners in bancors which would immediately define a positive deposit with the Fund. The surplus countries, the owners of this deposit, would thus be the real lenders, and the deficit countries would find themselves indebted towards the XIMF. Now, two questions can be asked at this stage of the argument, namely: is this a 'system of unlimited credit', and is it not already true in the actual system that surplus countries are automatically lending to deficit countries?

As for the first question, the answer depends on whether bancors are supposed to be issued as net assets by the XIMF or not. If it is the case, then Lutz would be right in pointing to its inflationary nature. Things would radically change, however, if bancors were conceived as pure 'empty' vehicles. The automatic lending by surplus countries would not require the creation of any international credit by the Fund, and would define the sale of financial assets (shares or bonds) by the deficit countries. Moreover, if the circuit of bancors were kept separate from the circuit of national currencies their entry on the asset side of the central banks' balance sheets would no longer entail the creation of domestic money as well as subsequent inflation. Lutz's objection that each country would try to take advantage of the system and have its deficit covered by the surplus of the other countries can be easily disposed of. In fact, it is simply not true that every country would be interested in running a current account surplus. LDCs need to increase their commercial imports as much as they can, and it is certain that industrial countries would not mind increasing their exports of goods and services. In so doing, they would also increase their purchase of financial assets from the LDCs, which would therefore benefit from a growing external investment. On the other hand, it is obvious that deficit increases would not be arbitrarily unlimited since they would depend on the decisions taken by the economic agents of each set of countries.

Let us now analyse the second question.

In his paper, Lutz maintained that the traditional system of international payments was characterized by the simultaneous presence of two sorts of lending, that of the 'neutral' type and that which creates international reserves for the lender. The lending of surplus countries through the IMF would pertain to the first category. Hence, Lutz considered as neutral a system in which the borrowing potentials of deficit countries could be increased by the automatic lending of surplus countries. The idea is of particular interest since it suggests the possibility of a system which would work perfectly well without requiring any international reserve whatsoever. As we already know, however, Lutz did not endorse this solution for fear that it could have been the cause of an inflationary policy of unlimited credit. But, if the automatic lending to deficit countries were to occur through the IMF creation of credit (instead of a mere 'vehicular' money), then world reserves would be increased to the benefit of surplus countries, and the system would obviously not be of Lutz's neutral type. We are led, thus, to the conclusion that under the present currency exchange standard the IMF lending does not pertain to Lutz's first category of lending. It is only if a new IMF were to channel the operation through the creation and use of an international *nominal* money that we would have a truly neutral system. Since the XIMF would no longer issue credit, it would also no longer add to international reserves, and the deposit with the XIMF earned by the surplus countries would simply define the deficit countries' sales of bonds, and not an additional amount of monetary assets.

As for the second category of lending, Lutz shows that a few countries, like the United States, benefit from the particular status granted to their currency and, although running a substantial commercial deficit, can additionally increase their borrowing potentials through the willingness of other countries to lend to them by accumulating key currencies balances. 'The United States, however, has in addition a borrowing potential which others do not have. It consists in the willingness of other countries to acquire dollar balances; and the acquisition of such balances is representative of the second type of lending, namely, that which creates international reserves for the lender' (p.242). Following Lutz, let us consider the American case. In the present system the USA pays for its commercial imports by sending dollars to the rest of the world. And, given the relationship existing between the growth of the American current account deficit and the accumulation of externally held dollars (eurodollars), it is easy to see that the USA does not need any explicit lending from the surplus countries. When the USA pays its net commercial imports in dollars, it does not sell any non-monetary financial asset to the rest of the world, and cannot be defined, therefore, as being a net borrower. It is true that surplus countries become the owners of dollar deposits, but it is also true that they will consider themselves as having been fully paid at the instant the accounts have been credited in dollars (and not in real shares or bonds).

Let us take the example of the USA paying its imports from country *A*. Book keeping entries relative to this payment would be as seen in Table 7.4. The payment by the American banking system to country *A* defines a simultaneous deposit by *A* into the US banks. Yet *A* does not receive any financial good from the USA, which does not allow us to conclude that a positive investment by *A* in the American economy has taken place. Moreover, if we remember that the dollars held offshore are the duplicata of those deposited with the US banking system, it becomes evident that surplus countries are not lending dollars to the USA but to international, speculative, capital. Under the present non-system the USA is not a net importer because the rest of the world is willing to lend to it, but because it is willing to be paid by the simple stroke of a pen. Hence, the dollar-exchange standard, which is characterized by Lutz as being a system in which lending creates international reserves for the lender, is, in reality, a system where international reserves are increased through the 'empty' payments of a deficit country whose domestic currency is erroneously thought to be much more than a mere acknowledgment of debt.

Table 7.4

U.S. banking system

Liabilities	Assets
Bank of *A* $x	

A's banking system

Liabilities	Assets
	US banking system $x

Although Lutz refused the solution based on the automatic lending of surplus countries, his analysis is highly stimulating, and worth continuing along the lines of a new definiton of international money which we are going to derive from the works of John Maynard Keynes.

Chapter Eight

Keynes's Clearing Union revisited

As is well known, the proposals advocated by Keynes at the Bretton Woods conference of 1944 were centred around the idea of having an international institution to provide the world with an international means of exchange and payment. In short, the purpose of Keynes's proposals was 'to establish a currency union, here designated an *International Clearing Union*, based on international bank-money, called (let us say) *bancor*, fixed (but not unalterably) in terms of gold and accepted as the equivalent of gold by the British Commonwealth and the United States and all the other members of the Union for the purpose of settling international balances' (Keynes, in Grubel 1963: 58). As is clearly stressed in the plan, officially presented by the Chancellor of the Exchequer to Parliament in April 1943 and reprinted in Grubel (1963), 'The idea underlying such a Union is simple, namely, to generalize the essential principle of banking as it is exhibited within any closed system. This principle is the necessary equality of credits and debits' (p.59). Starting from this principle, two alternative ways of interpreting Keynes's Clearing Union seem possible *a priori*. Let us analyse them successively.

1. The traditional interpretation

The necessary equality of international credits and debits has often be seen as the generalization of the earning-through-spending principle of income theory. In the same way as a given sum of national income can be repeatedly transferred from resident to resident — so it is claimed — international money would circulate among countries, the sole task of the Clearing Union being that of making sure that 'its members keep the rules and that the advances made to each of them are prudent and advisable for the Union as a whole' (p.59). According to this approach, money is seen as a net asset both at the national and at the international level, and banks — Clearing Union included — are supposed to be able to create positive purchasing power out of nothing.

The great majority of international monetary analyses developed since Bretton Woods are founded on this approach. Triffin himself, despite his efforts to put forth an alternative theory of world monetary economics, relies heavily on this net asset conception of money, and identifies the major problem of international transactions with the necessity of providing the countries with the amount of liquid asset required for the settlement of their reciprocal exchanges. As a matter of fact, the entire debate about the world liquidity problem is symptomatic of the way economists have considered international money, and the creation of the International Monetary Fund which followed the Bretton Woods conference was but the logical consequence of the pragmatic approach to monetary pathology which was going to dominate the international scene from then on. The articles of the first agreements and their following amendments denote the clear purpose of dealing with international monetary problems by taking for granted the existence of a fundamental analogy between national and international currency and by adopting a whole series of conjunctural measures coherent with this unquestioned assumption.

Keynes's plan was thus seen as an attempt to solve the liquidity problem by providing every member country with a given amount of overdraft facilities analogous to the amount of credit banks allow to national economies. Issued by the international Clearing Union in the same way as national currencies are issued by the domestic banking system, the bancor would be instantaneously deposited within this same Fund and be constantly available for the settlement of international transactions so that 'If no credits can be removed outside the clearing system, but only transferred within it, the Union can never be in any difficulty as regards the honoring of checks drawn upon it' (p.59). Each country would pay for its foreign purchases and would be paid for its international sales in bancors. The generalization of exchange and of the system of international settlements would avoid the one-to-one relationship between creditor and debtor countries and allow for the automatic lending of the surplus to the deficit countries.

Yet, according to the traditional interpretation of Keynes's proposals, the bancor is conceived as an international asset endowed with a positive purchasing power. Point 40 of the plan states, indeed, that 'it [the clearing union system] is capable of the abuse of creating excessive purchasing power' (p.77). Hence, the question arises of how the world purchasing power of bancor can be determined. The analogy with the working of national economies is of no help, since no international production is available to back the hypothetical value of bancor. Substitution can also not be invoked, for the quotas assigned to each member state (and which determine the issuing capacity of the Clearing Union) would be fixed by reference to the sum of each country's exports and imports so that bancors would not take the place, and value, of national currencies and gold. Total indeterminacy, if not absolute arbitrariness, is therefore the only possible answer to our question.

Now the problem would not be too serious if the reciprocal use of bancors had no repercussions at the national level. Analysis shows, however, that this is not the case. As we have already shown, the use of a net asset as international standard is bound to introduce several disturbing effects. In particular, if the bancor is defined as a positive amount of international purchasing power, its recording in the balance sheet of the creditor country immediately gives rise to an equivalent creation of national money, which pathologically inflates the amount of available domestic income. And the gravity of this situation is not diminished by the possibility of limiting the payment to the sum of outstanding balances, a possibility which seems to be necessarily implied in the nature of the system of international clearing advocated at Bretton Woods by the British government. 'The Clearing Union is set up, not for the transaction of daily business between individual traders or banks, but for the clearing and settlement of the ultimate outstanding balances between central banks' (p.69). The point is that, even if perfectly balanced, transactions between countries must be recorded as they occur, and the way in which they are recorded is all important for the working of an international monetary system.

Consider the case of two countries whose trade is perfectly balanced. If one exports *x* the other sells its goods and services for an equivalent amount. In this particular situation there would be no need for a clearing settlement between the two countries. Yet it would be wrong to infer that no problem could arise from this situation of equilibrium. Indeed, analysis shows that, although the equality between exports and imports is neutral on the exchange market, the same neutrality is not verified within the domestic monetary system of each country. Despite the trade equilibrium, transactions are all settled in bancor (or some other monetary asset), and because of this payment domestic banks enter a positive asset on their balance sheet, an asset which is immediately matched by an equivalent amount of national money which banks create precisely on the basis of the newly acquired asset. The inflationary nature of this creation does not need to be proved, and it is entirely related to the use of a net asset as international currency.

1.1. *The external debt problem within the traditional approach*

Another characteristic of the pragmatic approach which results from the traditional interpretation of Keynes's proposals for the creation of an international Clearing Union is related to the supposed reciprocity between surplus and defict countries. 'The system looks on excessive credit balances with as critical an eye as on excessive debit balances, each being, indeed, the inevitable concomitant of the other' (Keynes in Grubel 1963: 61). As a matter of fact, as in the proposals advanced by

Schumacher in his brilliant paper published by *Economica* in May 1943,[1] one of the aims of Keynes's plan was to restore unfettered multilateral clearing between member states in order to avoid the shortcomings of a decentralized system. 'These facilities are made possible by the constitution of the system itself and do not involve particular indebtedness between one member state and another. A country is in credit or debit with the Clearing Union as a whole' (p.66). Yet, though mediated by the Clearing Union, the relationship between surplus and deficit countries is still one of reciprocity and commercial equilibrium is still seen as a major objective of international economics. 'Thus each country is allowed a certain margin of resources and a certain interval of time within which to effect a balance in its economic relations with the rest of the world' (p.66).

Now, though apparently conforming to common sense, the claim that a country's surplus is necessarily matched by some other country's deficit should be submitted to closer examination and tested against facts.

A well-known argument against the necessary reciprocity of surplus and deficits is derived from taking into consideration the financial market. Through a positive sale of shares it is possible, in fact, to finance the net purchase of goods and services without getting into debt. At the international level this means that a country receiving foreign investment can increase its net commercial imports 'free of debt'.

But the necessary incurring of a debt is not the only anomaly which the traditional version of the Clearing Union does not handle. The double payment of external debt cannot be avoided by a system which is essentially founded on a net asset conception of international money. Let us consider the case of an indebted country trying to service its external debt by taking advantage of its international overdraft facilities. Since the country would be indebted towards the Clearing Union as a whole and not towards any particular foreign country, the servicing of external debt would have to be addressed to the Clearing Union itself. In order to do so, our country would have to earn a positive amount of bancors through its international transactions. Now, given the net asset nature of bancors assumed by traditional analysis, exporters would be paid by money creation and banks (either the Central Bank or any commercial bank) would record a deposit of international currency on the asset side of their balance sheets. This means that the bancors earned through net exports are not at the free disposal of the country's indebted residents. For these residents to honour their external debt it would be enough to pay a given sum of domestic currency, yet this payment would not be sufficient to discharge the country itself. It is true that, in the multilateral clearing system, the international credit earned by the indebted country can be used to decrease its previously accumulated debt. Yet, these deposits in bancors have to be paid for, even though they are already available within the domestic banking system. This second payment of the external debt is essentially the same which occurs under the present dollar-exchange standard and entails the same drastic consequence: the logical impossibility of external debt servicing.

The fundamental reason for this appalling result lies within the lack of distinction between money and real goods. Bancors are here still conceived as being essentially similar to real assets, and are consequently handled by the banking system. Thus, domestic money is being created on the basis of deposits with the Clearing Union and these same deposits are bought and sold in much the same way as goods and services are on the commodity market. As a consequence, the rate of exchange between domestic currencies and bancors would necessarily be submitted to disequilibrating pressures every time supply and demand did not match. The maintenance of fixed exchange rates would therefore be more wishful thinking than a feasible measure of international economics.

Within the traditional approach, international money is always identified with a positive amount of purchasing power. Keynes himself seems to conform to this generalized point of view when he claims, with regards to his plan, that 'the analogy with a national banking system is complete' (p.66). But, while it is perfectly licit to speak of domestic purchasing power, the concept of international purchasing power is not so evident as it may appear. In fact, it is the production of current output that accounts for the existence of national purchasing power. At the international level, however, no real production occurs so that the creation of international monetary assets, far from being justified either theoretically or pragmatically, artificially increases the amount of world purchasing power. Instead of considering the bancor as a pure international 'wheel of circulation' with no proper value, mainstream economists took up literally Keynes's analogy between his plan and the national banking system, and were therefore led to identify the bancor with a hypothetical international income of positive value.

The consequences of this confusion between pure vehicular money and income are already known; the inflationary creation of domestic money carried out on the basis of the credit with the Clearing Union earned through international transactions would add up to the double payment of external debt, and the entire system would be unable to prevent 'the contractionist pressure which might otherwise overwhelm in social disorder and disappointment the good hopes of our modern world' (p.66).

2. The modern interpretation

According to Keynes, the idea underlying the International Clearing Union was 'simple, namely, to generalize the essential principle of banking as it is exhibited within any closed system. This principle is the necessary equality of credits and debits' (p.59). Now, instead of considering this principle as proof of the existence of a necessary reciprocity between surplus and deficit countries, it is possible to take it as the starting point of a new analysis of international money.

Issued by banks as a spontaneous acknowledgment of debt, money can never define a credit without simultaneously defining an equivalent debit. The claim that 'no credits can be removed outside the clearing system, but only transferred within it' (p.59) is therefore derived from the application of the rule of double accounting to banking, so that the beneficiary of a payment becomes, necessarily and instantaneously, the owner of a bank deposit. Nationally, the credit of the payee is recorded in the banking system and defines his positive deposit; internationally, this means that each surplus country would have a credit (and therefore a positive deposit) recorded with the International Clearing Union. It is evident that, in these conditions, the Clearing Union would never be 'in any difficulty as regards the honoring of checks drawn upon it' (p.59). But what is the exact meaning of the debt incurred by the Clearing Union and how is it honoured?

In a national system, banks honour their debts simply by changing their form (they give you two five-pound notes in exchange for a ten-pound note, for example, or they credit your deposit account in exchange for banknotes). Likewise, in the international system the Clearing Union would never be asked to pay its debts except in bancor, i.e. by entering a debt in its accounting. According to the modern interpretation of Keynes's proposals the bancor would therefore be an IOU spontaneously issued by the International Clearing Union and supplied to the member countries as world monetary standard.

One of the main problems which was on the table at the Bretton Woods conference related to the supply of international liquidity. In this respect, the solution proposed by the British plan is quite satisfactory. In fact, given that every sum of bancor earned by a member country is immediately deposited how could it be possible for the circulation to be insufficient? As claimed by Keynes, money is issued by banks by spontaneously incurring a debt, and bancors would simply have to conform to this principle. The international IOUs thus created by the Clearing Union would be spent by, say, country *A* to the profit of country *B*, whose account with the Clearing Union would then be credited by the very amount of which *A*'s account is debited. The deposit earned by *B* would therefore be exactly offset by the debit of *A* to the international bank. Every time that a country needs to pay another it would take advantage of its overdraft facilities and this clearly means that the Bank would create the currency necessary to 'monetize' all international transactions. The debit of the paying country being necessarily and immediately covered by the credit of the country which is being paid, the Clearing Union could create all the money needed to carry out international transactions without there being any problem of liquidity.

It remains true, of course, that international economics is concerned only with pure exchange and, therefore, that the international standard issued by the Clearing Union cannot be associated with any real output. Thus, bancors never define a positive purchasing power; instead they are issued and used as a pure vehicular money. But what does it mean, then, to claim that a country pays its commercial purchases using a money of zero value? How can payments be positive if no purchasing power is transferred from the payer to the payee? Bound to remain unanswered if they are related to an economy of production, these questions can easily be handled if we bear in mind that no production can be accounted for in international economics. In order to explain how, internationally, payments can be carried on in a pure nominal money it is necessary to introduce the financial market into the picture. In reality, this market was already implicit in the analysis of Keynes's credit mechanism, for the deposit of credit countries with the Clearing Union defines their positive purchase of financial assets. Hence, countries which benefit from a surplus of their trade balance are simultaneously net purchasers of financial assets. In other words, through the financial market surplus countries are themselves financing the net commercial purchases of deficit countries. Since the financing comes from the exporting country itself, there is no need for the Clearing Union to create any additional purchasing power which, being deprived of any real base, would only result in a pathological increase of international speculative capital (through the same mechanisms which characterize the actual dollar standard system).

In the terminology of Ricardo, the bancor would therefore only be a 'nominal money' with no intrinsic value which, through its instantaneous circulation from the Clearing Union to the purchasing country, to the selling country, and back to the Clearing Union, would essentially guarantee the matching of trade deficits (surpluses) and surpluses (deficits) in the flows of non-monetary financial bonds. 'Countries having a favorable balance of payments with the rest of the world as a whole would find themselves in possession of a credit account with the Clearing Union, and those having an unfavorable balance would have a debit account' (p.59). Moreover, the automatic deposit of the bancors earned by a surplus country is a mechanism which guarantees the lending of this surplus to all the deficit countries without there being the necessity of putting any of them in a particular financial relationship with the lending country. 'A country is in credit or debit with the Clearing Union as a whole. This means that the overdraft facilities, while a relief to some, are not a real burden to others' (p.66).

Of course, this mechanism of international payments requires the national monetary systems to be reformed accordingly. The actual anomalous mixing of national and international circuits would no longer have to occur, and external transactions would have to be internalized in order to avoid the inflationary payment of domestic exports. In the plan elaborated by Keynes nothing was said about the structural changes to be introduced at the national level.[2] Yet, though the proposals for the establishment of a currency union are not entirely conclusive, they provide a new insight into the problem of international payments as well as the necessary elements for its basic solution. This conclusion is supported by the analysis of the way external debts would be serviced under the modern version of Keynes's plan.

2.1. *The reform of external debt servicing as implied in the modern interpretation of the Clearing Union system*

As the reader will certainly remember, the actual double payment of external debt is linked to the use of what is thought to be a net monetary asset (national currencies like the American dollar or internationally issued assets like the IMF special drawing rights) as the international 'wheel of circulation'. Since LDCs have to pay by means of these assets, external debts must be honoured twice, a first time by the residents who contracted them, and who have to part with an equivalent amount of their income, and a second time by the country itself which has to acquire the monetary vehicle necessary for the carrying out of its external payment and which, by so doing, suffers an equivalent loss of its internal resources. Moreover, considered as net assets, currencies are the object of speculative transactions which increase the degree of instability of the entire system. As Keynes already noted analysing the improvement in sterling exchange in 1925, 'speculative purchases of sterling in the expectation of its improving in value relatively to the dollar' (1972: 195) were one main cause of exchange rate variation, the other being the unilateral increase in demand operated by the debt servicing countries.

Now, the existence of a Clearing Union working on the basis of the modern principles of international money[3] would avoid the actual shortcomings of external debt servicing. The bancor, in fact, would not be issued as a net asset and countries would be able to use it as 'pure vehicle' without being asked to buy it. In order to service their external debt, countries would simply have to earn a deposit with the Clearing Union through their commercial exports. Nowadays, as we already know, this is not sufficient since the foreign currency available in the country still has to be bought by domestic money. Tomorrow, the payment of external debt would only be *in kind* (part of the exported goods and services), so that not a single unit of domestic income would be lost to the profit of international speculative capital. By crediting the debtor country with part of the bancors earned through external trade the debtor country would carry on the external debt servicing on behalf of the indebted residents. Thus, being essentially an intermediary, the country would have to earn the equivalent, in domestic money, of its external payment: the income spent by the residents would remain at the country's disposal and profit the economic system as a whole.

What Keynes noted relative to the indebted European Allies after World War II still applies perfectly well nowadays to the situation of LDCs: 'They may be expected, therefore, to make constant attempts to evade or escape payment, and these attempts will be a constant source of international friction and ill-will for many years to come' (1972: 25). As analysis shows, the situation is even more dramatic since, despite their willingness to pay, indebted countries are bound to operate within a structure of monetary payments which automatically invalidates the payment of their external debts. A reform of this structure is needed if the causes of the double servicing of external debt are to be definitively removed, and it is in Keynes's proposals for the establishment of an International Clearing Union that the fundamental elements of a new system of international payments can be partially found. The vehicular conception of money and the principle of double accounting are the corner-stones of the modern approach and it is from them that our search for a logical solution to the international debt crisis has to be pursued.

Part II

The Logical Impossibility of Positive External Debt Servicing

For clarity, in this second part of our investigation we shall separate the nations into two categories, the *North* and the *South*, according to the status granted their domestic currencies. We shall also distinguish between period p′, in which the South has progressively accumulated its debt towards the North, and period p when the South starts servicing its external debt, either in interest or in interest and amortization.

Even though the North and the South are groups of countries, we shall consider them as two different countries, and we shall analyse their mutual exchanges trying to prove that, in the absence of external debt servicing, no monetary disorder appears in their monetary relationship. Of course, this does not mean that the actual system of international payments is not the source of other kinds of monetary disequilibrium. As we have tried to show in the first part of this work, within the key currency exchange standard the settlement of international transactions leads to an inflationary emission of domestic money and to the 'deficit without tears' of the key currency countries. What we want to focus on here is the peculiarity of the problem related to the external debt servicing. In this respect it is worthwhile to show that, domestic disequilibrium notwithstanding, the servicing of external debts is the cause of a peculiar monetary disorder *among the countries*.

While in the first chapter we shall deal with the transactions characteristic of period p′, when the external debt is built up but not serviced, in the following chapters we shall analyse the nature of the formal anomaly arising in period p, when the debt is being serviced by the South. The main lines of a solution are given in the final chapter.

Chapter Nine

Save for External Debt Servicing No Formal Illogicality Affects the International Monetary System

1. Money neutrality in the case of trade balance equilibrium

Since, in this hypothetical case, the supply and demand of each country are equal, we can enunciate a twofold rule whose application is so important that we can name it the 'golden rule of international payments' (or, for short, the 'golden rule').

The golden rule of international payments:
1. every country pays with its own currency
2. every country is paid in its own currency

This 'golden rule' is of general application, but is it also always verified? Effectively yes, since the residents of a given country pay for their internal and *external* purchases (of either commercial goods or financial bonds) with the domestic money of the country even if a further operation on the exchange market is then required for the final payment of foreign exporters. If a transaction were to be paid *only* in the currency of the *exporting* country it would logically pertain to the category of *domestic* or internal transactions of this country. Being concerned with international monetary relationships, transactions can therefore be classified as domestic or international according to the distinction between national and foreign currencies. Moreover, it is clear that, in the absence of commercial surpluses, no country can increase its monetary reserves.

Apparently, the 'golden rule' is not fully consistent since, if each country pays with its own money this seems necessarily to imply that its partner is not paid in its own.

Yet, the alleged inconsistency of the 'golden rule' is avoided by the current working of the *exchange market*. In this market every unit of money spent by a country is converted into monetary units of the receiving country so that, although every country pays with its own currency, each country is finally paid in its own money.

Let us represent the payment, in money S (MS), of country's *S* imports (Figure 9.1). Two flows occur in opposite directions: the *monetary* flow (represented by a plain line) and a *real* flow (the dotted line). Country *S* spends a sum of money S in order to pay for its imports.

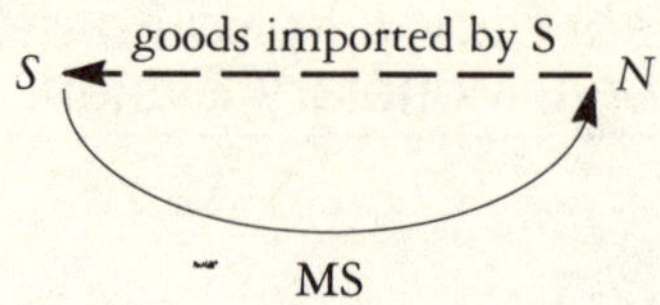

Figure 9.1

As we have already often recalled, the money paid to every economic agent is instantaneously deposited with the bank which issued it. Now, the whole of money S is deposited with the banking system of country *S*; from which we can induce that country *N* is debited, to the profit of *S*'s banks (where it sets up an equivalent deposit), in the very instant it receives a sum of money S (Figure 9.2). Flow 1 is the monetary payment of country *S*'s imports; flow 2 is the building up, by country *N*, of a monetary deposit with *S*'s banks. A real flow has therefore to be added to what is represented in Figure 9.2.: country *N* acquires a bank deposit in money, *real* payment of its exports. In fact, every bank deposit is a real good or, alternatively stated, 'really' defines a good (Figure 9.3). Finally, country *N* acquires a real good in exchange for the commercial goods it sells; the payment made by *S* is, therefore, *monetary in its form* and *real in its content*.

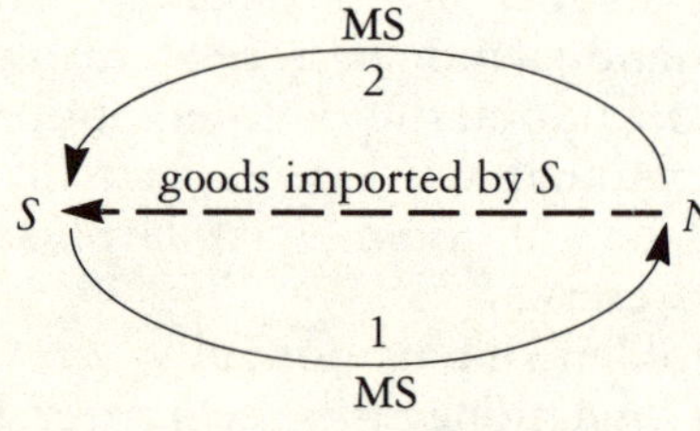

Figure 9.2

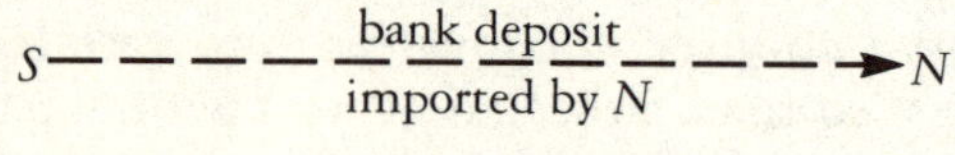

Figure 9.3

If we did not know the distinction between *nominal* and *real* money, we would consider the payment of *S*'s imports as an exchange between a sum of money and a given amount of commercial goods. In reality, the nominal payment (in money S) made by country *S*'s importers is immediately taken back by *S*'s banks, that convert it into a real payment in favour of country *N* (which becomes the holder of a deposit with country *S*'s banks).

From the payment of *S*'s imports it follows, in fact, that the two countries only exchange real goods: country *N* gives up commercial goods whereas country *S* yields up financial goods, i.e. bank deposits. Being logically necessary, the inclusion of bank deposits into the category of real goods proves that, as it is paid with a sum of money, country *N* is instantaneously paid with a sum of real goods.

Apparently, the payment made by *S* becomes effectively real only afterwards, when *N* is a net importer of commercial goods. In fact, *N*'s payment is real at the very instant the country is paid for its exports, even if what it gets is a sum of money and not a 'mass' or a 'volume' of commercial goods. Indeed, what *N* immediately (i.e. at the precise instant it is paid in money) gets, is the counterpart, in bank deposits (real goods *par excellence*), of the real goods it has given up.

We thus reach the conclusion that every payment in nominal money is a 'vector' of real goods. At the moment *S*'s commercial exports are paid, the two countries exchange real goods through the intermediation of a circular flow of money S. Finally, let us note that every real good carried by 'the great wheel of circulation' moves in the same direction as its vector. (Figure 9.4). In this 'monetized' exchange, we find simultaneously a sum of nominal money and an equivalent sum of real money:

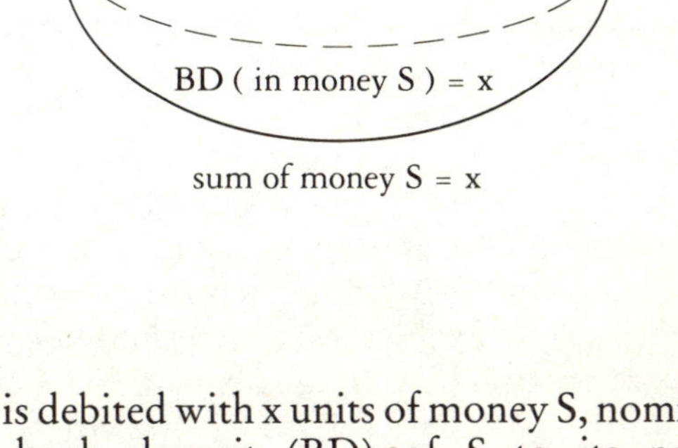

Figure 9.4

1. country *S* is debited with x units of money S, nominal flow which carries a bank deposit (BD) of S to its partner *N*; and

simultaneously
2. country *N* is debited with x units of money S, nominal flow which carries an equivalent volume of commercial goods to its partner *S*.

Usually, the equilibrium of a country's trade balance is represented in the commercial markets as the equality between the goods it exports and the goods it imports, an equality which can be verified only at the end of every given period. This method is clearly irreproachable, but it has the status of a pure convention. The choice of the periods of reference, in fact, is forcibly discretionary; is it a matter of a week, a month, a year? As soon as it becomes evident that bank deposits have to be included in the set of real goods, another class of equivalence is brought onto the stage: with each payment it carries out a country alienates an equivalent amount of bank deposits. It follows that, in our example, country *S* gives real goods in the same operation which defines the payment of its imports: in this sense balance of payments equilibrium is permanently verified, at whatever instant of chronological time. Hence, at the very instant country *S* pays its current commercial *imports*, it *exports* the exact counterpart of bank deposits.

Let us now consider what happens to country *N*. According to the hypothesis we are following here, within the chosen period *N* is also importing goods up to a value of *x* units of money S. However, according to the 'golden rule' country *N* pays for its purchases in money N, and not in money S. For simplicity let us suppose that, on the exchange market, 1 unit of money S is equivalent to 1 unit of money N. The payment of *N*'s imports thus conforms to the following representation as shown in figure 9.5. It is not necessary to explain this figure at length; the principle is known: spent by the importers of country *N*, money N flows instantaneously back to the banks which issued it. As a matter of fact, country *S* is not paid in money but in real goods since, in exchange for its commercial exports, it obtains an equivalent amount of deposits with the banks of country *N*. To reach the opposite conclusion — namely that *N*'s payment is *monetary* and not *real* — would mean to mix up erroneously money, a simple vector, and monetary deposits, the favourite real goods.

The first point of the 'golden rule' has thus found its full application. We now have to apply its second point: every country is finally paid in its own money even though it is first credited with the currency of its partner. What we have here is an operation on the exchange market where each country gives the other the deposit in foreign money which it had initially obtained in exchange (or as real payment) for its exports (Figure 9.6). The reciprocal flow of the deposits in foreign money takes place by means of monetary vectors of the same definition and of the

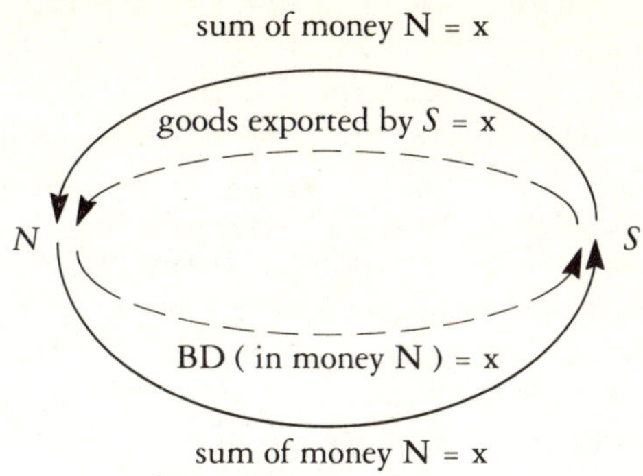

Figure 9.5

same direction. Thus, we can see that *N* is debited with money S to the benefit of *S*, and that *S* is debited with money N to the profit of *N*: these mutual credits amount to the retrocession, by each country, of the deposit first obtained in exchange for its commercial sales.

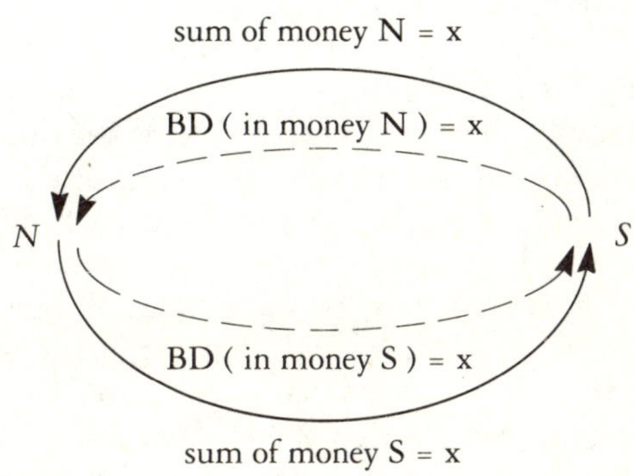

Figure 9.6

On the basis of the 'experimental' exchange we have just observed we can try to derive the (general) definition of every operation of foreign exchange.

The first point of the 'golden rule' applies independently of the exchange market since each country pays for its purchases in its own national currency just as if they were domestic transactions. The second point of the 'golden rule', however, directly involves the exchange market. Now, this involvement is double for a double reason: each country launches a vectorial (nominal) foreign currency to get a vectorial domestic currency, and, on the other hand, each country gives up a bank deposit made up in foreign money and gets, as counterpart, a bank deposit made up in its own money. Hence, to change a national currency into a foreign currency is to conclude an operation between vehicular monies of distinct 'denomination', and, therefore, between the corresponding bank deposits. Like every other monetary transaction, an operation of foreign exchange is, thus, simultaneously nominal and real.

An operation on the exchange market is either unilateral or reciprocal. Let us reason in terms of currency S and N. It is certainly possible that, at a given instant, a sum of money S is changed into a sum of money N *but money N is never changed into money S*. Yet, it remains true that no one could obtain a sum *x* of money N if somebody else did not give it up. This is, of course, a truism. And, given that a truism can never be dismissed, it is necessarily implied even in unilateral foreign exchanges. But what is the exact definition of a unilateral exchange? We are on the right track if we distinguish between two conceivable situations: at the instant the owner of money S asks for a sum of money N it is possible but not necessary that the owner of money N asks (simultaneously) for a sum of money S; if this happens, the transformation of money S into money N is reciprocal, if not, it is unilateral. But let us be more precise. Considered as an act, a monetary exchange is a *demand*. Suppose the exchange rate between money S and money N to be 1 MS for 1 MN. If the holders of money S *demand* x units of money N in exchange for x units of money S, the transaction will take place at this rate provided the holders of money N demand, simultaneously, x units of money S in exchange for x units of money N. The equality, in quantity and prices, of reciprocal desires or wants is the necessary condition for the exchange rate stability, money S being, then, neither appreciated nor depreciated in terms of money N. Now, it is not at all certain that the desire shown by the holders of money S, who demand x units of money N against x units of money S, will be met at this exchange rate; it will only be if the holders of money N simultaneously demand x units of money S against x units of money N. The measure of a demand for foreign money is given by the product of the price of one unit of this money and the number of units desired. This time the definition of the two kinds of exchanges, unilateral and reciprocal, is sufficiently clear: an exchange is reciprocal or unilateral according to whether the reciprocal demands of the two currencies are equivalent or not (these demands being determined and compared on the basis of the exchange rate resulting from the previous exchange operations).

The hypothesis of this section is the equilibrium of trade balances. Now, it can easily be shown that this condition defines perfectly reciprocal exchange operations.

It cannot be denied, however, that the simultaneity of the exchange operations called for by the final payment of each country's imports is not assured, except in one particular case (which we shall soon analyse). For the sake of clarity let us suppose that the holders of x MS in country *N* decide to change in one go — at instant *t* — the totality of this sum (into money N); let us also suppose that the holders of x MN in country *S* are able to offer this amount of money N (in exchange for money S) in just one operation — at instant t′. Now, there is nothing to indicate that instants t and t′ coincide. On the contrary, t precedes or follows t′ in chronological time. The case where t < t′ is sufficient to illustrate the general solution since t′ < t is its exact opposite. At instant t country *N*'s exporters bring x MS to the exchange market in order to obtain its countervalue in money N. The previous exchange rate being 1 MS for 1 MN, we observe that there is an appreciation of money N in terms of money S since the desired exchange is *unilateral*: money N is the object of a *net* (or *excess*) demand in money S. If this appreciation were effectively to take place at instant t, a counterbalancing depreciation would occur at instant t′, where a *net* demand of exactly the same proportion characterizes the purchase of money S. Yet, these 'rebounds' would occur only on a 'blind' exchange market, with no forecast and no time transactions. Modern techniques can easily smooth all the differences whose sum is nil in the short term. It is therefore correct to conclude that everything happens as if instants t and t′ did perfectly coincide.

This result is experimentally verified when the Central Banks of the two countries 'take back' the foreign currencies earned on both sides: it is then in one and the same operation that *S*'s Central Bank gives up x MN and that *N*'s Central Bank gives up x MS, which is a rigorous definition of a *reciprocal* exchange.

It seems therefore to follow that only the equilibrium of *trade* balances can account for the neutrality of exchange market operations. Now, what we are going to verify is the exact opposite: if the overall balances are equilibrated in periods p′, in which no external debt is serviced either in interests or amortization, the foreign exchanges *induced* by the mutual imports of commercial or financial goods are *reciprocal*, and, therefore, *neutral*, so that they rigorously preserve the external value of both currencies.

2. When trade balances are out of equilibrium monetary order is maintained by offsetting capital flows disequilibria

Let us suppose that, in period p′, the South imports commercial goods up to a value of x + y units of money S while the North's commercial imports amount to x units of money N, and let the previously determined exchange rate be equal to 1 MS for 1 MN.

Up to x units of money S country *S* finds in its own commercial exports the monetary resources necessary for the payment of its commercial imports. But from where can it derive the balance? As it is, we may think this is a false problem since every country has always at its disposal, in *its own money*, the resources necessary for the payment of its foreign purchases. Thus, what would prevent *S* from spending (x + y) units of money S to the profit of *N*'s commercial exporters? Yet, we should not forget the second point of the 'golden rule': the final payment of *N*'s exporters has to take place *in money N*. Consequently, it would seem that the South will exert a demand equal to (x + y) MS relative to the money of the North while the demand exerted by the North relative to the money of the South will only be equal to x MN. The difference would define an excess demand for money N in terms of money S, a disequilibrium that would lead to a depreciation of country *S*'s currency.

The disequilibrium that we have just pointed out is groundless. In fact, the South has to acquire y units of money N in order to pay its net commercial imports; this is a true *purchase* whose counterpart is necessarily *real*, a condition which is verified for every purchase. But what is this counterpart? It is made up of non-monetary financial bonds that country *S*'s residents sell to country *N*'s capital lenders. The South's need to sell bonds to the North simply shows the fact that a sum y of money N has to be found by *S* on the financial market given that it cannot be derived from the commercial market. Let us represent the two real terms of the exchange taking place on the financial market as shown in Figure 9.7. This scheme complies with the first point of the 'golden rule': the South pays in its own money (y MS) for its external purchase of bank deposits (BD = y MN); symmetrically, the North also pays in its own money (y MN) for its external purchase of non-monetary financial bonds (for a global value of y MS).

However, the first point of the 'golden rule' finds another application when country *S* exchanges the bank deposit it has acquired in money N against commercial goods imported from country *N*. In fact, every country pays for its external purchases in its own money; we can thus induce that *S* pays for its net imports in money S, and that *N* buys back, in money N, the monetary deposits built up in its banks to the benefit of country *S*'s residents (Figure 9.8).

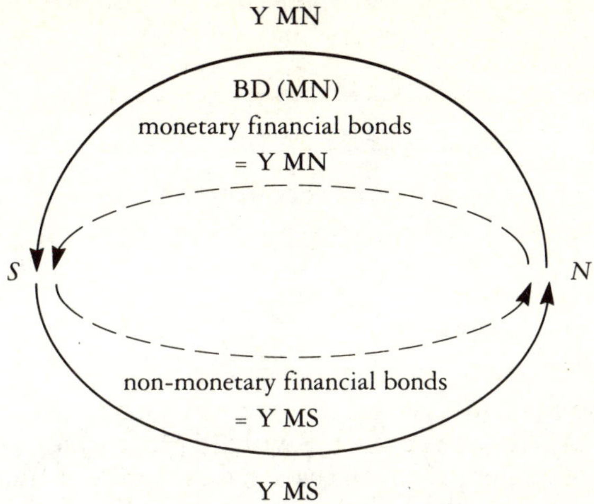

Figure 9.7

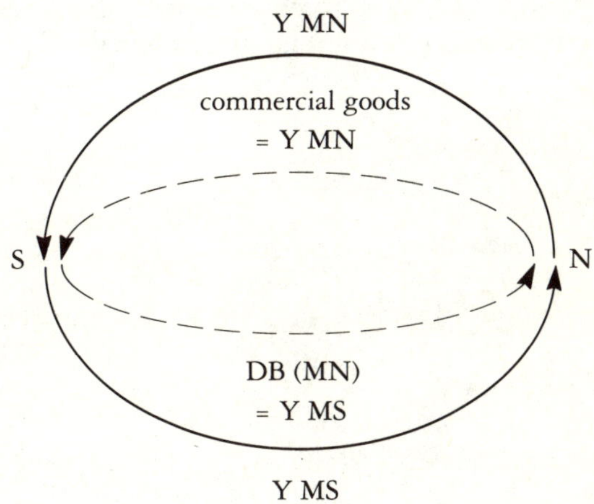

Figure 9.8

Even before the second point of the 'golden rule' applies it appears that from a real point of view the operation is reduced to the transfer of financial bonds (= y MS) by *S* and to the reciprocal transfer of commercial goods (= y MN) by *N* (Figure 9.9).

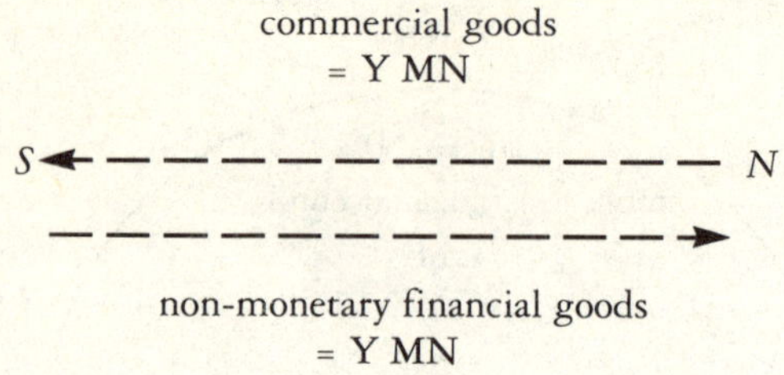

Figure 9.9

The second point of the 'golden rule' being now applied, country *N* is debited with 2y MN and country *S* with 2y MS, each one to the profit of the other. The operation (international exchange of financial bonds against commercial goods) finds its final completion in a circuit of vehicular money formed by a debit of 2y MS incurred by country *N* and a debit of 2y MN incurred by country *S*. Each country is thus finally paid in its own money; *S* gets 2y MS because it has exported non-monetary financial goods equivalent to y MS and, by recovery, bank deposits equivalent to y MS; symmetrically, *N*'s earnings are globally equivalent to 2y MN since it exports bank deposits (then recovered) for y MN and commercial goods for y MN (Figure 9.10).

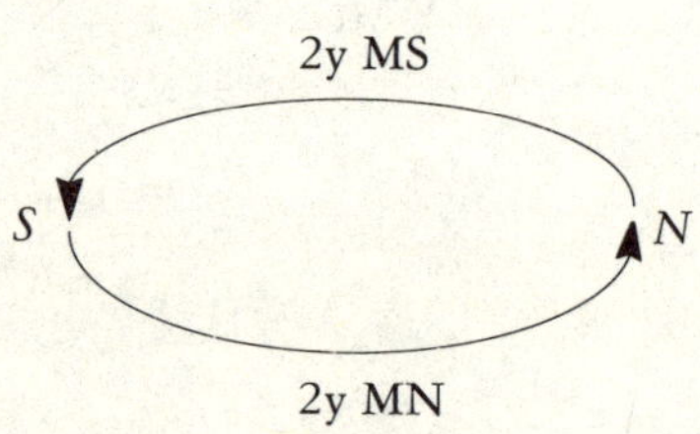

Figure 9.10

If we abstract the reciprocal transfer of y units of money N as bank deposits we can see that, internationally, each country offers and demands real goods for the same amount; country *S* offers non-monetary financial bonds and demands commercial goods to a value of y MS whereas country *N* offers commercial goods and demands non-monetary financial bonds to an amount of y MN.

The international exchange we have just described is neutral on the exchange market despite the deficit of country *S*'s trade balance (in periods p′). Let us give a further and more direct proof of this neutrality.

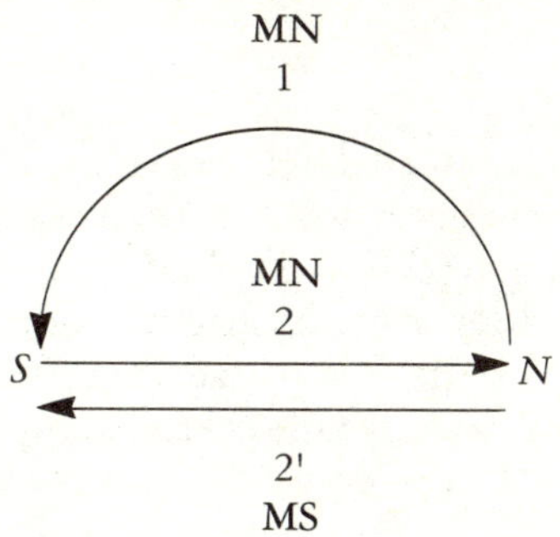

Figure 9.11

Country *N* pays in its own currency (flow 1) but country *S* is eventually paid in its own: this means that country *S* exerts, in money N, an excess demand for money S (flow 2 and 2′) (Figure 9.11). Yet, country *S* pays in money S whereas country *N* is eventually paid in money N. It then follows (without it being necessary to represent the phenomenon) that country *N* exerts, in money S, an excess demand for money N. Now, since the two excess demands of opposite sign are equivalent, it can easily be induced that, in themselves, the international transactions of periods p′ have no repercussions on the *external* value of national currencies; in particular, country *S*'s money does not experience the negative rebound of its net commercial imports.

This nice harmony, however, will be inexorably shattered starting from period p; in the following chapter we shall establish that the external debt servicing undertaken by country *S* has a disruptive and unavoidable consequence for the external value of its domestic currency.

Chapter ten

External Debt Servicing: the Source of a Formal Anomaly

We shall first prove that external debt servicing breaks the 'golden rule' of international payments (section 1). Then we shall analyse the exact meaning of this anomaly (section 2). And finally, in section 3 we shall try to highlight the hidden vice; its effect is gravely disruptive since it counters the efficacy of the heavy sacrifices imposed on the South, whose commercial imports remain literally unpaid for.

1. External debt servicing (principal and interests) breaks the 'golden rule' of international payments

To service a debt is to pay an interest or part of the capital due. Whichever it is, creditors are serviced through a *transfer*: they obtain a fraction of their debtors' savings.

Strictly speaking, a transfer is a *unilateral* flow; its beneficiary gets a positive payment but does not make one. To be precise, transfers are defined by the *real* payment of creditors, who give nothing in exchange, neither commercial or financial goods nor bank deposits.

It will be remembered that, relative to periods p′, we did not find any unilateral payment; the South had effectively *obtained* commercial goods without any *commercial* counterpart but it had also *given up* (non-monetary) financial goods without any *financial* counterpart: equivalently negative and positive these two net transactions expressed a global equilibrium, in which debt and credit payments of each partner were perfectly matched.

Thus, if it is confirmed that external debts are serviced by the unilateral payment (in amortizations and interests) of the countries whose residents are indebted, it will be because a novel situation appears after period p, during which all payments followed the logic of *exchanges*.

Now, it is possible to conceive of the external debt servicing as being no exception to the general regime of *exchanges*. Let us suppose, in fact, that in period p the North sells (non-monetary) financial bonds to the South in order to obtain an equivalent sum of deposits with *S*'s banks; the purpose of the operation being the payment by *N* of its net commercial imports. Let us represent these two successive operations schematically as in Figure 10.1.

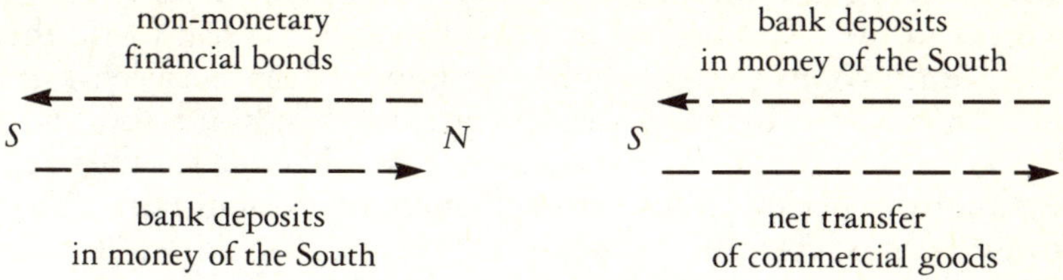

Figure 10.1

Under these circumstances the North makes a real payment to the South since it first gives up financial bonds in order to get an equivalent amount of *S* bank deposits; it then follows that real payments are reciprocally equal: the South gives up commercial goods and the North gives up (non-monetary) financial bonds. Despite the perfect reciprocity of real transactions, the South services its external debt, for it cancels out the financial obligations, which the North underwrites in its favour to pay for its net commercial imports. The 'golden rule' of international payments is complied with in the successive exchanges (which we have just been representing), and the South's external debt servicing is the result of a *compensation* (Figure 10.2).

Clearing

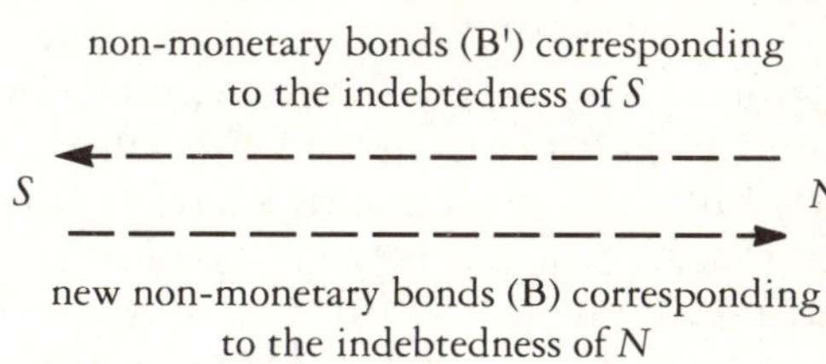

Figure 10.2

Factual evidence shows, however, that external debt servicing is not carried out through compensation. The fact is that the North does not have to make a *financial* payment of its net commercial imports *except under the form of a transfer of bank deposits in money N*. As a consequence, the South obtains *no amount of non-monetary bonds* as payment for its commercial exports surplus. In the real world there is therefore no room for the slightest compensation between financial bonds first issued by the South (in periods p′), bonds B′, and new financial bonds, bonds B, that the North would issue for the payment (starting from periods p) of its own net commercial imports; bonds B are purely hypothetical.

The anomaly inherent to every external debt servicing, thus, takes the form of an *asymmetry*: in p′ the South finds it necessary to contract a (non-monetary) financial debt towards the North (emission of bonds B′); otherwise the South would not find the purchasing power, in money N, needed to match its commercial deficit. And this situation is not reversed at all in period p; on the contrary, in every period in which the North's commercial imports are net, it pays the South simply by giving up equivalent net sums of bank deposits defined in money N: the North does not cover its commercial deficits by the emission of non-monetary financial bonds (bonds B′). It follows that the South is never in a condition to compensate its bonds B′ with other bonds B′ (since no bond B′ is obtained by *S* in exchange for its commercial exports).

Another demonstration leads to the same conclusion. The 'golden rule' is not respected since every external debt servicing carried out by the South defines a 'non-purchase' of the South: in order to service its debt, the South abstains from purchasing commercial or (non-monetary) financial goods from the North. The North purchases a surplus of commercial goods from the South while the South purchases nothing from the North (except, of course, monetary financial goods, bonds B): it is to the extent that the purchases of the North are not correlated to any purchase of the South (of commercial goods or non-monetary financial goods) that the South services its external debt.

Let us develop the analysis of the last paragraph. In paying for its commercial surplus the South *purchases* an equivalent amount of bank deposits previously built up in the banking system of the North; in this sense the South purchases real goods from the North. Yet, in order to service its foreign creditors, the South does not purchase any *non-monetary* real good; in exchange for its trade surplus the South gets neither commercial goods nor non-monetary financial bonds. On the contrary, as we have seen, in periods p′ the North obtains a sum of non-monetary financial bonds as final payment for its commercial exports surplus. Let us again call B′ the non-monetary financial bonds and B the monetary financial bonds. In periods p′ the South gives up bonds of type B′; starting from period p the North gives up only bonds of type B (its own bank deposits)(Figure 10.3). We have already shown that if, since period p, the North had to contract non-monetary financial debts (bonds B′) in order to cover its excess commercial purchases, everything would be 'normal', for the South and the North would be placed in a symmetrical situation as to the financing of their trade deficits: North and South would be on the same footing. However, observation reveals a totally different reality: while the South has to issue bonds B′, the North confines itself to the emission of bonds B.

Figure 10.3

The 'golden rule' of international payments allows every country to pay, as well as be paid, in its own money. This permutation is possible for only one reason, namely that every country buys from the other an equivalent amount of non-monetary real goods. Now, in the new situation characterizing the external debt servicing the South does not purchase any non-monetary real good from the North. The 'golden rule' is thus broken.

Let us retain here only the purchases of non-monetary real goods. The object of the analysis can be further simplified by abstracting the commercial exports which are compensated by commercial imports. The essential object of our inquiry is therefore identified with the commercial exports surplus whose payment is devoted to external debts servicing. Let us represent the type of exchange we are interested in by referring, first, to real flows alone as shown in Figure 10.4. In this scheme the first point of the 'golden rule' is applied *to country N alone*: *N* pays for its excess purchases of commercial goods (as it does for the totality of its commercial imports) in money N.

It is true that we still have to account for the service of *S*'s external debt (Figure 10.5). The complementary transaction that we have just represented is not a purchase but a unilateral transfer: country *S* gives up, to the benefit of its foreign creditors, the bank deposits in money N which it had initially obtained as payment for its excess commercial exports.

Operations would follow a completely different path if country *N* contracted a *non-monetary* financial obligation in view of the payment of its excess commercial imports. In this case the first point of the

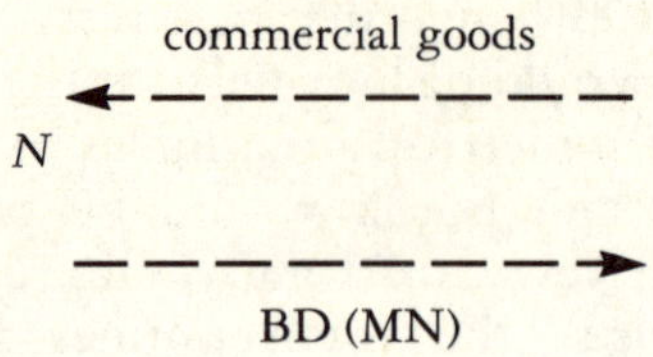

Figure 10.4

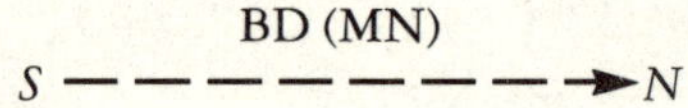

Figure 10.5

'golden rule' would apply *also for country S*, which would pay, in its own money, for the new non-monetary bonds (B′) issued by country *N* in view of the payment of its excess commercial imports. In comparison with the North, a net *commercial* buyer, the South would be, to the same extent, a net *financial* buyer.

Yet, the world is such that the North pays for its net purchases by issuing *monetary* obligations: it pays directly in bank deposits and not by issuing *non-monetary* obligations.

It logically follows that every external debt servicing of country *S* defines a *purchase of S equal to zero*. The country has therefore to undergo the sheer loss of the bank deposits in money N initially earned through its net commercial exports.

We now reach the conclusion; country *N* pays for its (net) purchases in money N; correlatively country *S* does not purchase anything but limits itself to the transfer of deposits in money N to its foreign creditors. In one word, and contrary to the 'golden rule', the pertinent international transactions call for only money N, of which we can now represent the flows both in their nominal and real aspect(See Figure 10.6). Operation 1 is the purchase, by (the importers of) country *N* of country *S*'s trade surplus, which thus obtains a sum of deposits with *N*'s banks. Operation 2 is not a purchase; country *S* does not therefore spend any sum of money S; it is a deposit in money N that *S*'s debtors unilaterally transfer to their foreign creditors.

The indebted country (*S*) first tries to gain key currency bank deposits, an objective which it attains via a trade surplus; the country thus has the possibility of paying, to the benefit of its foreign creditors,

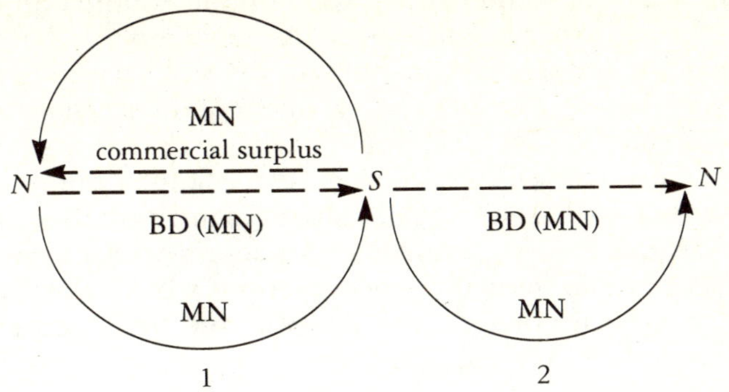

Figure 10.6

interests and amortization of its external debt (in money N). This clearly means that country *S* finally transfers to its creditors the whole (or part) of the monetary product, deposited with the banks of the North, which it first obtains as payment for its commercial surplus. Operations 1 and 2 of Figure 10.6 are then confirmed. It follows that, always to the extent of its current external debt servicing, the South pays the North in money N and is paid by the North with this same money: this lack of symmetry, money S not being associated with operations 1 and 2, defines the vice inherent in external debt servicing.

We now have to discover the exact meaning of this vice.

2. The exact meaning of the anomaly inherent in external debt servicing

Let us remind ourselves that, consistently with the first point of the 'golden rule' of international payments, in periods p′ the North pays for its external purchases of non-monetary financial goods in money N; symmetrically, country *S* pays for its (net) foreign commercial purchases in money S. Thus, each country earns the currency deposits required to cancel out non-residents' deposits in its own banks (second point of the 'golden rule').

In the case of external debt servicing, country *N* pays for its (net) commercial purchases in money N; but country *S* is bound to give up every payment in money S, and this is for the double reason that its foreign creditors require payment in money N and that country *N* does not sell any new *non-monetary* obligation that country *S* would purchase (in money S). Let us repeat, in fact, that if, in order to match its trade deficits (since period p), the North were required to export non-monetary financial bonds, country *S* would pay for them through the expenditure of an equivalent sum of money S: the non residents' deposits created in money S in country *N* and in money N in country *S* would verify, therefore, the first point of the 'golden rule', a necessary and sufficient condition for the enforcement of the second point of this rule. In fact, since the North *and the South* pay the entire external debt servicing *in the money of the North only*, the South cannot in the least impose on the North a measure of money S equivalent to the money N which it has to accept as payment for its commercial surplus.

Let us try again to show the way operations would take place if each country were authorized to impose on its partner, either symmetrically or within the equivalence of exchanges, a measure of its own money.

Country *S* would purchase from *N* new *non-monetary* financial obligations for a sum of x MS. For its part country *N* would purchase from *S* a commercial surplus for a sum of x MN. These two purchases and the way they are paid would conform to the first point of the 'golden rule of international payments'.

The second point of the 'golden rule' would then apply: *N* would buy back from *S* the deposit of x MN; reciprocally *S* would buy back from *N* the deposit of x MS.

Finally, in the application of the two points of the 'golden rule' we would ascertain that the goods exchanged between the two countries would eventually include no bank deposit: *N* would give up *non-monetary* financial goods, and *S* an equivalent surplus of commercial goods.

We are thus approaching the exact meaning of the disorder inherent in external debt servicing. *A contrario*, no disorder appears when the transfers of bank deposits are finally replaced by equivalent transfers of non-monetary real goods. It follows that the vice inherent in the servicing of external debts can be thus expressed: the indebted country (*S*) is bound to accept a final payment under the form of currency deposits. The order would be safe only if *S* received, as final payment for its trade surplus, a *non-monetary* foreign good.

Let us go back to the terms of the symmetry with which we are dealing here and which, according to our analysis, are not complied with in the case of external debt servicing.

In periods p′ neither the North nor the South get, as final payment, a sum of deposits with foreign banks; the North gets non-monetary financial bonds and the South an equivalent volume of net commercial imports. Since period p the South cannot avoid receiving, as final payment, a sum of deposits, which is equal to the servicing of its (previously accumulated) external debts, made up of *N*'s money. Hence, periods p′ show the perfect symmetry of international payments, since *non-monetary* real goods are transferred by *S* to *N* and by *N* to *S*, whereas *S*'s external debt servicing, carried out in period p, is the source of asymmetrical obligations for the two countries: *S* has to give up a commercial surplus while *N* only gives up, as 'counterpart', an equivalent sum of bank deposits (in money N), i.e. *monetary* real goods (bonds B).

We could even speak of a double symmetry; every external debt servicing creates an asymmetry in the very period (since p) in which it takes place; but every asymmetry of this kind is identically verified between the period (in p′) in which the corresponding debt is formed and the period (since p) in which it is serviced. Inevitably with all the weight placed on the indebted country alone, the asymmetry arising from the servicing of its foreign creditors is illustrated by the fact that the country is bound to accept simple currency deposits as unique and final payment of its trade surplus (unless it gives up servicing its external debt).

Let us resort to a series of simplified representations of the events occurring during periods p′ and, *mutatis mutandis*, since period p (Figure 10.7). It will be noted that we have introduced an indifferentiated vehicular money (MV); according to the 'golden rule' of international payments, vehicular currencies of different countries are in fact interchangeable. In the circuit of an 'abstract' vehicular money the North and the South are thus exchanging commercial surpluses and equivalent financial bonds, by which we mean, of course, *non-monetary* financial bonds (bonds of type B′).

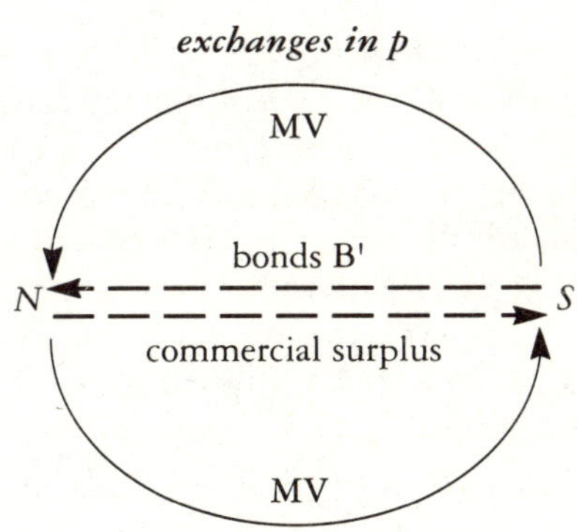

Figure 10.7

In period p country *S* starts servicing its foreign creditors, an operation which presupposes that *S* has a positive margin of net commercial exports (Figure 10.8) If the bonds given up by the North in period p were of type *non- monetary*, the order would be preserved since the two countries could then compensate bonds B′, currently obtained by *S*, by bonds B′ previously obtained by *N*. We would verify, then, that the 'golden rule' of international payments applies equally well in period p and in period p′.

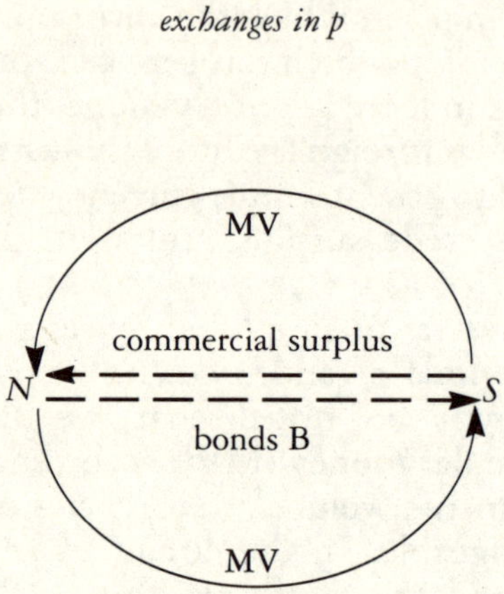

Figure 10.8

In reality, however, the North gives up bonds of type B, i.e. simple deposits with its banks. A reciprocal cancellation (compensation) of bonds B′ on the asset side of both countries is therefore not possible. The only available alternative for the indebted country is to transfer to its foreign creditors (totally or only partially) the bonds B (mere bank deposits) obtained as payment for its commercial surplus. Now, to transfer means to 'transport': a vehicular money is thus involved in the transfer of bonds B (from *S* to *N*) (Figure 10.9) This time the target has almost been hit. In so far as it services its external debts, the indebted country (*S*) is the object of a NET debit in vehicular money.

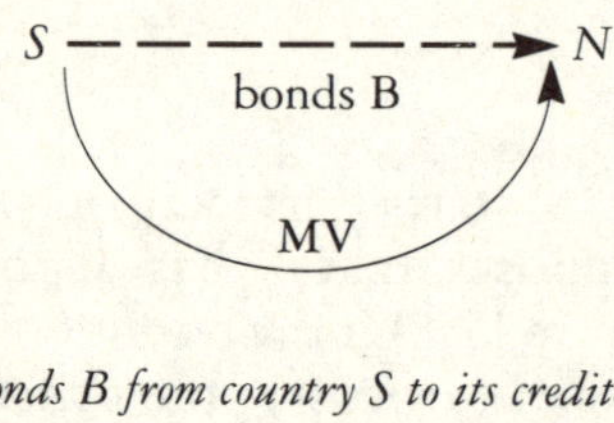

Figure 10.9 *Transfer of bonds B from country S to its creditors in N*

The same target is perfectly hit if we add a specification which, as a matter of fact, is evident: the nature of the vehicular money is clearly determined since the payment can only be carried out in money N. Insofar as it services its external debts, the indebted country (*S*) is the object of a NET DEBIT in VEHICULAR MONEY of COUNTRY N.

Given the intrinsic difficulty of the subject it is worthwhile to re-examine it *ab initio*. Let us reason again starting from 'principles'. The instant country *S* gets paid for its current net commercial exports country *N* is debited with a given amount of its own money, x MN. However, *S* immediately transforms this payment into an equivalent deposit with *N*'s banks. This is because money N is a *bank* money and because every payment carried out in bank money flows instantaneously back to the very bank which issues it. To reason differently would amount to mixing up money, as such, with monetary deposits. The beneficiary of a payment obtains, finally, the possession of a bank deposit: it is proof that it spends, without delay, the money which it gets in order to build up an equivalent deposit with the bank which carries out its payment. Hence, the instantaneous circuit which is defined by every flow of bank money is a *vehicular movement*. In the case we are analysing here, country *S* instantaneously sends back to country *N*'s banks the payment in money N which it gets as payment for its commercial surplus; we thus note that country *S* is instantaneously credited *and debited* with x units of money N, 'debit-credit' which is the definition of a circular movement of x units of money N or, identically, of x units of vehicular money N. Let us represent this circuit once again(See Figure 10.10).

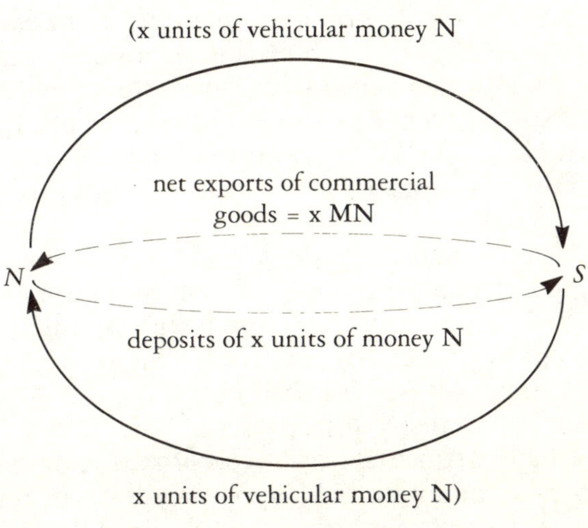

Figure 10.10

In the operation represented in Figure 10.10 the North gives up a sum of real goods under the form of deposits with its own banks (*monetary* financial bonds) up to x MN; reciprocally, the South gives up a surplus of commercial goods whose value is equal to x MN. It is certain, of course, that the bank deposits given up by *N* are as much real goods as are the commercial goods given up (as surplus) by *S*. Now, this payment is a 'monetized' exchange, that is to say a transaction taking place by means of a *monetary circuit*: nobody should mix up, therefore, the circuit described by x units of money N with the goods exchanged through the intermediary of this circuit. Represented by plain arrows, the vehicular money instantaneously 'passes through' the assets of *N* and *S*, whereas the real goods given up by both sides define positive deposits: a bank deposit of x units of money N is entered on the asset side of *S*'s balance sheet and an equivalent sum of commercial goods is entered on *N*'s asset side.

To summarize we see that the exchange of bank deposits (in money N) and commercial goods (produced by *S*) calls for the circuit of x units of money N: country *S* is thus simultaneously credited and debited with the sum of x units of money N. Country *S* is credited with x MN as payment for its commercial surplus, and *S* is immediately debited with x MN in order to create an equivalent deposit in its favour with the banks of country *N*.

Everything is all right up to here. But a serious disorder appears when country *S* starts servicing its external debts: to this purpose *S* is *debited* with x units of money N, a *net debit* by which *S* transfers to its creditors the ownership of equivalent bank deposits with the banks of the North. And how could *S* transfer to its creditors a bank deposit in money N *if not through the debit of its accounts with the banks of country N*? Once the distinction between a '*flow of debit*' (*vehicular* money) and the object of this debit (bank deposit or *real* money) has been understood it becomes clear that every time it services its external debt country *S* suffers from *two distinct sacrifices* since it undergoes a VEHICULAR NET DEBIT of x units of money N simply to transfer unilaterally a DEPOSIT of x units of money N to its foreign creditors. (Figure 10.11)

Figure 10.11 represents the *double debit* of country *S*, which transfers a *deposit* of x units of money N to its foreign creditors (Figure 10.12) and which, moreover, is debited with x units of *vehicular* money, x MN, to the benefit of country *N* (Figure 10.13).

It is logically impossible to transfer a bank deposit — a sum of *real* money — if not by the debit of its present holder and the credit of its new owner, which defines a flow of *vehicular* money; and, since country *S* transfers a deposit of x MN to its creditors in country *N*, *S* is debited with x MN. In a few words, country *S* provides both the vector of the transfer and the object to be transferred: the vector is the sum of

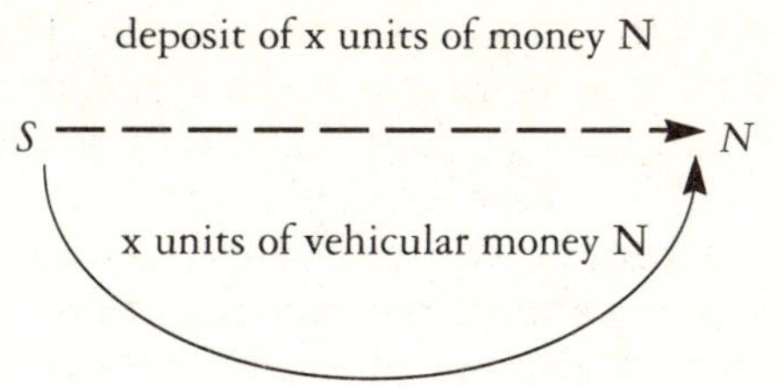

Figure 10.11

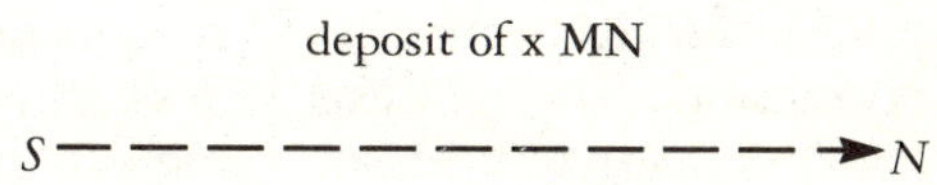

Figure 10.12

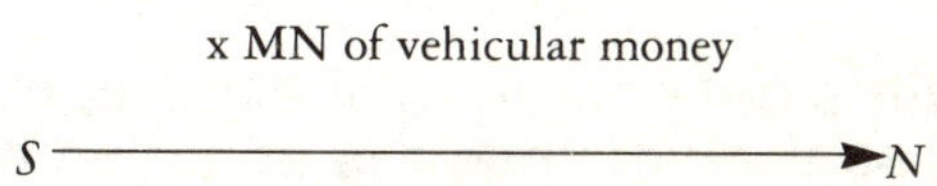

Figure 10.13

x units of money N which carries an equivalent deposit in money N to *S*'s creditors.

The distinction of the two monies, nominal and real, is not at all mysterious; on the contrary, it can be found everywhere, even within domestic transactions. Let us suppose *n* and *s* to be residents of the same country, and MN to be the currency of this country. To transfer a deposit of x MN to his correspondent, *s* has to ask for his bank account to be debited with x MN: correlatively, *n* is credited with x MN. As soon as we distinguish between the actions and their results we can see that the action or the operation defining the debit of *s* and the credit of *n* is the necessary and sufficent condition for the transfer of a deposit of x MN from *s* to *n*. Considered in itself this transaction is a movement of *vehicular* money; its result is a sum of *real* money newly deposited with *n*.

We have just seen that it is perfectly 'normal' for every 'payer' to be debited *twice*, that is, in *vehicular* money and in *real* money. Given this, where can be found the alleged anomaly which would afflict the indebted country (*S*)? Despite appearances to the contrary, it is certainly there. To discover it, it is enough to look more closely at the comparison between domestic payments and international payments. In order to transfer a *deposit* of x MN to his correspondent, *s* is effectively *debited* with x units of *vehicular* money; however, in the same movement, that is instantaneously, *s* is *credited* with x units of vehicular money; globally, therefore, *s* is faced with *no net debit* in vehicular money: in the operation under investigation *s* is *debited only once*, namely through the *negative* transfer (to the profit of *n*) of x units of *real* money. As far as country *S* is concerned, relative to international transactions, the analysis is less smooth: *S is debited without being credited* with x units of vehicular money (x MN); it follows that *S* is submitted to two distinct debits since its debit is net in money N both in terms of *vehicular* money and in terms of *real* money.

The vice we have just been discovering is of the utmost gravity since it nullifies the payments of country *S*'s commercial surplus as long as these are employed to service its foreign creditors.

3. The South's net commercial exports remain unpaid in so far as their payment is annulled when transferred to foreign creditors

Let us first enunciate a truism: an economic agent cannot keep owning the sum of money which he has just given up to his creditors. If, within the period we have been considering, the South gains a deposit of x units of money B from its commercial surplus, it would be absurd to claim that *S* can simultaneously retain this gain and use it for the servicing of its external debt. However, is it really true that the South is deprived of the payment of its net commercial exports since it gives it up to its creditors? In fact, such a conclusion would be wrong. Like every physical or moral person, the South has to honour its obligations: it is therefore perfectly licit for the South to sacrifice at least part of its net external gain in order to service, in interests and amortization, its foreign creditors. The following scheme illustrates this truism, as shown in Figure 10.14.

The payment of its current commercial surplus gives to the South the ownership of a deposit with the banks of the North, of an amount of x MB; successively the South has this deposit transferred to its creditors

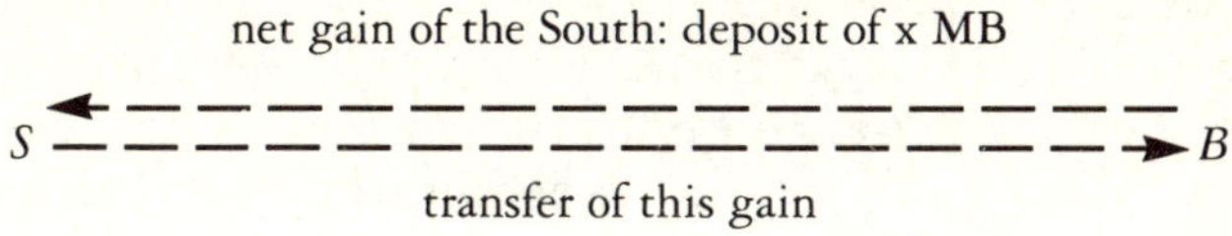

Figure 10.14

in the North: is it logical, in these conditions, to conclude that the South has not obtained, finally, *any payment* for its trade surplus? The correct answer is, obviously, that the South has fully obtained the countervalue of its net exports, from which it has definitively gained x units of money deposited with the banks of the North. In other words, the external net gain of the South is *not in the least under dispute* at the instant it is transferred to *N*'s foreign creditors; on the contrary, *S*'s external income is *confirmed* since nobody could positively transfer an income which had been cancelled. The external gain of the South remains net since the South gives it up to the benefit of its creditors in the North. 'The one who pays his debts gets richer'. The South is therefore the beneficiary of the gain which it derives from its trade surplus *even after having used it for the servicing of its external debt*.

Transposed into more *formal* language the preceding truism reads as follows: the transfer of an external income of *S* is an expenditure which does not at all diminish the initial *formation* of this income. In other words, the formation of *S*'s income and the subsequent expenditure of this income are opposite flows which cannot neutralize each other.

Let us develop this analysis further, and call IF the formation of *S*'s external income and IE the expenditure of this income to the profit of the foreign creditors of the South. In a given period the South witnesses the positive formation of an external income, derived from the payment of its trade surplus: IF = x MB. In the same period the South spends this income on the current service of its external debt: IE = x MB. It would be totally illogical to *merge* these expenditures of opposite sign as if the formation of *S*'s external income were positive only for *the difference IF − IE = 0*. In reality, the expenditure concerning the *formation* of *S*'s external income is *net* relative to every expenditure concerning the *disposition* of this income; if this were not the case, every income formation would be neutralized by the subsequent expenditure of this income, so that the economic agents would systematically nourish positive expenditures out of non-existent incomes! This absurdity is avoided when, relative to *S*, the *positive* expenditure IF and the *negative* expenditure IF are kept separate; empirical observation shows that these expenditures do not 'fuse' together. It is true that, in this respect, not every 'fusion' is definitively avoided: the *result* of expenditure IF (= + x MB) and the *opposite result* of expenditure IE (= − x MB) define one and the same reality, positive and negative, i.e. a sum equal to zero (+ − x MB). Finally, the *expenditures* of opposite sign remain net relative to one another but the *results* of these expenditures are fused together and verify the cancellation of opposites.

Our analysis has been developed here at the level of a simple truism. Now, truisms are obvious truths in every *logical system*; we are therefore compelled to speak of a *non-system* each time that a truism is not complied with. And this is precisely what we are going to verify in the case of external debt servicing: in the actual regime of international payments the very formation of the indebted country's external incomes is retroactively cancelled out at the moment *S* services its foreign creditors.

It is difficult to break down a truism. The fact is that it is particularly embarrassing to treat as self-evident the invalidation of evidence. This is, however, the task we are confronted with; not to face it would amount to avoiding what should be the duty of every economist who becomes aware of a fundamental disorder affecting the world economy. Nothing is more serious than the denial of a truism within the world of real transactions: in the case we are analysing, the resulting illogicality is the source of an international payments disorder which endangers the well-being and even the survival of a great number of people.

As a matter of fact, the demonstration that we have to provide here is already well on its way; taking advantage of our preceding arguments we have merely to conclude.

Let us first consider the application of the 'golden rule' of international payments to the case of external debt servicing. If the 'rule' applies this means that the *negative* expenditures, the transfer of country *S*'s income to the benefit of its foreign creditors, do not modify the *positive* expenditures, the formation of the corresponding external income of country *S*; the 'truism of payments' is thus safe.

Now, if the 'golden rule' applies to the external debt servicing, thus confirming the truism of payments, this also means that the North, instead of paying for its net imports in money, pays for them by selling non-monetary financial bonds (B′) to the South. We are then confronted with two perfect circuits of vehicular money (Figure 10.15). In this first circuit country *S* purchases non-monetary financial bonds (B′) up to the amount of x MS from the North; which, thus, obtains deposits with the banks of the South up to a value of x MS, an exact counterpart of the bonds given up by the South. It is therefore important to distinguish carefully the circuit of x units of money S (vehicular movement represented by plain lines) from the real objects, deposits and bonds, transported from one side to the other (two flows

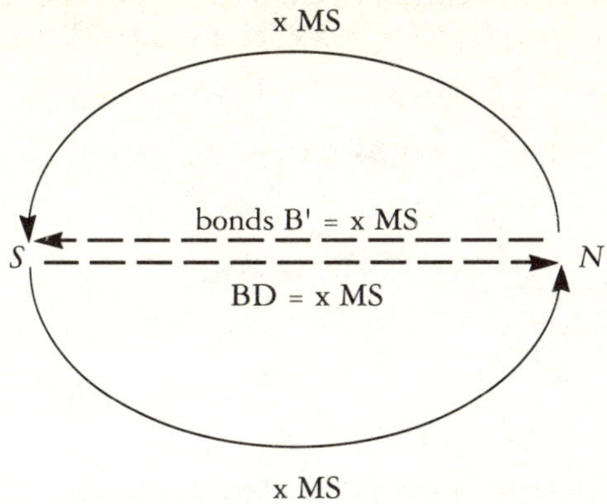

Figure 10.15 *First circuit of vehicular money*

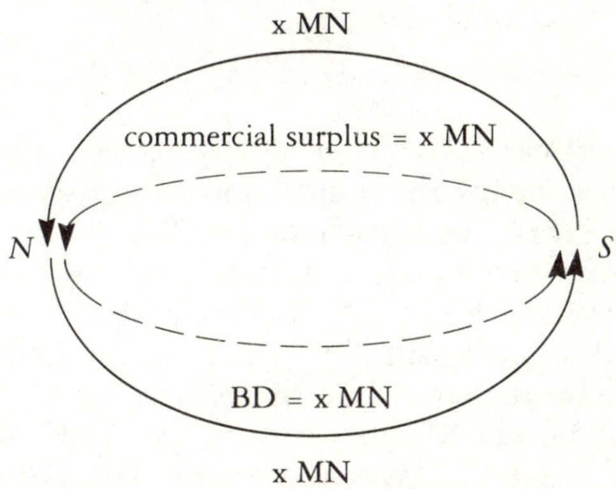

Figure 10.16 *Second circuit of vehicular money*

of opposite direction represented by dotted lines: See Figure 10.16).

This second circuit confirms the application of the first point of the 'golden rule', since every country pays for its imports in its own money. The South pays for the bonds (B′) issued by the North (first circuit) in its domestic money; the North pays the net commercial exports of the South in its national money (second circuit). Hence, the circuit of x units of money N (plain lines) allows the reciprocal transfer of real goods (dotted lines), the transport of a bank deposit of x MN to the benefit of the South and, as exact counterpart, of a commercial surplus to the profit of the North.

These two circuits bring a deposit of x MS to the North and a deposit of x MN to the South; now, these two countries are finally paid in their own money by the application of the second point of the 'golden rule'; a third circuit carries out this task (See Figure 10.17).

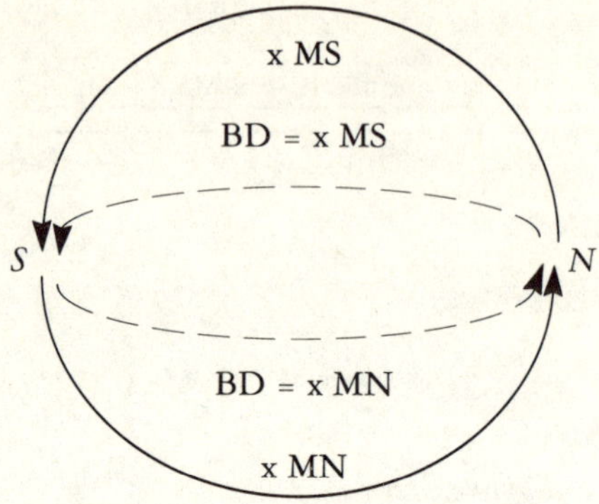

Figure 10.17 *Third circuit of vehicular money*

Each country, South and North, has finally been paid for its exports (of commercial goods, as for the South, and of non-monetary financial bonds, as for the North) in its own money. What has to be 'organized' now is the South's current external debt servicing. Two amounts of non-monetary financial bonds (B′) face each other. The South has at its disposal bonds B'_N newly issued by the North in order to finance its current commercial deficit, while the North can count on a whole accumulation of bonds B'_S previously issued by the South when (periods p′) its external debt was formed. The argument develops following the same path as before; three new circuits are formed, which are perfectly similar to those we have just represented: the South buys back from the North bonds B'_S up to a value of x MS, and, reciprocally, the North buys back from the South an equivalent amount of bonds B'_N newly created in the current period. From then on the 'golden rule' of international payments applies (without there being any need to represent it with new schemes, which would merely be repetitive).

Now, as we have already established, reality shows that the application of the 'golden rule' in the case of external debt servicing is impossible. We can therefore deduce that *every external debt servicing is an expenditure of the indebted country's external income disposition, IE, which affects the corresponding expenditure of income formation, IF*. According to the truism, IF is net relative to IE, since every person, natural or juridical, benefits from an income formation which is not modified by its subsequent expenditure; the external debt servicing case is therefore highly original and worrying: the indebted country (*S*) verifies a decrease — not only of its external income already formed (which is consistent with the truism) — but also of the very *formation* of its net external gains. In other words, the instant the indebted country sacrifices part of its external gains (invariably due to its trade surplus) to service its foreign creditors, its decision affects retroactively the formation of these gains, which are *purely and simply cancelled out*. Let us repeat that it is the FORMATION of the gain which is under dispute and not (according to the truism) the gain itself. For an indebted country, the formula expressing the formation of its net external income is, in every period, the difference between IF and IE_s (where IE_s is the current service of its external debt, in interests and amortization). In period p (for example) country *S* realizes a trade surplus of x MN; if it sacrifices this external income in order to service its foreign creditors, *S* provokes — against its own will, of course — the retroactive cancellation of its international gain, so that its net commercial exports literally bring *nothing* to it. In fact, the formula IF - IE_s gives x MN − x MN as a measure of the current formation of country *S*'s external income. It is clear that the truism gives a different solution, the formation of *S*'s external income remaining equal to x MN despite the fact that this income is successively sacrificed in the payment of interests or amortization due from *S*. It is the truism which conforms to reason; how could this be denied? but it is the draconian and leonine formula (IF - IE_s) which unfortunately applies in the real world. What we all have to do first is to 'read' the facts and accept them as they are; it would be to easy to declare 'normatively' that the truism is correct and that its application is therefore warranted.

Let us add some information which, although already implicit in the previous argument, is worth making explicit. Let us suppose that in our example country *S* is able to credit its foreign creditors with a sum of x MN. As a consequence, we get the impression that everything is, eventually, going to work well. In reality, however, this is not so: the *formation* of *S*'s external income is inevitably diminished, cancelled out up to the amount of x MN. If the current servicing of *S*'s external debt amounts, nevertheless, to x MN this is because *S gets instantaneously into a new debt of the same amount*. In fact, since its external trade brings a gain invalidated at source, country *S* has no net external income at its disposal which could nourish the current servicing of its external debt; if it can none the less pay its creditors up to x MN this is because it finds this sum in the financial market: this means that *S* gets into a new debt simply in order to get rid of a previous debt which it could have paid entirely thanks to its trade surplus if (consistent with the truism) the latter had given it a definite gain. The system is such that country *S* is a helpless witness to the retroactive cancellation of its international gain formation. This gain, due to its trade surplus, will have finally brought it a *net loss* of commercial goods, i.e. a '*loss without cause*'.

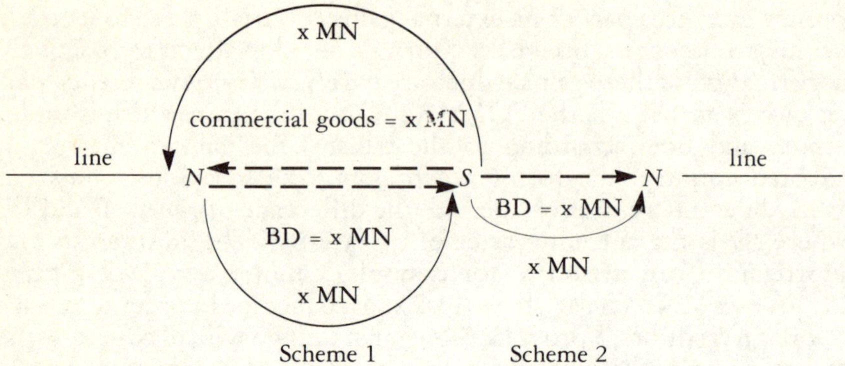

Figure 10.18

Let us propose a simpler demonstration on the basis of the schemes to which the reader is already accustomed (Figure 10.18). Scheme 1 represents *N*'s payment of country *S*'s current trade surplus: through the circuit of x MN country *N* transfers a bank deposit of x MN to its partner in exchange for an equivalent amount of net commercial goods.

Scheme 2 represents the current external debt servicing of country *S*, which unilaterally transfers to its creditors the deposit of x MN which it had obtained as payment for its trade surplus.

We have added a 'line' in order to be able to reason separately about the flows occurring above and below the 'line'.

Let us first note that scheme 2 is only concerned with flows situated below the 'line'; how should this be interpreted? The fact is that scheme 2 refers to *two additional debts* of *S*, one defined in *vehicular* money (plain line) and the other in *real* money (dotted line). From this we can make a very important induction: *S* is debited both at the level of its *formed* income (loss of a deposit of x MN) and at the level of its external income *formation* (net debt of x MN in vehicular money).

Let us now reason by taking into account both schemes, 1 and 2, again below the 'line'. Relative to *real* flows, i.e. the movements of a bank deposit of x MN, we notice that *S* loses (scheme 2) the external income formed in its trade surplus (scheme 1) ; this loss is 'normal' and conforms to the truism: it would be inconceivable for a debtor (*S*) to keep hold of the very income which it transfers to its creditor (*N*). But this is not all; in fact, we have not yet considered the *vehicular* flows, *S* being, in this respect, credited with x MN first (scheme 1 below the 'line') and then debited with x MN (scheme 2): globally, therefore, *S* is subjected below the 'line' to a debit-credit of x units of vehicular money. This clearly means that *S* is not the beneficiary of any *net formation* of external income below the 'line': this time the withdrawal takes place at the level of *S*'s external income FORMATION and not only (as the truism would require) at the level of its income FORMED in the international market. As the analysis has already established, the external debt servicing of country *S* defines an income expenditure, IE_s, which logically affects the formation of its corresponding income, IF, so that *S* only benefits from *zero formation* of its external income, $IF - IE_s = x\,MN - x\,MN = 0$. This result holds good for the simple reason that the external debt servicing (scheme 2) does not entail any credit of *S* in vehicular money (total absence of flows above the 'line' in scheme 2).

If we now consider what happens above the 'line' we can easily see that this conculsion is not modified, since above the 'line' country *S* is debited both in *real* and in *vehicular* money. The truism would prevail only if the indebted country (*S*) could maintain the benefit of a positive formation of external income proportional to its trade surplus; in reality *S* suffers from the retroactive cancellation of its external income formation as soon as it transfers it to service its foreign creditors (See Figure 10.19). Scheme 3 shows the depth of the vice: although it has sacrificed the monetary counterpart of its net commercial exports (deposits of x MN), *S* still has to face the same external indebtedness since it has to provide for the *net debit of x MN*, of which it is the object in vehicular money.

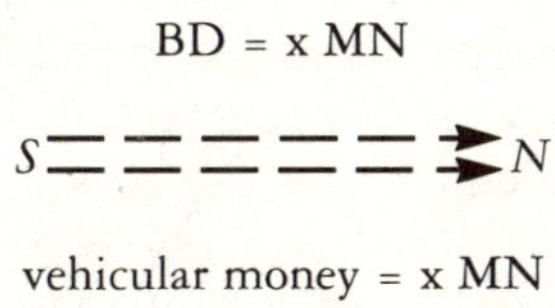

Scheme 3

Figure 10.19

If country *S* did not sacrifice its external gain for the servicing of its foreign creditors, its trade surplus would define the final formation, to its profit, of an international income. We can thus see that the net commercial exports of a *non-indebted* country define the *final formation* of a positive external income (to its benefit). It is the indebted country (*S*) which suffers from the vice; it is only to this country that the formal anomaly of international payments applies and deprives it of the external incomes which it so greatly needs in order to face its international obligations.

The disorder characterizing the actual system of international payments can be illustrated by means of the distinction between intermediary and final goods. Let us note, however, that vehicular money are not goods at all; it would be totally wrong, therefore, to classify them as *intermediary* goods. But bank deposits are goods, and it is at this level that the analysis has to be further developed.

Every time the 'golden rule' of international payments applies, transactions show that each country first obtains a deposit with the banks of its partner; country *S* thus obtains a deposit in money N and country *N* a deposit in money S. This is the direct consequence of the first point of the 'rule': each country pays for its imports in its domestic money. Now, the second point of the 'rule' has a univocal meaning: each partner 'repatriates' the deposits in its own money formed abroad. Once these repatriations have been carried out it becomes clear that the terms of the exchanges considered here are real, and that they do not imply any bank deposit but are only made up of commercial goods and non-monetary financial bonds. In periods p′, when the 'golden rule' is complied with, the South finally gives up non-monetary financial bonds as payment for *N*'s trade surplus: first formed 'face to face', the bank deposits of *S* with *N* and of *N* with *S* will have played the role of intermediary goods, eventually leaving their place to the single category of non-monetary goods (either commercial or financial).

It is true that the case of *non-indebted* surplus countries also seems to be problematic. If country *S* were not indebted, would it not receive as *final* payment deposits with the banks of country *N*? If this were so, the 'golden rule' would not be complied with even in this case, i.e. even in the absence of any external debt servicing. In reality, however, the 'rule' applies. Let us prove it.

Proof of the application of the 'golden rule' to the case of a non-indebted surplus country Let us suppose *S* to be a non-indebted surplus country.

Country *N* first pays its net imports of commercial goods in its own money (Figure 10.20).

Country *S* also pays in its own money its net purchases of bank deposits in money N (Figure 10.21).

We note that country *S* finally obtains a sum of deposits in money N because it *purchases* them; it *imports* them in exactly the same way as country *N* imports a surplus of commercial goods.

The first point of the 'rule' has therefore been applied; but, then, the second also applies since each country eventually 'repatriates' the bank deposits, in its own money, owned by its partner.

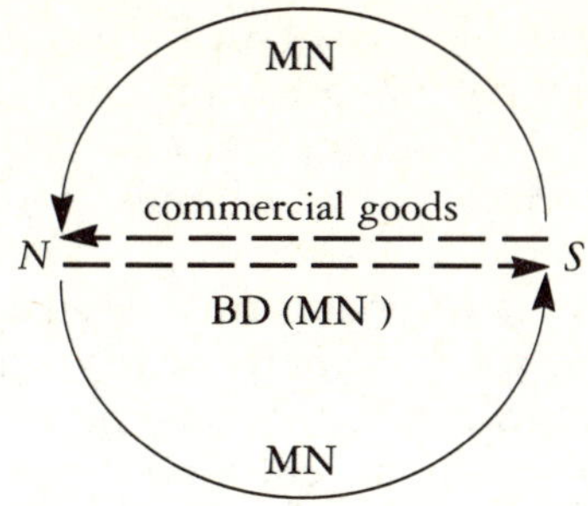

Figure 10.20

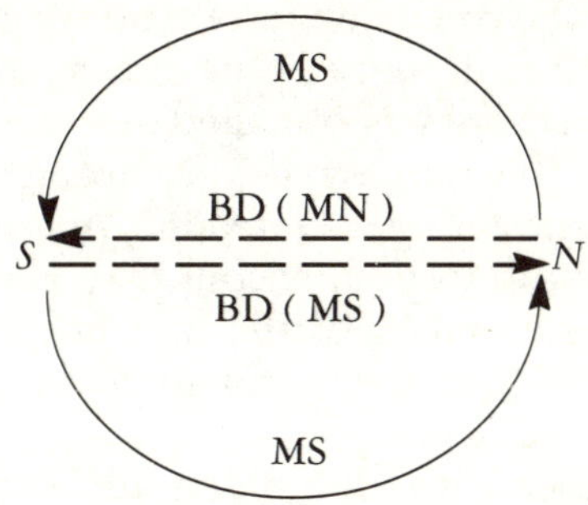

Figure 10.21

The essential thing is to note that the bank deposits reciprocally given up by each partner in its own money merely play the role of *intermediary* goods; the 'golden rule' is therefore perfectly complied with. If it happens, as is the case here, that a deposit in money N is finally owned by country *S* it must be clear that this deposit is not the one which country *N* had initially lost in the payment of its net commercial imports; the cross-expenditure of bank deposits followed by their 'repatriation' undoubtedly corroborates the free working of the 'golden rule': each country purchases final goods through the intermediation of bank deposits; for country *N* these goods are commercial goods while for country *S* they are financial, and take the form of bank deposits; but it would be illogical to induce from this that the same deposits in money N play both the role of an intermediary good and of a final good. In reality, every deposit finally owned by the surplus country (*S*) defines either an increase in its capital or an increase in its reserves, that is to say the increment of a *real* quantity.

In this respect everything would be perfectly clear if the 'golden rule' were verified on condition that for each partner in the transaction there were an equivalent outflow-inflow of bank deposits in its own money: this circular movement having been verified, it is not important whether or not the surplus country chooses to hold its net financial enrichment under the form of 'normal' bonds (B′) or under the 'liquid' form (bonds B).

We can now turn our attention towards the analysis of the only case which interests us in this work, namely the payment of a trade surplus of the *indebted* country (*S*). In fact, this is the *only case* in which the 'golden rule' is effectively infringed. Country *S* does not obtain a deposit in money N which it could later exchange against a deposit in its own money formed to the credit of country *N*; as a matter of fact country *S* does not exchange a deposit in money S against a deposit in money N: from the beginning of the operation country *S* exchanges its commercial surplus against a deposit in money N; this deposit in money N never plays the role of an *intermediary* good, since country *N* never obtains a deposit in money S as 'means of exchange'; on the contrary, the deposit in money N obtained by country *S* in payment of its trade surplus is finally transferred to its foreign creditors *without country N ever purchasing it against deposits in money S*. The 'rule' is therefore infringed in both its points: country *S* alone obtains deposits in foreign money (infringement of the first point of the 'rule') and, consequently, country *N* alone is finally paid in its own money (infringement of the second).

The lack of compliance with the 'golden rule' entails a very concrete consequence; let us work it out.

Every transaction between country *S* and country *N* which conforms to the 'rule' first implies the international exchange of a deposit in money S against a deposit in money N and ends up with the opposite exchange, i.e. with the 'repatriation' of these deposits (See Figure 10.22). Each of these exchanges implies a perfect circuit of vehicular money.

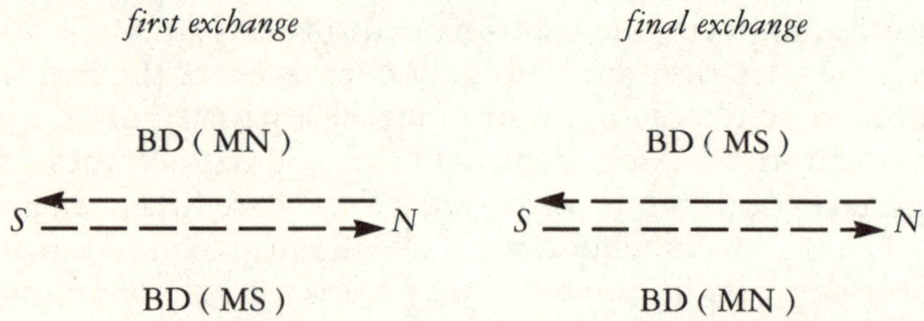

Figure 10.22

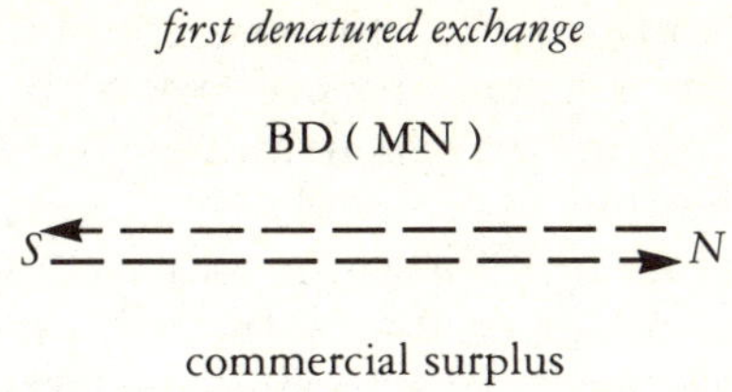

Figure 10.23

Every monetary transaction taking place between country *S* and *N* complies with this description *except one*.

In order to service its external debts, country *S* has to exchange a commercial surplus — and not a deposit in money S — against a deposit in money N. Thus, even the 'first exchange' is denatured (Figure 10.23).

At this stage of the analysis the vice does not seem too serious since the denatured exchange that we have just represented implies a perfect circuit of vehicular money.

Yet, starting from the next stage, the effective servicing of *S*'s external creditors, country *S* has to give up, *without any reciprocity* (on the side of *N*) a positive amount of deposits in money N. This unilateral transfer is the mark of a *maimed* exchange from which the second term is missing. The symmetry would be preserved only if country *N* gave up an equivalent deposit in money S (as is represented in Figure 10.22). Things being what they are, country *N* does not give up any deposit in money S in exchange for the deposit in money N given up by country *S*. This serious asymmetry spreads the disorder within international payments Figure 10.24.

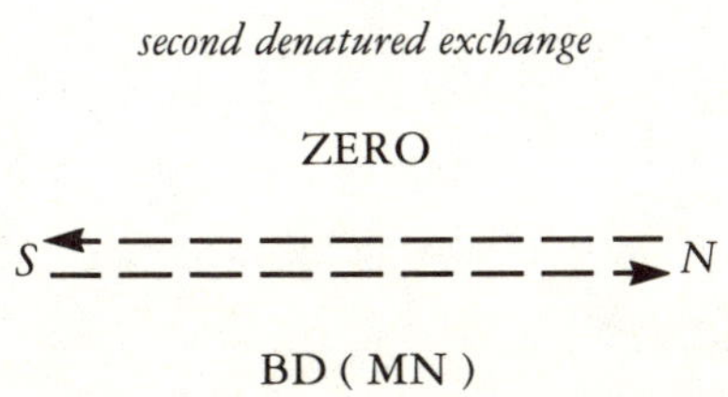

Figure 10.24

From Figure 10.24 it appears that country *S* is *debited* in money N without being *credited* in money N; it is 'normal', as we have repeatedly pointed out, for the indebted country (*S*) to lose a bank deposit to the benefit of its creditors. Every bank deposit is a sum of real money; and debtors owe real money — savings — to their creditors. Hence, the flow represented by a dotted line conforms to logic: country *S* can face its obligations only by transferring part of its current income to its foreign creditors. Indeed, it is quite 'normal' for a country to draw on its purchasing power in order to service its external debt (interests and principal). Yet every servicing of an external debt is a truncated exchange for a totally different reason: namely because it does not provide any credit in vehicular money to the indebted country. Country *S* cannot avoid transferring part of its income to its foreign creditors: what is inconsistent is the fact that, in order to carry out this transfer, the indebted country has to suffer from a net debit in vehicular money.

To state this another way, we can see that it is absurd — but it is an absurdity of the real world — for the indebted country (*S*) to be faced with the obligation to *purchase at a cost* (significant pleonasm) a monetary VECTOR in order to transfer a monetary deposit to its creditors.

Diagnosis of the vice inherent in international payments: the indebted country has to buy the vector of the transfer it addresses to its creditors.

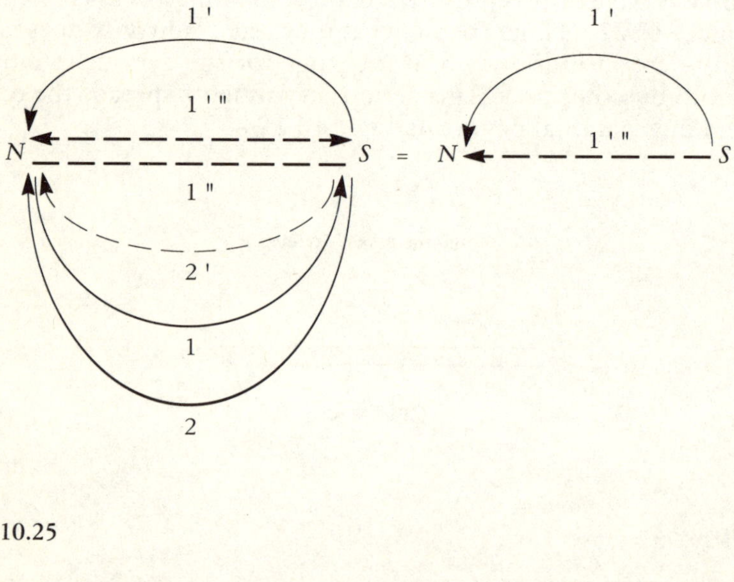

Figure 10.25

Let us repeat our argument referring to two new schemes, very similar to the previous ones but 'purged'. Only money N is present (both as a vehicular object and a real good deposited with the banks). As usual we represent the vehicular flows by plain lines and the real flows (even monetary: i.e. the 'displacements' of bank deposits) by dotted lines (See Figure 10.25). Let us analyse these flows one after the other.

1. Flow 1 is the monetary or *nominal* payment by *N* of *S*'s net commercial exports.
2. Flow 1' is the instantaneous deposit of the sum of money N obtained by *S* (in flow 1); the corresponding deposits are in *N*'s banks; this is the reason why flow 1', which starts in *S*, ends up in *N*.
3. Flow 1" is the 'displacement' of a deposit in money N; in fact, by depositing money N (flow 1'), *S* obtains an equivalent sum of deposits in *N*'s banks.
4. Flow 1'" is the counterpart of flow 1": *S* gives *N* an amount of commercial goods equivalent to the bank deposits given up by *N*.
5. Flow 2 is the monetary or *nominal* debit that *S* assumes in view of the transfer of bank deposits to its creditors in *N*.
6. Flow 2', consequence of flow 2, is the 'displacement' of a deposit in money N; *S* is therefore effectively able to transfer a sum of deposits in money N to its creditors in *N*.

All these flows come down to only TWO flows, represented by the 'half-circle' and the corresponding real movement. We thus end up with flow 1', monetary or *nominal*, vector of flow 1'": in just a few words *country S is simultaneously — that is ADDITIONALLY — debited in money N (flow 1') and in commercial goods (flow 1'")*.

The indebted country (*S*) would be paid for its net commercial exports only if these net exports saved it from the obligation to purchase (and pay for) the monetary vector of the deposits transferred to its creditors, *which is not the case in the real world*.

Chapter Eleven

Experimental Verification of the Vice Inherent in External Debt Servicing

The division of the real world into country *S* and country *N* is a simplification that we can maintain as long as it is agreed that *S* is the set of the indebted countries and *N* the set of the corresponding creditor countries; these sets are both made up of a great number of countries; however, we shall go on referring to the money of the South and the money of the North considering both money S and money N as being homogeneous.

The asymmetry we have pointed out in the previous chapters has a direct impact on the exchange market where money N is the object of an excess demand in terms of money S; the measure of this excess demand is precise: in each period it concerns the total amount of money N earned by the South through its net commercial exports and thrown into the current servicing of its external debt.

It is obvious that the South should not be forced to purchase and pay for, at the expense of the external value of its own money, the currencies which it earns through its trade surplus. Yet, in fact, the South is subjected to the double charge of its external debt servicing: the currencies transferred to the foreign creditors of the South are paid for twice by the South, a first time through the net export of commercial goods and a second time through the purchase, in money S, of the currencies thus earned.

Even if the South were able to cover the final servicing of its foreign creditors by transferring an equivalent amount of money S to them, the problem would not be solved since every sum of money S held by the residents of the North defines a debt of the South towards the North (section 1).

The final servicing of *S*'s external debt can therefore only be carried out in money N; this is the reason why, in every period in which it can service its external debt, the South has first to realize a net external gain; logically, this gain (in foreign currencies, i.e. in money N) can only come from its trade surplus. Factual observation confirms the constraint faced by the indebted countries (*S*) who have to realize a net export of commercial goods in order to gain the amount of foreign currencies necessary for the servicing of their external debts (section 2).

The currencies (of the North) earned by the South through its net commercial exports should be at its disposal for the servicing of its external debt, free of cost; now, it is clear that the residents of the South who are indebted with the external world cannot obtain the currencies held by their country free of cost (section 3).

The indebted residents of the South can service their foreign creditors only in so far as they purchase, through the expenditure of their income (formed in their domestic money), the currencies earned by their country (as counterpart of its trade surplus); these purchases define an equivalent excess demand for money N in terms of money S (section 4).

1. The South cannot carry out its external debt servicing in money S

Let us suppose that in period p the residents of the South who are indebted to the Rest of the World are able to save 2 million units of money, 2 MS (in million). Let us also suppose that 1 MS = 1 MN (except in the case where the external value of *S*'s money is modified by the influence of the current servicing of its debts). The indebted residents honour their obligations when they transfer this sum to their creditors in the North, (Figure 11.1). What we have just represented is a *real* flow, since *bank deposits* to a total value of 2 MS are given up by the indebted residents of the South and are recorded among the assets of their creditors in the North.

2 MS

residents of the South — — — — — — — → creditors in the North

Figure 11.1

There is no doubt that the indebted *residents* suffer a loss of 2 MS at the instant their bank deposits are decreased by this amount; in this respect everthing happens as if their correspondents were residents of the South. It is true that money S has no 'liberating power' in the North; but this is only a legal argument. The economic sacrifice imposed on the indebted residents is equal to 2 MS; and since a monetary loss is always accompanied by a correlative monetary gain, it is certain that the North finds a real payment in the bank assets it gets from the South in money S.

The observation of real events constantly shows that the creditors of the South finally demand to be paid in money N. It follows, therefore, that the sum of 2 MS first received by the creditors of the South is finally converted into money N. At this stage of the analysis it seems that the creditors' requirement to convert money S into money N is 'descriptive' and, therefore, deprived of any fundamental significance. It would be a matter of 'behaviour' and not an economic constraint. If this were effectively so, we would be allowed to conclude that the payment of the creditors in money S is perfectly valid in itself.

In reality, however, there is an economic law which is at work here: in fact, even if the creditors agreed to hold their assets indefinitely in money S, the indebted country *would still owe the entire sum of 2 MS transferred by its indebted residents*. The reason is that every sum of money deposited with a bank defines the bank's acknowledgment of debt to its customer. The banks of the South thus owe the sum of 2 MS deposited by the creditors of the North. It therefore appears that *S*'s debt has remained unchanged since new debtors have taken the place of the early debtors: the indebted residents have decreased their debt by 2 MS, the amount of their transfer, but the banks of country *S* are now indebted for the same amount to the creditors of the North (Figure 11.2). Let us recall that bonds B′ are *non-monetary* obligations while bonds B are credits with the banks. As results from this representation, country *S*'s servicing of its external debt in money S ends up with the simple substitution, in the assets of the North, of bonds B′ with an equivalent sum of bonds B.

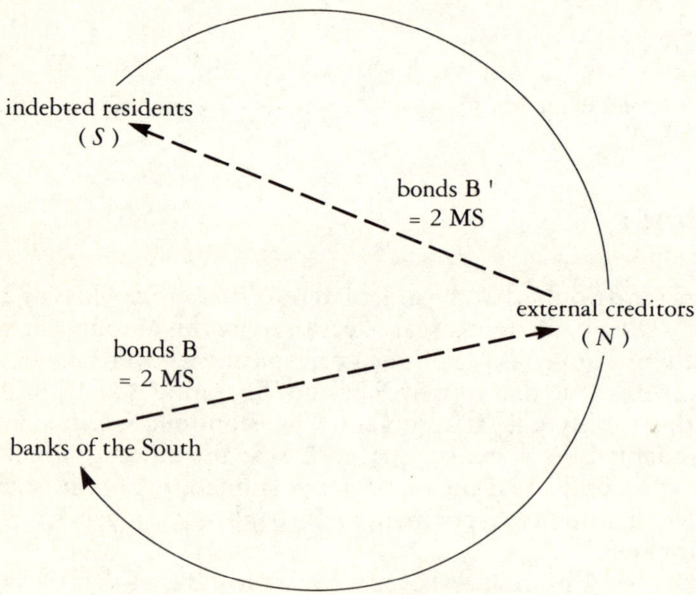

Figure 11.2

If we were allowed a neologism we would say that the experience we have just described is *counterproductive*, to the detriment of country *S*. The total of this country's external debt remains *unchanged* even though it has sacrified a saving of 2 million units in money S to the payment of its foreign creditors. The loss is *net*: country *S*'s banks are now carrying the burden of that part of the country's external debt which its residents have paid for through the sacrifice of 2 MS. We can clearly see here how important it is, if we want to observe facts as they really are, to distinguish the residents of the indebted country from the country itself: the initially indebted residents are able to run away from their debt through the transfer of 2 MS to the profit of their foreign creditors; however country *S* considered as a whole does not benefit from the operation since the external indebtedness of its banks grows by 2 MS. The distinction between the residents of *S* and country *S* applies again: *S*'s banks are not at all damaged since their internal indebtedness decreases to the very extent that their external indebtedness grows; yet it remains true that country *S* as a whole suffers a net loss of 2 million units of money S since its external debt does not decrease despite the transfer, to its foreign creditors, of the sum of 2 million units of money S.

External debt of country S
BEFORE the transfer of 2 MS to its
foreign creditors:
z million units of money S

External debt of country S
AFTER the transfer of 2 MS to its
foreign creditors:
z million units of money S

It is certain that logic and order would be respected only if the current transfer of 2 MS to the creditors of the North decreased the external indebtedness of the South, which, in millions, would thus be reduced from z MS to (z − 2) MS. The observation of facts, on the contrary, shows that the new indebtedness of country *S* remains at the *unchanged* level of z MS.

The exact principle which guarantees the full success of an external debt servicing is the following: the operation is fair to the indebted country (and to the rest of the world) on the necessary and sufficient condition that the indebted residents and their countries free themselves from debts *in parallel*; by contrast, if the residents free themselves only in so far as their debt is carried over to their countries it is clear that the latter suffers an equivalent set-back since its debt remains unchanged despite the real loss incurred by its residents, whose savings are transferred without there being any counterpart for the indebted country itself.

Let us take advantage of the previous observations by 'formalizing' the distinction between the two levels at which external debts declare themselves: they first relate to the indebted *residents* but they also imply their *countries*.

Let us consider an indebted country R taken as a whole (set) and its indebted residents R', also taken as a whole. Let us analyse the case of the South. Country S is seen as set R as soon as it is considered within the space of international transactions; by contrast, this same country defines a set R' every time that its transactions are concerned with the area of domestic payments. Set R' includes, therefore, the residents who are indebted towards the external world precisely because they get (when their debt is formed) and spend (to service their creditors) their own national or domestic money. The distinction between sets R and R' is univocal since, in the real world, every country has its own autonomous banking system. The 'dollarization' of some national economies does not alter, therefore, the 'clear and distinct' character of the separation between sets R and R'. Relative to every payment implying S's banks alone, the South is a set R'; *a contrario*, for every payment implying both S's and N's banks, the South is a set R. It could still be thought that an external payment of the South would not imply the country as set R if the sum of money S received by the non-residents is not deposited with the banks of the North. Only the careful observation of facts can settle the question. Now, in almost all cases the non-residents are paid through the intermediation of the banks of their own countries; and in the unusual cases in which they are paid *directly* in foreign currencies, they still maintain their quality of non-residents for the simple reason that they can at any moment convert their foreign currency assets into equivalent sums of money issued by the banking system of their own countries. Hence, every payment to a non-resident implicates the country of origin in its function of set R.

Carried out in the domestic currency of the indebted residents, the external debt servicing of country S lies first on its set R'; but every sum of money S deposited with the banks of S by *non-residents* defines a debt of country S's set R.

Distinguishing between the two sets, R and R', of the indebted country (S), let us show the succession of the operations relating to the servicing, in money S and up to 2 MS, of S's foreign creditors (See Figure 11.3). Scheme 1 shows the transfer, by the indebted residents of the South, of 2 million units of money S to their foreign creditors.

Scheme 2 show the deposit of this sum of money with the banks of the South; in the real world it is impossible, in fact, for a sum of money S to be deposited with institutions totally distinct from the banking system of country S.

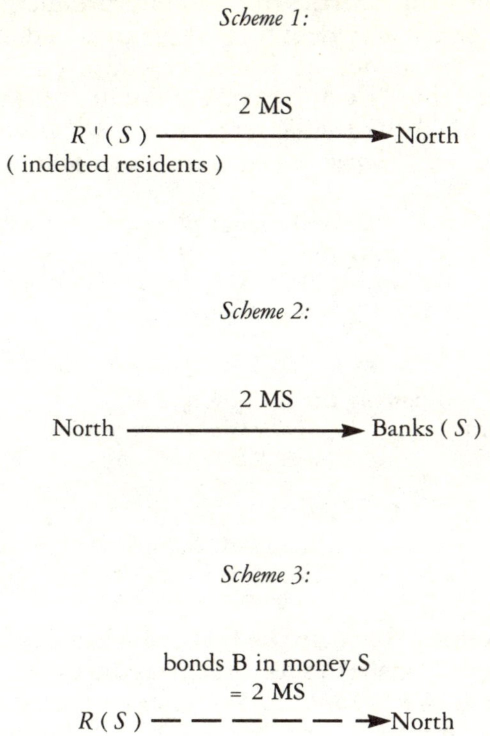

Figure 11.3

Scheme 3 represents the transfer, by the South, of financial bonds (bonds B) up to a value of 2 MS; three considerations apply here: these bonds are transferred by the banks of the South; to the benefit of the external world, which implies country *S* in its function of set *R*; and the North finds in the bonds B the exact financial compensation of the bonds B′ which it gives up to its debtors in *S*.

It would be logical for the indebted country's set *R*′ to be able to get out of its debt without being detrimental to set *R*. Now, the observation of facts shows that every external debt servicing carried out in the domestic money of the indebted country, *S*, allows set R'_s to get out of its debt, but only in so far as it lays the debt upon set R_s. At the moment the indebted residents of country *S* (*R*′) transfer 2 million units of money S to their foreign creditors, *S*'s debt goes from z units of money S to z units of money S; this is because the deposits newly formed by non-residents with *S*'s banks, equal to 2 MS, define a new external indebtedness of country *S*.

Thus every indebted country which chooses to service its foreign creditors in its own money carries out a counterproductive operation. In the case of country *S* it is evident that, by giving up a domestic saving of 2 MS in order to service its foreign creditors, it carries out a self-defeating policy since, by doing so, it maintains its external debt at the previous level: the debt of set R'_s *goes from* z *MS to* (z − 2) *MS but, at the same instant, set R incurs a new debt equal to 2 MS.*

Debt of the set R'
following the transfer of 2 MS
to the foreign creditors of country S:
z MS − 2 MS

Debt of the set R
following the transfer of 2 MS
to the foreign creditors of country S:
+ 2 MS

New debt of country S
relative to its two sets R and R':
z MS − 2 MS + 2 MS = z MS

Since the debt of country *S* remains unchanged whatever the amount of its domestic savings it transfers to its foreign creditors, it is urgent for it not to make *any payment in money S*; if, none the less it did this its sacrifices would be in vain. According to logic, the indebted country realizes net gains in foreign currencies (money of the North) in order to service its foreign creditors using these gains and not its own domestic money.

2. Trade surpluses in the South, a prerequisite of its external debt servicing

As it is, nobody denies that, with the present organization of international payments, the indebted country has to realize net commercial gains in its transactions with the rest of the world; if it did not succeed in doing so it would not be able to service its creditors who would not even obtain the payment of the interests.

The constraint we have just pointed out is the expression of a truism: if an indebted person currently purchases commercial goods up to the total amount of his commercial sales, he does not realize any net saving and is therefore formally unable to carry out any financial transfers to the benefit of his creditors. This evident truth applies to every individual or nation. Thus, as a simple 'individual', country *S* can own an external saving, which it can later transfer to its foreign creditors, only if it realizes a net gain in its commercial trade with the rest of the world.

To understand the analysis clearly we must reintroduce the distinction between sets R_s and R'_s.

If only the set R' of country S were implicated in the external debt servicing of S, then only one condition would be necessary to fulfil this task, namely that R'_s realize a positive saving which can be transferred to its foreign creditors. Now, every service of an *external* debt necessarily implicates both set R' and set R of the indebted country.

Experimental observation confirms the necessity of this double implication.

Implication of set R'. Every external debt of a country has been contracted by its residents, whether of the private or public sectors. Even the State of a country is a resident of this country. It is invariably the set R', therefore, which first bears every external debt of the country. We note that R' is involved since only a saving formed within the indebted country can nourish the servicing, of the principal and interests, of its creditors.

Implication of the set R. The proof of this second implication is given by the fact that even a country whose indebted residents manage to realize sufficient savings is not able to service its foreign creditors without also having to earn a *net external income* at least equal to the sum currently due to its creditors.

In view of the external debt servicing the coexistence of two distinct savings is required; if the indebted residents did not carry out any *internal* saving they would have no transferable funds at their disposal; but if, on its side, the indebted country did not earn any *external* income, it would be unable to transfer the required amount of *foreign currencies* to its external creditors; and, as we have established, it is only in money of the North that the South can service its foreign debt.

To summarize we can see that every external debt servicing of country S requires both:

1. the formation of an *internal* saving by set R'_s; and
2. the formation of an *external* saving by set R_s.

If one of these savings were missing — set R'_s being solvent (in domestic money) while set R_s is not (in foreign currencies) or, conversely, set R_s being solvent (in foreign currencies) while set R'_s is not (in domestic money) — no external debt servicing could be carried out.

We thus verify, *de facto*, that the distinction between sets R and R' of the indebted country (S) applies even in the case when the external debt servicing is carried out in foreign currencies.

As will be remembered, we did not find any anomaly in the external debt servicing when it is carried out in foreign currencies. On the contrary, the operations develop very logically: set R'_s transfers its savings to set R_s which then transfers them to the foreign creditors (Figure 11.4).

Figure 11.4

Those who carry *S*'s external debt (set R'_s) transfer their savings, up to a value of 2 million units of money S, to country *S*. *S*'s set *R* gets these savings and finally transfers them to the foreign creditors after having converted them into foreign currencies (money of the North); the current rate of exchange being of 1 unit of money N for 1 unit of money S, 2 million units of money N are thus transferred to the creditors of the South. But, how is this expenditure of foreign currencies fed by the South? The answer is already known: the South earns 2 million units of money N through its trade surplus.

Let us identify set R_s with the Central Bank of country *S*. The development of the operations conforms to the following representation as in Figure 11.5.

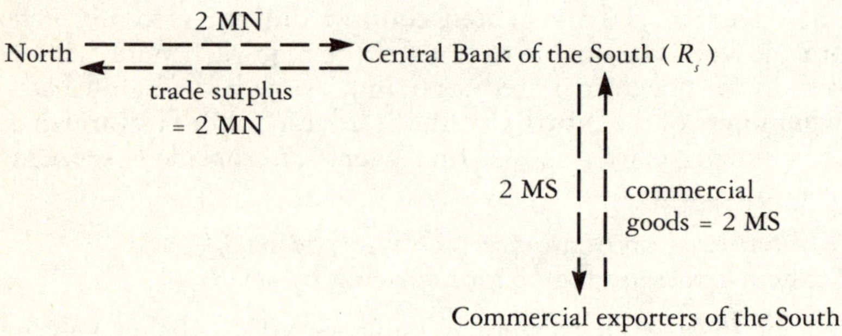

Figure 11.5 *External savings of country S*

As counterpart of *S*'s net commercial exports (in period p), the central Bank of country *S* (representing set R_s) obtains a net gain of 2 million units of money N; it then pays an equivalent amount of domestic money to the exporters, who get, therefore, 2 million units of money S.

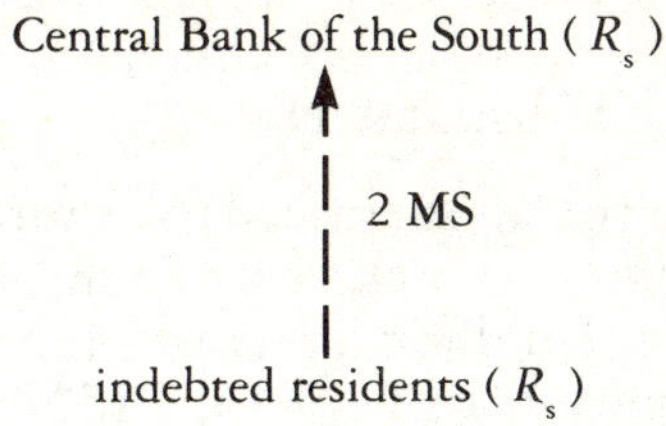

Figure 11.6 *Transfer of an internal saving of the indebted residents of country S*

Those who carry the external debt of country *S* have saved 2 million units of money S and transfer them to their central Bank (See Figure 11.6) which transfers them to the foreign creditors (See Figure 11.7).

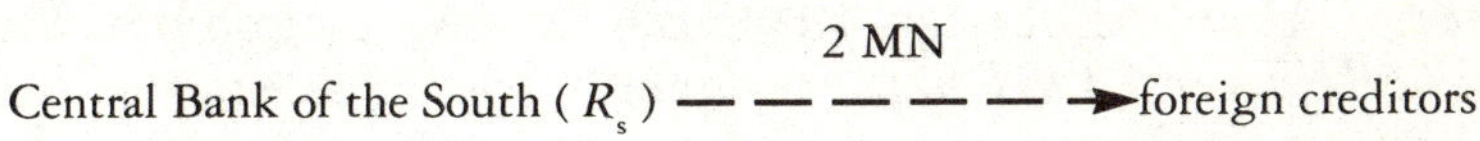

Figure 11.7 *Final transfer of an internal saving to the foreign creditors of country S*

This time everything seems to have been explained: set R'_s has just transferred 2 million units of money S to set R_s which has converted this sum into 2 million units of money N, which is the current commercial gain of country *S*: country *S*'s external creditors have thus obtained interests and amortizations of 2 MN.

Now, despite appearances to the contrary, things works quite differently.

3. Foreign currencies earned in the South trade surplus should be available free of cost for its external debt servicing

When an indebted person has a commercial surplus he pays his debt IN KIND. It would obviously be iniquitous to deny him the gain corresponding to the decrease of his debt arguing that he would still have to compensate it by a payment in MONEY.

In the domestic relationships of a country it never happens that an economic agent has to pay his creditors both in KIND and in MONEY: one of these two payments is enough.

But let us consider country *S* in period p: it currently sacrifices a surplus of commercial exports equivalent to 2 MS; in addition country *S* sacrifices an internal saving, also equivalent to 2 MS. The two following facts are both indisputable:

1. the external saving of *S* is sacrificed to its foreign creditors, under the form of foreign currencies earned through its trade surplus and equivalent to 2 million units of money N (that is, at the supposed exchange rate of 1 MS for 1 MN, to 2 million units of money S);
2. the internal saving of country *S*'s indebted residents, carried out in period p, is also sacrificed for the external payment of interests or amortizations up to 2 million units of money S.

Logically, these two sacrifices imposed on country *S* should 'merge' and define a unique sacrifice equal to 2 MS. It would be totally absurd to expect country *S* to have to pay a total of TWICE 2 MS in order to service the sum of 2 MS to its foreign creditors ONLY ONCE. It then follows that the two sacrifices are reduced to a unique sacrifice of 2 MS *on condition that the foreign currencies earned by country S are available FREE OF COST to the residents servicing its external debt.*

Can it be denied that in the real world country *S*'s indebted residents are bound to PAY for the foreign currencies earned by *S* in its foreign trade?

The distinction between sets R_s and R'_s is of a great help here. Set R_s sacrifices a commercial surplus equivalent to 2 MN. Set R'_s sacrifices an internal saving equivalent to 2 MS. Only two possibilities are open to us: the saving transferred by R'_s is picked up by set R_s (that is, by its central Bank on behalf of country *S*'s public); or, alternatively, the saving realized in money S by the indebted residents of country *S* is lost in a *sinking fund* so that *S* suffers both the loss of the domestic savings carried out by its indebted residents and, in addition, the loss of the commercial goods exported without counterpart.

How can we choose between these two possibilities? The right method is to observe facts. In today's world a central Bank never earns the sum of interests or amortizations paid by the country's indebted residents to their foreign creditors. Thus, the expenditures of a set R'_s are invariably thrown into a *sinking fund.*

Let us represent schematically, for country *S*, the two terms of the alternative (See Figure 11.8). How is it possible to explain the existence of TWO flows of payment going from set R_s to the rest of the world? The expenditure of 2 MN is self-evident. But what about the ADDITIONAL expenditure of 2 MS? And yet in the real world this

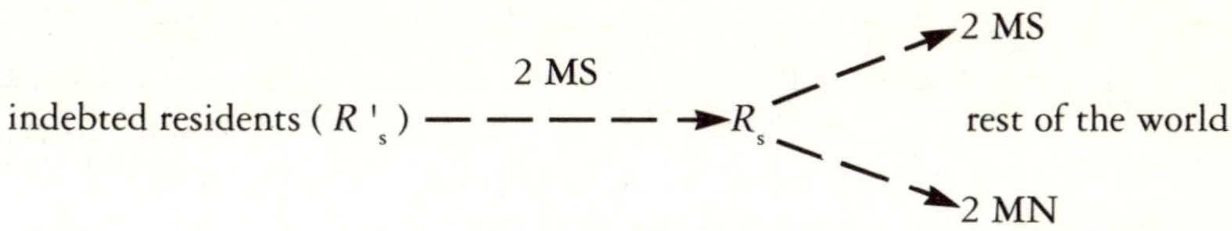

Figure 11.8 *Sinking capital expenditures of* R'_s

second expenditure is undoubtedly present: since the indebted residents of country *S* currently sacrifice their domestic savings, up to 2 million units of money S, WITHOUT IT BEING PICKED UP BY COUNTRY S, this means that this payment *is lost in the current servicing of S's external debt*. It is sometimes difficult to reason logically, and this is particularly true here; it is not at all clear, in fact, how the rest of the world could be paid TWICE, that is how it could simultaneously get 2 MN *and 2 MS*. This being what effectively happens in the real world, the determining principle is the following: does the country lose the indebted residents domestic savings or not? Now, as experimental evidence irrefutably shows, the country does not earn what is spent by its residents. All the rest is simply a question of induction: country *S* currently loses a saving of 2 million units of money S, a loss which has to be ADDED to its current sacrifice of 2 million units of money N. To reach a different conclusion would be going against facts.

Relative to the rest of the world, the indebted country (*S*) would have to give up ONLY the gain corresponding to its net commercial exports if, and only if, the expenditures carried out by its indebted residents were the source of an equivalent net profit (Figure 11.9).

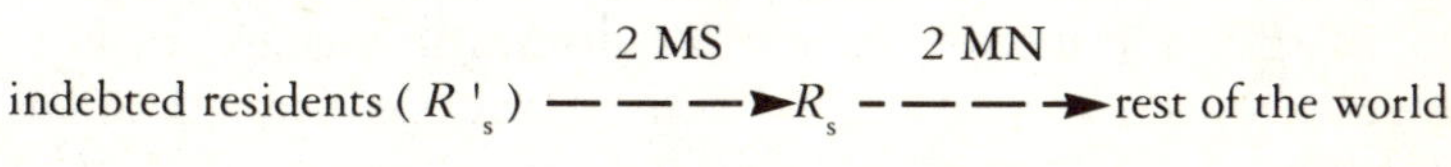

Figure 11.9 *Expenditures carried out by* R'_s *to the profit of set* R_s

To say that set R_s does not transfer the expenditure of 2 MS carried out by its indebted residents to the rest of the world (since R_s would only be transferring 2 MN abroad) is the same as saying that the operation brings a profit or a NET GAIN of 2 million units of money S to this set.

The pertinent question is therefore the following: in the real world do central Banks get a sum of NET PROFITS equivalent, in their own domestic money, to the savings transferred abroad by their indebted residents or not? The correct answer is indisputably NEGATIVE. This means that each time it services its foreign creditors every indebted country suffers a DOUBLE SACRIFICE since it loses a MONETARY domestic saving IN ADDITION to the loss IN KIND corresponding to its net commercial exports.

Even though we have proved by inductive reasoning that the indebted country (*S*) has to carry out *two concurrent expenditures* in period p, 2 MN + 2 MS, it remains true that one of these expenditures seems to 'disappear into nothing': even if the 'source' of the expenditure of 2 MS is clearly defined, where does it end up? After reflection the answer seems clear: in our example the 2 million units of money S 'disappear' on the exchange market.

This is represented in Figure 11.10 in which 2 million units of money S 'enter into' 2 million units of money N as 'nourishment' coming from the current external debt servicing of country *S*. Let us explain this

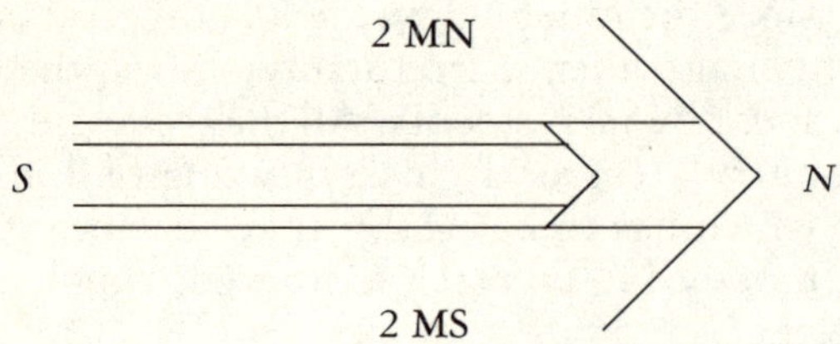

Figure 11.10

curious flow of 2 million units of money N *which includes* a flow of 2 million units of money S. Things are less bizarre than they first appear. The fact is that a sum of country *S*'s domestic money would never 'reinforce' country *N*'s money if the operations carried out on the exchange market were balanced. Now, in the present situation, where the external balance of payments of country *S* includes the servicing of its foreign creditors up to 2 MN, savings of 2 MS are lost by *S* to the profit of the rest of the world: this loss manifests itself on the *exchange market*. This clearly means that 2 million units of money S are used on the exchange market for the unilateral (excess) purchase of money N: it is perfectly correct, therefore, to say that 2 million units of money S disappear into money N, which is thus proportionally 'strengthened'.

Let us analyse further this net excess demand for money N in terms of money S.

4. Every external debt servicing of country S entails an excess demand for money N in terms of money S

Let us recall that an exchange operation is *unilateral* when one of the two currencies concerned is demanded without the other being simultaneously demanded.

Let us look at period p, when country *S* pays 2 million units of money N to its foreign creditors. If country *N* were also to pay 2 million units of money S to the residents of country *S* the equilibrium of the overall balance of each country would have as corollary the stability of their currencies on the exchange market.

In reality the South is a net debtor to the rest of the world; and the 2 million units of money N currently serviced to the foreign creditors of *S* correspond to the *net* indebtedness of this country towards the North; it can therefore be said that this flow of 2 MN is by definition *unilateral*. It is true, however, that the overall balance of payments of country *S* is in equilibrium despite this transfer of 2 MN. This is because 2 million units of money N, as payment for its trade surplus, form a *net* credit of country *S*. And, according to a rule expounded in every textbook, the neutrality of the operations taking place on the exchange market is guaranteed only when there is an overall balance of payments. Taking place within the South's overall balance of payments, the current servicing of its external debt, equal to 2 MN, would not lead, therefore, to an exchange market disequilibrium.

Now, textbooks are not always correct. Even though 'included' in an equilibrated overall balance of payments, external debt servicing is the cause of a disequilibrium on the exchange market.

This 'disequilibrium within equilibrium' is a phenomenon of great theoretical interest. Yet, this chapter being mainly concerned with experimental verification, let us limit our analysis to a few considerations. Given the actual system of international payments, the external debt servicing always implies an equivalent transfer to the benefit of the creditor country: thus, in period p the North effectively pays for its commercial imports from the South only within the limits of its own, concomitant, commercial exports; as for its net commercial imports, no payment is due by the North: the payment of its commercial deficit is not required by the South which is supposed to service its external debt currently through *compensation*. However, we already know (Part II, Chapter 10) that this kind of procedure hides a serious vice: in the absence of an effective payment for its trade surplus the South does not benefit from the formation of a positive external income, and has, therefore, to resort to a non-existent international income in order to find the resources in foreign currencies necessary to nourish the current servicing of its debt towards the North. In short, the South is forced to *purchase* the foreign currencies which it has already *earned* as counterpart for its trade surplus. The careful observation of facts makes it possible to verify the reality of this serious disorder.

In period p the sum of 2 million units of money N defines the net commercial gain of country *S* in international transactions. Country *S*'s reserves in foreign currencies are subjected, therefore, to a net increase, which is recorded on the asset side of its Central Bank's balance sheet. The corresponding liability is an equivalent sum (according to the effective exchange rate) of money S, created for the payment of the commercial exporters, whose complementary payment comes from the income spent by the commercial importers of *S*. Let us consider only the *excess* trade of country *S* (Table 11.1).

Table 11.1

Central Bank of country *S*

	Liabilities	Assets
1.	Countervalue: x MS	+ 2 MN

The first important question is whether this net entry of foreign currencies exerts a pressure on the external value of money S, which would, thus, be made to increase. The factual answer is negative since *S*'s Central Bank does not look to the *financial markets* for the countervalue in domestic income of its new assets in foreign currencies; on the contrary, the sum of x MS is *created* by the central Bank of *S*, which thus 'monetizes', in its own units, the sum of foreign currencies which it adds to its reserves (2 MN). It follows that the payment in money N of country *S*'s trade surplus *does not define a net demand for money S in terms of money N*.

Let us now consider the current servicing of country *S*'s external debt; it amounts to 2 MN: this means that *S*'s Central Bank gives up *at a cost* or *sells* the sum of 2 MN to the indebted residents of country *S* (Table 11.2).

Table 11.2

Central Bank of country *S*

	Liabilities	Assets
2.	2 MN	External debtors x MS

To summarize we can see that the Central Bank of country *S* intervenes in two operations: in the first (1) it creates the sum of x MS, in the second (2) it *gives up* the sum of 2 MN.

Every creation of money shows that the supply is infinitely elastic: the price of the money concerned is not at all affected, therefore, by money creation. The Central Bank of country *S* does not purchase any (pre-existent) sum of money S in order to nourish the payment in domestic money of *S*'s commercial surplus; the sum of money S necessary to this purpose is, in fact, entirely created by the Central Bank of country *S*.

When MN is entered in the books of *S*'s Central Bank NO sum of money S is purchased in money N.

The indebted residents of country *S* purchase from their Central Bank the foreign currencies obtained as payment for *S*'s trade surplus.

When MN is cancelled from the books' of *S*'s Central Bank, a POSITIVE sum of money N is purchased in money S.

We have just *observed*, looking at the *actual* working of international payments, that the formation of a positive excess demand for money N in terms for money S is equal to the exact amount of country *S*'s current external debt servicing.

Yet, before carrying on our analysis let us dispose of an objection which, though futile, could be advanced at this stage of the argument.

Objection. The payment of every commercial export of country *S* increases the foreign currency assets of its banking system; if we consider that commercial banks also create money, it follows that the *global* amount of foreign currencies earned by country *S* as counterpart for *all* its commercial exports is the cause of a net creation of money S. Hence, when all these foreign currencies, amounting to x′ million units of money N, enter country *S*, money S is the object of no net demand in terms of money N. Now, *S*'s commercial importers add their expenditures to the expenditures carried out by the indebted residents of country *S*. In these conditions the excess demand for money N in money S amounts, so it seems, to the total of the expenditures in money S, carried out by the commercial importers as well as by the indebted residents of country *S*. The vice inherent to external debt servicing would therefore extend to the payment of country *S*'s commercial imports; the absurdity of this conclusion would call in question the reality of the vice.

Futile character of this objection. Relative to the commercial exports of country *S* which correspond to the commercial imports of this country, the South and the North are in a perfectly *symmetrical* position: within the equilibrium of the balance of trade every excess demand for money N in terms of money S is thus perfectly compensated by an excess demand for money S in terms for money N. The *symmetry* of the international transactions carried out by the South and by the North is broken only in relation to the unilateral external debt servicing of the South towards the North. The vice that we have denounced, confirmed by the observation of facts, is therefore strictly confined to the South's external debt servicing.

Let us give a numerical example of the asymmetry which we have found in the reality of observable facts. In period p the South exports commercial goods up to a value of 10 million units of money S (10 MS); at the same time the commercial exports of the North amount, globally, to 8 million units of money N (8 MN). The exchange rate *before* taking into account the South's current external debt servicing is of 1 unit of money S for 1 unit of money N. In p the South gives up the total of its current external income, that is the sum of 2 million units of money N (= 2 MS), to the servicing of its foreign creditors.

In these conditions an excess demand for money N in terms of money S to the exact amount of 2 million units of money S (2 MS) is observed. In every theory (whatever the 'schools') excess demand ends with an increase in the price of goods. In our case the new exchange rate is of 10 million units of money S for 8 million units of money N.

Initial exchange rate
before current servicing of country S's external debt
1 unit of money S for 1 unit of money N

New exchange rate
after reabsorption of the excess demand due to
the current servicing of country S's external debt
1.25 units of money S for 1 unit of money N

Let us remember that the balance of external payments of every country, *S* and *N*, is in equilibrium in period p: *S* gives up bank deposits in money S to a value of 8 million units; as complement *S* gives up bank deposits in money N to a value of 2 million units; as for country *N*, it gives up bank deposits in money N to a value of 10 million units. The deposits transferred from both sides have the same value, which is the condition for the perfect equilibrium of the overall balance of payments of both countries. Now, it is within this same equilibrium that the vice linked to the external debt servicing is hidden; the residents of country *S* sacrifice a sum of 10 MS to pay for money N, whereas country *N*'s residents only spend 8 MN to purchase money S. It follows that the exchange market is in *disequilibrium* even though the overall balance of payments of each country is in *equilibrium*. It is this disequilibrium within equilibrium which makes up the vice we keep denouncing.

Before taking up again this question of a disequilibrium in the exchange market within the equilibrium of the overall balance of payments, let us look once again at facts as carefully as possible.

Within the limit of each country's commercial equilibrium, *S* pays for its imports in money S and *N* pays for its own in money N; we thus observe an exchange of bank deposits amounting to 8 MS on one side and to 8 MN on the other, the exchange rate being still 1 unit of money S for 1 unit of money N (since the effect of country *S*'s external debt servicing on the external value of its money has still to be taken into account). Since each country is finally paid for its exports in its own money, the exchange market records the demand for 8 MN by 8 MS and, reciprocally, the demand for 8 MS by 8 MN. These reciprocal demands define two equivalent actions of opposite sign taking place on the exchange market which reconfirm the initial exchange rate of 1 unit of money S for 1 unit of money N. As can be observed, this result is reached even though each country 'monetizes' within its banking system the foreign currencies earned by its residents: the sums of domestic currencies thus additionally created by each country is the mark of an infinitely elastic supply, so that the external value of national currencies is not at all affected by the 'inflows' of foreign currencies into the two countries, as payment for their commercial exports. But the 'outflows' of foreign currencies, as payment for the corresponding commercial imports, are the effect of net purchases of foreign currencies in domestic currencies: the importers of the North exert, in the money of the North, a net demand for money S while the importers of the South exert, in money of the South, a net demand for money N. Since these net demands for foreign currencies are equivalent, their opposite effects neutralize each other on the exchange market.

But the essential point must be remembered; the situation is interesting relative to the international monetary flows taking place *outside the equilibrium of the balances of trade*. Now, the analysis of the true problem could still be postponed. It could happen, in fact, that the trade deficit of the North is compensated by a net export of non-monetary financial bonds (of type B′) by *N*. According to the logic of the mechanism of international payments, bonds B′ mass with commercial goods, so that we again reach our previous conclusion: the sum of international transactions is still neutral on the exchange market.

At present we can no longer avoid the basic problem: is the equilibrium preserved on the exchange market when (as in periods p) a commercial surplus of the South is compensated by the current servicing of its external debt? Throughout this chapter the answer is given by observing facts. Let us follow our numerical example. The residents of the North demand, in the money of the North, the sum of 8 MS, the value of their current commercial imports. Now, the residents of the South demand, in money of the South, a sum of 10 MN, namely 8 MN for the payment of their commercial imports and 2 MN for the current servicing of their external debt. That the two terms of the comparison have the exact value we have just given them is an indisputable fact. The residents of the North do not demand a sum of 10 MS, since their current international expenditures are limited to the sum of 8 MS; on the other side, the residents of the South could not stop their expenditures at the level of 8 MN, since the indebted residents of *S*, like the commercial importers, have to purchase the foreign currencies necessary to pay their foreign creditors.

The terms of the comparison are eloquent; a sum of 10 MN is demanded in money S while a sum of only 8 MS is demanded in money N: there is thus, at the initial exchange rate, an excess demand for 2 MN in money S. The ensuing exchange rate variation is easy to calculate: at a price of 10 MS for 8 MN the reciprocal demands are equalized on the currency market.

Let us confirm this new exchange rate.

First we have to determine the exchange rate variation due to the transactions taking place within the balance of trade equilibrium; this variation is nil, and the exchange rate of 1 unit of MS for 1 unit of money N remains unchanged (See Figure 11.11). Being of equal intensity these two demands of opposite sign neutralize each other in their effects.

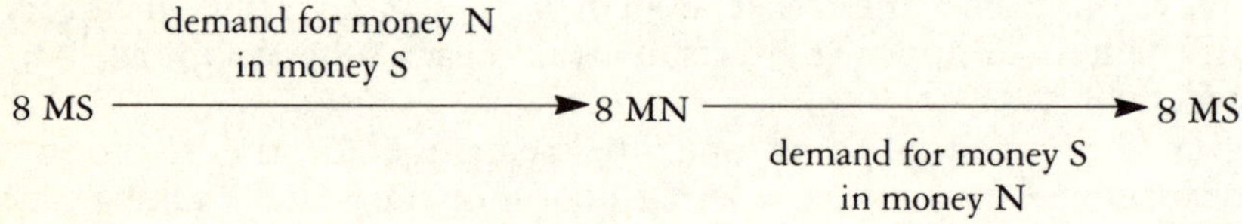

Figure 11.11

But now we have to consider the transactions which take place outside trade equilibrium: country *N* imports a surplus of commercial goods equivalent to country *S*'s external debt servicing. These transactions would not have any net repercussion on the exchange market if they gave rise to the following demands, as shown in Figure 11.12.

Yet, in the real world, outside trade equilibrium, the demand for money S in money N is NIL; the residents of the North demand the

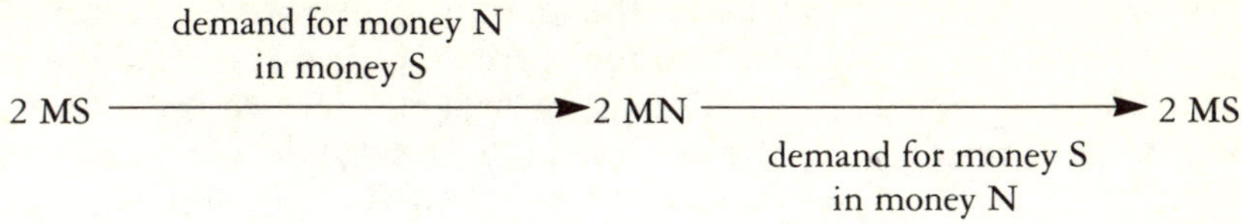

Figure 11.12

money of the South up to the value of their commercial imports; beyond this their demand for money S is NIL. The additional demand for money N carried out by the externally indebted income holders of country *S* is, therefore, not matched by any supply of money N. Let us also note, since it is important, that if the demand for money S in money N is nil once the commercial imports of the North have been financed, this fact does not in the least depend upon the exchange rate between the two currencies. From this it can directly be induced that the 2 million units of money S additionally spent on the exchange market do not displace any sum of money N. Hence, the new exchange rate is effectively 10 MS for 8 MN.

External debt servicing invariably gives rise to a disequilibrium in the exchange market whenever the overall balance of payments is equilibrated. In period p country *S* sacrifices, for the servicing of its external creditors, the exact sum, in money N, it earns in its net commercial exports; in p *S*'s overall balance of payments is thus in equilibrium; despite this, money S is subjected to a devaluation whose proportion is the ratio between the value of the current servicing, in interests and amortization, of country *S*'s foreign creditors and the value of its commercial imports.

Ratio of money S's devaluation:

$$\frac{\text{value of current external debt servicing}}{\text{value of commercial goods current imports}}$$

Relative to period p, money S loses its external value in the ratio of:

$$\frac{2\ \text{MS}}{8\ \text{MS}};$$

which means that in period p money S loses a quarter of its external value.

This disequilibrium comes from the fact that, in order to service their creditors, country *S*'s externally indebted residents are bound to sacrifice a domestic income for the purchase of foreign currencies already earned by *S* through its trade surplus. One question alone has therefore to be asked: is it true that, in order to service their foreign creditors, the residents of the indebted country (*S*) do not receive the net external income of their country *free of cost*? It is absolutely certain that in no country of the world are foreign currencies given up gratis by the Central Bank. Hence, it is also certain that every time they service their external debts countries lose in the exchange market the exact amount they gain on the commercial markets. In our example country *S* suffers from a deterioration in the terms of international exchange which swallows up and cancels, on the exchange market, the reality of this net commercial gain: while it derives a trade surplus of 2 million units of money S from its domestic output, country *S* suffers a straight loss of 2 million units of money S on the exchange market. If nevertheless country *S* is able to service its foreign creditors in period p this can only mean that it *gets into a new equivalent debt*. If the current servicing of its external creditors amounts to 2 MS, in period p we are faced with the following situation:

1. country *S* realizes a net export of commercial goods equal to 2 MS;
2. country *S* gets into a new external debt equal to 2 MS;
3. country *S* services its external creditors by an amount of 2 MS.

Finally, victim of the vice inherent in every external debt servicing, country *S* does not get any benefit — any positive payment — from its trade surplus, since its net external income of 2 MS is cancelled on the exchange market, so that it can no longer get out of debt except by getting into a new debt.

All the trouble comes from the fact that, in the actual regime of international payments, the indebted country (*S*) carries TWICE the load of its external debt servicing: it first pays in KIND interests and principal, since it exports a surplus of commercial goods; but it also pays, additionally, in MONEY or in MONETARY INCOME, since its indebted residents can honour their obligations only by forfeiting their savings in a sinking fund to the benefit of international speculative capital.

The careful observation of facts reveals the absurdity characterizing the servicing of external debts; the indebted country (*S*) shoulders a double load, both in *kind* and in *money*; now, nobody has ever observed the *double* payment — in kind and, additionally, in money — of the creditors. How is it conceivable then, that debtors pay twice while creditors are only paid once?

A question of this kind can easily be disposed of, since it misses completely the true nature of the problem. In the actual real world, the residents carrying the country's external debt have invariably to get foreign currencies by *paying* them; they never get them *free of charge*, which is enough to prove our point. The South makes sacrifices which are *doubled* by the residents who carry its external debt. But, then, how is it that the creditors of the South are entirely satisfied if they get paid *only once*? It never happens, as we have already said, that the creditors are paid both in kind AND in money: they are paid in kind OR in money. Now this contradiction is specious. It is on the *exchange market* that the indebted country (*S*) suffers its second sacrifice: in period p the 2 million units of money S lost in the exchange market do not fall into the hands of the creditors of the South.

After all the only solution is to give gratis — to the set of the country's indebted residents, more precisely to set *R'* — the foreign currencies earned by the country through its trade surplus and assigned to the servicing of its foreign creditors. Before establishing that this solution is not at all paradoxical let us first show that the rest of the world would be entirely paid, in interests and principal, if the South did not bring to the exchange market the income, in domestic money, saved by the residents carrying its external debt and transferred to their creditors.

Chapter Twelve

A Further Proof of the Double Servicing of External Debt

It could be thought that the arguments developed in the preceding chapters are not always positive, yet it is a fact, already fully verified in the actual real world, that the North is paid in (money) income of the North (section 1).

If, as is obviously the case in the actual system of international payments, the indebted residents of the South forfeit their own income to pay their foreign creditors, this clearly shows that the South's external debt servicing is carried out both in income of the North and in income of the South (section 2).

Finally, a numerical example will illustrate the double load shouldered by the South and show that it results in a foreign currencies deficit (section 3).

1. Creditors in the North are paid by importers in the North

The South can service its external debt only by giving up a positive margin of its external income. Let z units of money N be the amount of net external income earned by the South and let us suppose that the totality of this income is currently devoted to the external debt servicing of the South. In these conditions the residents of the North, creditors of the South (CS), get, in interests and principal, the totality of the income that their co-residents forfeit to pay for the excess commercial imports of the North, z MN. As a general rule, every transfer carried out to the benefit of CS is nourished by the income that country *N* spends in paying for its commercial imports.

Let us represent the transfer of z units of money N, from the commercial importers of the North to the creditors CS, as shown in Figure 12.1 We can see that the creditors of the South (CS), residents of the North, are effectively the final beneficiary of the income spent by their own co-residents, as payment for their commercial imports (Figure 12.2). It is true that the transfer that we have just represented is not *direct*; it also true, however, that the income obtained in money N by the creditors of the South (CS) comes entirely from their domestic economy, or to be more precise from the commercial importers of the North.

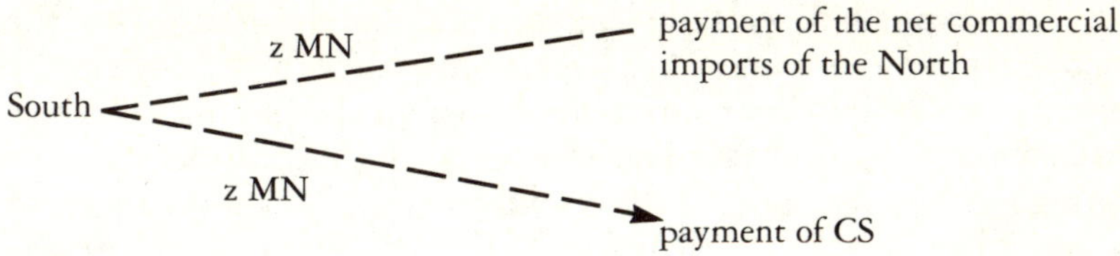

Figure 12.1

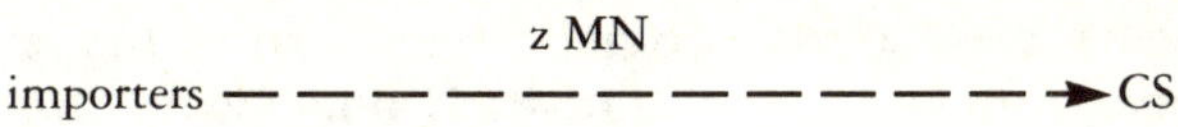

Figure 12.2

But is the situation we have just described, which conforms to reality, not anomalous? Why should the North be constrained to find within its own national income the resources necessary to the servicing of *S*'s external debt? Would it not be logical, on the contrary, to ask the South to transfer to its foreign creditors a sum of income formed within *its own economy*?

After reflection, however, it is perfectly *correct*, both from a logical and an equitable point of view, that a sum of income produced in the North — and not a sum of income produced in the South — should make up the payment, in interests and amortizations, of CS, the residents of the North creditors of the South.

In fact, the South sacrifices a net amount of commercial exports. In the example it earns the net sum of z units of money N, which means that up to z MN the South *does not compensate*, on the commercial goods market, its exports with its imports. Hence the South services in KIND its external debt: it gives up commercial goods up to a value of z MN *without getting anything back*. For its part, the North does not make any sacrifice: on the contrary it gains, in KIND, the amount of its excess imports (= z MN); in MONEY its sacrifice is nil, since the sum of its domestic income forfeited to pay for its net commercial imports (z MN) is recovered by its residents, creditors of the South.

It remains true, of course, that in order to service its foreign creditors the South has to give up a sum of foreign currencies earned in its trade surplus; but this loss means the transfer to its creditors of the income *in money of the North* spent in the payment of its net commercial imports.

Finally, observation reveals the constant fact that the creditors of the South, CS, get paid in *money of the North*, since they invariably get the sums of income which their co-residents spend in paying for their excess commercial imports. Therefore, it is not a question of maintaining that the servicing of the creditors of the North by means of the income of the North is a NORMATIVE proposition; it is, on the contrary, a matter of a pure and simple fact.

From an impartial point of view it should be easy to admit that if the creditors of the South get, as total payment of interests and amortizations, part of the income produced in the North, the South should be exempted from servicing its external debt out of its domestically produced income. This time we are on the normative level: it is outrageous for the South, which already pays in money of the North, to be made to pay another time in its own money. Yet, this is what happens in fact; let us illustrate once again the additional character of the two burdens lying on the South, which, while sacrificing the foreign currencies earned in its net commercial exports to the profit of its foreign creditors, suffers concurrently an equivalent loss in its own domestic income.

2. Two distinct incomes (internal and external) are forsaken by the South in each payment of its external debt

It is interesting to note that the resident *s*, indebted to co-resident *n* within a given national economy, can only take advantage of an extrinsic income in the exact sense that it cannot earn a positive income on its own. Things are quite different for country *S* with regard to country *N*; it is clear, in fact, that every country benefits first from an intrinsic or *internal* income formed within its own domestic relationships. Debt servicing, therefore, poses a specific problem as long as it implies a country in its relationships with the rest of the world. As opposed to the indebtedness of *s* to *n*, the debt of the South relative to the North is defined with regard to the duality of income, internal and external, intrinsic and extrinsic, of *S* and *N*.

Let us look at the following example: if *s*, an indebted resident, paid its creditor *n* in kind it would take a real good out of its real income; now purely real incomes are formed in the autarchic economy of every agent: they are, thus, *internal* incomes. It then follows that in order to service its creditor (*n*) agent *s* would sacrifice an equivalent part of its *internal* income; consequently, no *monetary* sacrifice would be asked of s in these conditions.

The indebted country (S) finds itself in a much more uncomfortable situation: its indebted residents (set R') could not pay interests and amortizations to their foreign creditors except by giving up an equivalent amount of *internal* or domestic income; having given this up, country S should not also have to sacrifice its *external* income. Now, in the actual real world it can easily be observed that, every time it services its external debt, the indebted country (S) has to give up both an *intrinsic* income and, additionally, an equivalent *extrinsic* income.

The only equitable rule is the following: no economic agent, individual or country, should be compelled to service its debt by drawing both on its intrinsic income and on its extrinsic income.

It is true that it is unavoidable for the indebted country (S) to suffer a loss in foreign currencies every time it services its foreign creditors: this means that it is unavoidable for the external debt servicing to be carried out by drawing on the *extrinsic* income of the set of the indebted countries (S). But then it must be concluded that the debtor countries (S) should logically be exempted from drawing on their *intrinsic* income.

Yet, it cannot be denied that in the real world of today the South services its external debt both in money of the North — that is by drawing on its *extrinsic* income — and in money of the South — by drawing on its *intrinsic* income.

3. A numerical example of the double load borne by the indebted countries

We shall first show that the payment of the net commercial exports of the South would be positive if, and only if, the foreign currency earned through this surplus were not thrown into the servicing of the external creditors of the South. Then, we shall verify that the only uncertainty in this matter regards the distribution of the loss between the decreased price of exports and the increased price of imports of the South on the external commercial markets. And finally we shall conclude that the true nature of the loss unjustly inflicted on the indebted countries (S) is such that the loss inevitably takes the form of a deficit in FOREIGN CURRENCIES.

3.1. *The net commercial exports of the South remain totally unpaid in so far as they correspond to the servicing of its external debt*

Let us represent, with two rectangles, the commercial exports and the commercial imports of the South in a given period (See Figure 12.3).

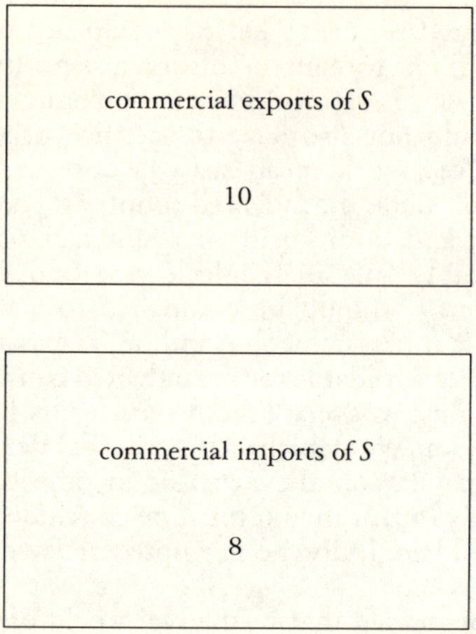

Figure 12.3

These amounts are in billions of American dollars.

Let us follow successively two hypotheses, depending on whether the external income of 2 billion dollars is accumulated in the (official or private) reserves of country *S* or thrown into its external debt servicing.

Increase of the South's foreign currency reserves In this case it is undeniable that the *totality* of the commercial exports of the South (for the given period) brings a positive payment to the country. Up to 8 billion dollars, the commercial market compensates the sales of *S* with the purchases of *S*; as regards the surplus, the goods exported by country *S* are the source of a net gain in foreign currencies: a financial good, namely the sum of 2 billion dollars, has thus taken the place of an equivalent amount of commercial goods. The South is therefore treated with logic and equity, since its total gains reach the exact level of its total losses.

Use by the South of its gain in foreign currencies for the servicing of its external debt It is important to reason in pure logic first, up to the limit of absurdity. The *external* gain of the South is equal to 10 billion dollars; its *external* expenditures are of the same amount: everything seems to be all right. Yet, we have also to take into account the *internal* income of country *S*, irrespective of whether this income is expressed in domestic money or in foreign currencies. It cannot be denied that the residents of the South who are indebted to the rest of the world make the sacrifice of an *internal* or *intrinsic* income of 2 billion dollars. Globally we verify that:

1. the *external* income of *S* is cancelled, which is logical since nobody could pay its creditors and retain the income thus transferred;
2. an *internal* income of *S* is similarly cancelled, which is illogical since, in order to transfer 2 billion dollars to its foreign creditors, the South has to make a sacrifice of a total value of 4 billion dollars. In other words, when it succeed in transferring 2 billion dollars to its creditors in the North, the South gets into a *new debt* of the same amount.

Let us corroborate the results of the previous paragraph by referring to country *S*'s national book-keeping.

The *internal* effect — within the domestic economy of country *S* — of the payment (in foreign currencies) of its net commercial exports is as shown in Table 12.1. Within the given period the South realizes an internal income equivalent to 100 billion dollars and an external income of 2 billion dollars. In practice, as well as in theory, the external income of each country adds up to its internal income: in this example, the total income (internal and external) of country *S* amounts to 102 billion dollars. If the value of the domestic output still available after net exports amounts to only 98 billion dollars it is precisely because a domestic output of *S*, of a value equal to 2 billion dollars, has already been sold (through exports). But an equivalent sum of foreign currencies *replaces* the product which has been sold, so that an internal income of a value of 100 billion dollars faces a product of 98 billion dollars plus an increase of reserves of 2 billion dollars.

Table 12.1

Banking system of the South

Liabilities		Assets	
Domestic income	100	Domestic output	100
Domestic income	2	Foreign currencies	2
Domestic income	100	Domestic output	98
		Foreign currencies	2

This description is valid in every case, whether country *S* sacrifices its external gain to pay its foreign creditors or not.

Before carrying on, let us analyse further the meaning of the bookkeeping relationship between an internal income of a value of 100 billion dollars and an internal output, still to be sold, of a value of 98 billion dollars. The point is that the *macroeconomic price* of this output has a value of 100 billion dollars. Let us note that this conclusion is universally admitted; it follows from a simple reading of the books of account: being confronted with an internal monetary income of a value of 100 billion dollars, the internal price of the domestic output still available grows, in domestic money, from a value of 98 billion dollars to a value of 100 billion dollars.

It is starting from these facts that the boundary line between logic and absurdity can be drawn.

1. If the South were to keep the foreign currencies earned through its trade surplus in its bank reserves, its residents would then have at their disposal the purchasing power necessary to buy the remaining output, since the value of 100 billion dollars would define the domestic income which they would still have at their disposal after payment of country *S*'s trade surplus.
2. But the situation is worrying in the case in which country *S* was sacrifying its external income to the current servicing of its foreign creditors. In this case, in fact, the internal income would finally reduce to the value of 98 billion dollars only (See Table 12.2). Entry (1) represents the expenditure of domestic income carried out by the externally indebted residents of country *S*. Entry (2) shows the result of this payment, the internal income being reduced from 100 billion dollars to 98 billion dollars. *Now, we must not forget that the macroeconomic price of the domestic output to be sold within country S amounts to 100 billion dollars*: in fact, this 'price differential' is the result of *S*'s trade surplus, a result which is not modified by the way the foreign currencies thus earned are successively disposed of.

Only one way remains open to the indebted country: the global economy of country *S* can compensate its lack of purchasing power only through a *new debt* incurred by the set of its residents (See Table 12.3). Entry (2') now shows the purchasing power available within country *S* which is just sufficient for the final purchase of the domestic output still unsold after its net commercial exports have been taken into account.

Table 12.2

Banking system of the South

	Liabilities		Assets	
	Domestic income	100	Domestic output	100
	Domestic income	2	Foreign currencies	2
	Domestic income	100	Domestic output	98
			Foreign currencies	2
(1)	Foreign currencies	2	Domestic income	2
(2)	Domestic income	98	Domestic output	98

Table 12.3

Banking system of the South

	Liabilities		Assets	
(3)	Domestic income	2	New debt	2
(2')	Domestic income	100	Domestic output	98
			NEW DEBT	2

Let us now take just a glimpse at the logic behind the reform which is called for by this state of affairs. Its full description is given in entry (1') of Table 12.4. If — but only if — the transfer of country *S*'s external income to its foreign creditors defined an equivalent asset in the form of a decrease in *S*'s external debt, the external debt servicing of country *S* would be carried out only by drawing on its *extrinsic* income, that is without decreasing its *intrinsic* income.

We thus find again the rule by which the actual disorder relative to external debt servicing has to be ascribed to the fact that the indebted countries have to sacrifice, besides their EXTERNAL gains, an equivalent fraction of their INTERNAL incomes.

Table 12.4

Banking system of the South

	Liabilities		Assets	
	Domestic income	100	Domestic output	100
	Domestic income	2	Foreign currencies	2
	Domestic income	100	Domestic output	98
			Foreign currencies	2
(1)	Foreign currencies	2	Domestic income	2
(1')	Domestic income	2	Decrease of country *S*'s external debt	2
(2'')	Domestic income	100	Domestic output	98
			Decrease of country *S*'s external debt	2

3.2. *Debt servicing has a negative impact on the exchange rate of the indebted country's money*

Let us reconsider our numerical example and its representation in two rectangles (See Figure 12.4). The essential elements of the argument we have been developing can be summarized, following this example, in two points:

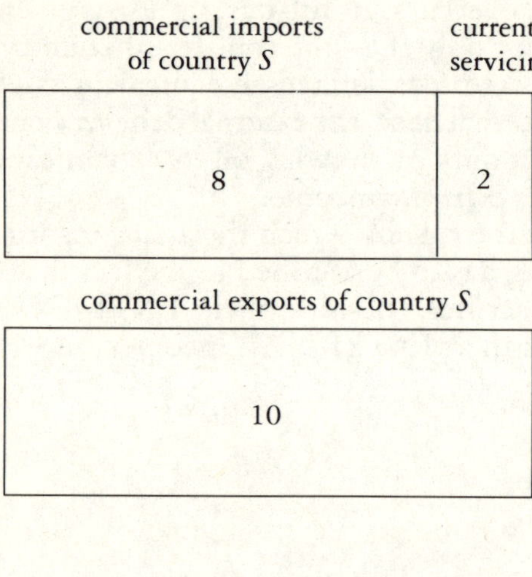

Figure 12.4

1. if country *S* set aside the 2 billion dollars gained as counterpart of its trade surplus, no excess demand for dollars (money of the North) would occur in money S;
2. given that country *S* gives up its net external gain, a value of 2 billion dollars, to service its foreign creditors, an excess demand appears to the profit of the dollar and to the detriment of *S*'s domestic money, a net demand which can only be reabsorbed through *the equalization of the current price of S's commercial exports and the current price of its commercial imports*.

As far as country S's EXTERNAL income is concerned, 10 billion dollars are *demanded* by *S* (payment of its commercial imports + current servicing of its foreign creditors) and 10 billion dollars are gained by country *S* (foreign payment of its total commercial exports): these transactions are balanced on the exchange market.

As far as country S's INTERNAL income is concerned, 2 billion dollars are *demanded* by *S* and no *additional* sum of dollars is gained by *S*.

As far as country S's INTERNAL and EXTERNAL income is concerned, 2 billion dollars are therefore the object of an excess demand in terms of money S. According to every theory (neoclassical, Marxist, Keynesian) it follows necessarily that the current external debt servicing of country *S* is the cause of a depreciation in its domestic money's external value, which brings the price in foreign currencies of its commercial imports to the exact level of the price in foreign currencies of its commercial exports.

Let us first suppose that only the price of country *S*'s commercial exports suffers from the repercussions due to the current servicing of *S*'s external debt. In this case the commercial exports of the South, whose value would have been 10 billion dollars, reach a total value of 8 billion dollars, the exact price of its concomitant commercial imports: no net surplus in foreign currencies is thus earned by country *S* whose only way to service its external debt is to get into a new equivalent debt.

But now let us suppose that it is the price of country *S*'s commercial imports which suffers from all the repercussions relative to the current servicing of *S*'s external debt. Then, the price of *S*'s commercial imports, initially equal to 8 billion dollars, rises to 10 billion dollars, which is the exact value of its commercial exports relative to the same period: again the conclusion is that country *S* can only find through a new external debt the resources necessary for the current servicing of its external debt.

Every country which fixes the price of its commercial exports in terms of dollars is affected by the mechanism described in the previous paragraph: but no country can avoid the logical consequences of excess demand for foreign currencies in terms of its domestic money. Hence, these countries see the price in foreign currencies of their commercial imports increase to the exact amount of the current servicing of their foreign creditors.

It is true that it is easy to get it wrong: does the price in *dollars* of the country's commercial imports increase because of its external debt servicing? Obviously not. But the question is a different one: *translated into dollars, does the price in domestic money of the country's commercial imports increase because of its external debt servicing*?

From what we have just been arguing it seems that the South suffers a loss in its own *domestic income* every time it services its external debt; in no single case, at least according to the stage reached by our analysis in this chapter, is the loss suffered by the South made up in foreign currencies (dollars). Yet, as we shall argue in the next section, it is precisely in foreign currencies that the loss of the South takes place.

3.3. *Finally, each time it services its external debt the indebted country suffers from an equivalent loss in FOREIGN CURRENCIES*

It can be admitted that if the indebted country were to lose only its domestic money, the deficit would easily be made up. A country, in fact, can freely — and also free of cost — issue positive amounts of its own money.

In reality, however, the vice inherent in the country's external debt servicing is much more serious since, in the absence of a fundamental reform, it cannot be eradicated. As it is the indebted country suffers a net loss in FOREIGN CURRENCIES.

Let us reason within the framework of our previous numerical example. In the period of reference the price in money S of the South's commercial imports is multiplied in the proportion of 8 to 10. If the index of the nominal income generated by the domestic production of *S* were adjusted accordingly, the problem would remain, but the coefficient would pass from 1 to 1.25. It is therefore ineluctable that the holders of the macroeconomic income defined in money S suffer a loss in domestic purchasing power equivalent to 2 billion dollars. For a trade surplus of this amount (provided its product in foreign currencies is totally sacrificed to the servicing of *S*'s foreign creditors) the loss suffered by the domestic income holders of country *S* is effectively equal to the money S equivalent of 2 billion dollars. Hence, in order to maintain the domestic purchasing power at the macroeconomic level of national output, it is necessary for the whole population to contract a new debt of a value equal to its trade surplus with the rest of the world. But is it not possible for this additional debt to be defined in money S? As a matter of fact, if it were so defined the purchasing power of country *S*'s population would remain *curtailed*. The fact is that we are confronted with TWO DISTINCT FACTORS in the growth of prices within the economy of the indebted country: on the one hand the macroeconomic price of the output to be sold within the country exceeds the value of this output up to the amount of the country's net commercial exports (we have shown this earlier); on the other hand, the price of the imported goods grows because of the country's external debt servicing. Confronted with these two price increases, the population can only maintain its standard of living through a *supplementary import of commercial goods*, which supposes that country *S* runs up a new EXTERNAL debt to the very extent it services its foreign creditors. Finally it is effectively in FOREIGN CURRENCIES that the loss, which the indebted country suffers through its external debt servicing, occurs.

The vice inherent in the countries' external debts servicing can be expressed in a simpler way: in each period the South, in order to maintain the standard of living of its population, has first to sacrifice the new amount of foreign currencies arising from its freshly contracted debt. If the vice were removed the new debt could be used for the investment — and not for consumption.

Part III

Proposals For the Individual (Country) Solution to the Problem of External Debt Payments

Chapter Thirteen

The Logic of Indebted Countries' External Accounts

1. General principles

Once the 'diagnosis' has been clearly worked out, the solution to the international debt problem is essentially a matter of application. In short the fundamental principle is the following: it is necessary and sufficient to endow the indebted countries with a book-keeping system which does not nullify their net gains in foreign currencies even when these gains are used for the payment of interests and principal to their foreign creditors. And this is, let us repeat it, for the simple reason that the decrease in the South's external debt logically defines an equal gain realized by the South relative to the rest of the world.

In other words, the solution requires the working out of a monetary (book-keeping) system allowing for the total neutrality of the 'vehicle' used in the settlement of international transactions. In the case we are analysing, the money playing the role of international currency should be given gratis to the South, so that *S* could transfer to its foreign creditors the income earned in its trade with the rest of the world without being forced to purchase the vehicular money required for this transfer. But how could this project be adopted without having to call an international conference whose aim would be the substantial reform of the actual system and the creation of a truly international money? To put it another way, would it be possible for a single country to avoid the negative consequences of the system of non-payments? According to our analysis, the problem is not of a political order, since, if a country only had to service its external debt once, no country would suffer from it. Only international speculative capital would experience a decrease in its sources of growth, but this is far from representing a negative factor for the equilibrated development of the world economy. It remains to be seen whether an analytical solution can be applied in the real world.

As has already been shown, the double payment of external debt servicing has its source in the lack of distinction between the country as a whole (nation) and the sum of its residents. To avoid the simultaneous loss of the country's external *and* internal income corresponding to external debt servicing it is thus necessary to call into a book-keeping existence the nation itself and to credit it with the gain resulting from the decrease of the country's external debt. At the international level, monetary neutrality implies that no currency plays the role of a final good, and in order to avoid every commercial transaction having money as its object it is enough to guarantee the total separation between the national and the international monetary circuits. In the absence of a true system of international payments this means that the external transactions of the South have to be taken up by a specific institution (which could be the Treasury, the Exchequer, the Hacienda or a special department of the Central Bank) which would have to receive and carry out all external payments in foreign currencies. On the other hand, the internal department of this institution would have to receive and carry out all the payments in domestic money inherent to *S*'s international transactions. Hence, the importers of country *S* would have to pay the internal department, and the exporters would be paid by it. As far as the external debt servicing is concerned, the indebted residents of the South would pay the internal department while the creditors of the rest of the world would be paid by the external department. Up to the amount of external debt servicing there would be, therefore, a transfer of foreign currencies (to the external world) and an equivalent inflow of domestic money; this obviously conforms to common sense since, if the country plays the role of intermediary and takes upon itself the payment of foreign creditors, it has to find its counterpart in its relationship with the indebted residents. What is today definitely lost to the profit of speculative capital would tomorrow be picked up by the country, without the creditors of the rest of the world being deprived of the slightest part of their credits.

Since the problem is of monetary origin (and not of financial origin), the solution is also monetary. Hence, given the nature of banking money, in order to avoid the double servicing of external debt it is useless to resort to aberrant economic policies; a simple reform of the system of external payments is enough. What has to be avoided, in fact, is the purchase of a vehicular money instead of that of the goods and services of which the less developed countries are so much in need and which the industrialized countries would be so keen to sell. Let us stress the fact that the vice of the actual system goes far beyond the countries' behaviour, to reach the structural framework within which international transactions are carried out. The neutrality of this framework is the fundamental condition for the sound development of international trade, and the reform outlined here aims only at modifying a structure which, far from being neutral, negatively influences the external debt servicing of the great majority of countries (the South) compelling them to a double payment for which it would be pointless to look for any justification whatsoever.

As a last general remark let us note again that the gain is justified only to the extent that the external department takes up all the foreign debt accumulated by the country. Logically, only the residents should be indebted, and not the country as such. Today the logic of international transactions is not complied with, and countries themselves are indebted. This is why the payment of external debt is doubled, and this is also why, being a barrier to the second payment, the external department earns an amount equivalent to the current servicing of the country's external debt. Having in fact proved that, according to logic, nations as such should not be indebted in addition to the indebtedness of their residents, it appears that, under the actual non-system of international payments, countries have accumulated an undue external debt that has heavily hampered their economic development. In other words, indebted countries are suffering a continuous loss having to service their debt under a monetary system that doubles their burden. Now, it is clear that the new order of international payments should allow each of these countries to stop giving away undue positive amounts of their domestic resources to the rest of the world. Under these circumstances it should not be surprising, therefore, to find that the plan proposed here would bring a net gain that derives from the possibility given to each country to service its debt only once (that is, the possibility of effectively decreasing its external debt when servicing it).

In a sound system, the country would act as a pure intermediary between its residents and the rest of the world, which means that the residents' foreign debt would be carried by their country and that the country itself would become a creditor towards its own residents. Acting as intermediary the country would therefore borrow from the rest of the world only in order to lend to its domestic residents, and would then service its foreign debt on their behalf. In this respect the new plan avoids the loss of internal resources which characterizes the servicing of external debt in the actual non-system of international payments, and would allow the indebted country (*S*) to make an equivalent profit whose *raison d'être* would persist until the world reformed the entire non-system and adopted a pure vehicular money as international currency.

2. Synthetical rules of the reform

The rules we are introducing here refer to the changes that any single country (here called *S*) should adopt in order to avoid the negative consequences of the actual disorder of international payments. Book-keeping modifications are reduced to the essential, and the function of mediation is ascribed to the Central Bank. It goes without saying that any other national institution — the Treasury, the Hacienda, the Exchequer — could equally well carry out this function, and that the reform does not in the least depend on the political status of the institution itself or its use of the gain which the country would derive from the new system. For the sake of simplicity, reference to foreign currencies is limited to the dollar, and the exchange rate between the dollar and the indebted country's domestic money, MS, is supposed to be 1 MS for $1.

As will immediately be clear, book-keeping accounts are named according to their specific function, and the specialist should easily be able to translate them into more traditional terminology, bearing in mind, however, that the new accounts cannot be merely rehashed old ones. In particular, the accounts of the nation's external debt do not exist, as such, in traditional book-keeping, and it would be useless, and wrong, to incorporate them into already existing structures. Note that when operations are stated in a given order they may in fact be simultaneous as occurs below (for example, although apparently separated entry 1 and entry 8 of Case A are simultaneous since they refer to the same transaction).

1. The Central Bank is divided into two departments: the internal department (I), carrying out and receiving all payments in national money relative to imports, exports, loans and external debt servicing; and the external department (II), carrying out all payments in dollars to the rest of the world.
2. At the beginning the second department of the Central Bank takes up the country's external debt accumulated during the previous periods, and balances its account by entering an equivalent amount of reserves and imports on the asset side of its balance sheet (See Table 13.1).

Table 13.1

CB II

Liabilities		Assets	
External debt	X	Imports	X - y
		Reserves	y

3. The gain realized by the second department, due to the decrease in the country's accumulated external debt, is transferred to the first department which monetizes it in the country's domestic currency and uses it to pay the exporters.
4. The domestic payment carried out by the country's indebted residents in order to service their external debt is collected by the Central Bank's first department on behalf of the country's Treasury.

Chapter Fourteen

Analytical Representation of the Reform

1. Summary of the different Case-studies

A. Imports and exports equality

Imports = 10
Exports = 10
New loan = 2
Debt servicing = 2

The internalization of the external debt servicing brings the Treasury a gain in domestic money, MS, while the new loan is borne by the residents alone, and increases the country's external debt only to the extent that it increases its internal credit.

B. Net imports

Imports = 10
Exports = 8
New loan = 4
Debt servicing = 2

Even though the new loan is now equal to 4 units of MS the conclusion is the same as in the previous case: the external debt servicing benefits the Treasury whose assets increase by a corresponding amount of domestic money.

C. Net exports

Imports = 8
Exports = 10
Debt servicing = 2

In this case the gain derived from external debt servicing — and which results in the decrease of the debt carried by the Bank's second department on behalf of the country — goes together with the decrease in the resident's indebtedness. The country's net exports are paid for by the first department of the Central Bank which benefits from a transfer from the second department. The amount of money S paid by the indebted residents is transferred to the Treasury.

2. Analysis of the different case-studies

Case A

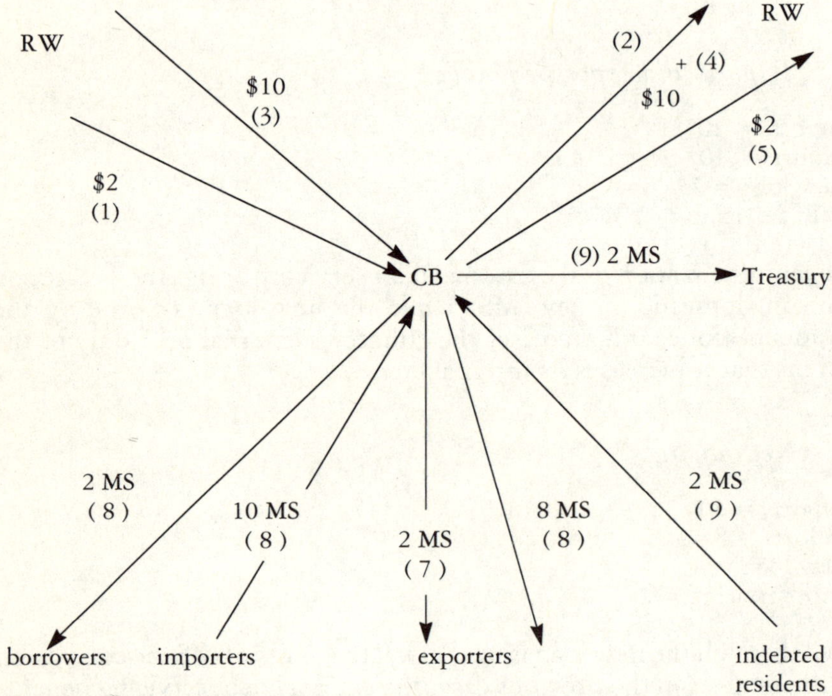

Figure A

Analytical Accounting

Table 14.1

CENTRAL BANK

Internal department I

	Liabilities (MS)		Assets (MS)	
(7)	Exporters	2	Department II	2
(8)	Exporters	8	Importers	10
	Borrowers	2		
(9)	Treasury	2	Indebted residents	2

Table 14.2

CENTRAL BANK

External department II

	Liabilities ($)		Assets ($)	
	External debt	$X	Imported goods	X - y
			Reserves	y
(1)	Capital	2	Reserves	2
(2)	Reserves	2	Capital	2
(3)	Capital	10	Reserves	10
(4)	Reserves	8	Capital	8
(5)	Reserves	2	Capital	2
(6)	Department I	2	External debt	2

The operations defined by each entry are the following:

(1) new loan of $2 granted by the rest of the world.
(2) imports financed through the loan of $2.
(3) exports equivalent to $10.
(4) imports equivalent to $8.
(5) external debt servicing of $2.
(6) transfer to the first department of the Central Bank of the gain due to the decrease in the external debt carried by the country.
(7) monetization in MS of the gain relative to external debt servicing and partial payment of *S*'s exporters.
(8) payment in MS carried out by country *S*'s importers which is partly transferred to the beneficiaries of the new loan, 2 MS, and partly used to pay the exporters, 8 MS.
(9) payment in MS carried out by the country's indebted residents and transfer of the sum to the Treasury.

Having to carry out the whole of country *S*'s external transactions, the second department of the Central Bank is paid in dollars by the rest of the world and so pays *S*'s foreign creditors in dollars. Thus, the country's exports and the loans it gets from abroad give rise to a positive inflow of dollars into the second department, whereas *S*'s imports as well as its external debt servicing are the cause of a positive outflow of dollars. The loan of $2 necessary for the balancing of imports and exports (of goods, services and bonds) increases the Central Bank's reserves in dollars and represents capital that the Bank will lose as soon as these reserves are spent in order to pay for part of the country's imports; the residents' indebtedness alone will remain as counterpart of the new debt incurred by the country on their behalf. Besides, the payments for country *S*'s exports made by the rest of the world increase the Central Bank's reserves; they are also recorded in the form of capital. When the Bank pays for *S*'s imports, the reserves are decreased and the capital disappears. What remains is a reserve of 2 dollars, which the Bank employs in the servicing of the country's external debt. The result of these operations is therefore a decrease in *S*'s accumulated debt which is recorded as an equivalent gain that the second department transfers to the first. Here the operations are recorded in domestic money and relate to the payments made by the indebted residents and the importers, as well as to the payments carried out by the Bank to the profit of exporters and borrowers. It appears that the country's importers pay the borrowers and part of the exporters while, relative to the external debt servicing, it is the Central Bank which (by money creation) pays the exporters directly. This creation has no effect on the exchange rate and is not inflationary, since it corresponds to the domestic monetization of the country's external gain. On the other hand, the amount paid by the indebted residents in order to service their debt is entirely earned by the Bank on behalf of the Treasury. It is this amount which defines the gain due to the new system and which directly derives from the positive payment of the country's accumulated external debt, which changes from X to X − 2 dollars, that is, if we consider also the payment of interests, from X + i to X + i − i − (2 − i).

The entries corresponding to this first case are the following.

CENTRAL BANK

Department I

depart. II in $

l.		a.	
(7)	$2	$2	(6)

transfer from depart. II

l.		a.	
(6)	$2		

depart. II

l.		a.	
		2 MS	(7)

importers

l.		a.	
		10 MS	(8)

exporters

l.		a.	
(8)	8 MS		
(7)	2 MS		

borrowers

l.	a.
(8) 2 MS	

indebted res.

l.	a.
	2 MS (9)

Treasury

l.	a.
(9) 2 MS	

clearing

l.			a.		
	$	MS	$	MS	
(7)		2	2		(7)

CENTRAL BANK

Department II

accumulated external debt

l.	a.
$X	
$(X + i)	
	$2 (6)

reserves

l.	a.
	$y
(2) $2	$2 (1)
(4) $8	$10 (3)
(5) $2	

imports

l.	a.
	$X - y

capital

l.	a.
(1) $2	$2 (2)
(3) $10	$8 (4)
	$2 (5)

CB dep. I

l.	a.
(6) $2	

borrowers

l.	a.
	$2 (1)

new external debt

l.	a.
(1) $2	

TREASURY

transfer from CB

l.	a.
(9) 2 MS	

CB dep. I

l.	a.
	2 MS (9)

INDEBTED RESIDENTS

external debt

l.	a.
$X	$2 - i (9)

CB dep. I

l.	a.
(9) 2 MS	

interests on external debt

l.	a.
$i	$i (9)

clearing

l.	$	MS	$	MS	a.
(9)	2 - i			2 - i	(9)
(9)	i			i	(9)

IMPORTERS

CB dep. I

l.	a.
(8) 10 MS	

imported goods

l.	a.
	$10 (8)

clearing

l.	$	MS	$	MS	a.
(8)	10			10	(8)

EXPORTERS

CB dep. I

l.	a.
	2 MS (7)
	8 MS (8)

exported goods

l.	a.
(7) 2 MS	
(8) 8 MS	

BORROWERS

CB dep. II
external debt

l.	a.
(1) $2	

CB dep. I

l.	a.
	2 MS (8)

clearing

l.	$	MS	$	MS	a.
(8)		2	2		(1)

Case B

Analytical Accounting

Table 14.3

CENTRAL BANK

Internal department I

	Liabilities (MS)		Assets (MS)	
(7)	Exporters	2	Department II	2
(8)	Exporters	6	Importers	10
	Borrowers	4		
(9)	Treasury	2	Indebted residents	2

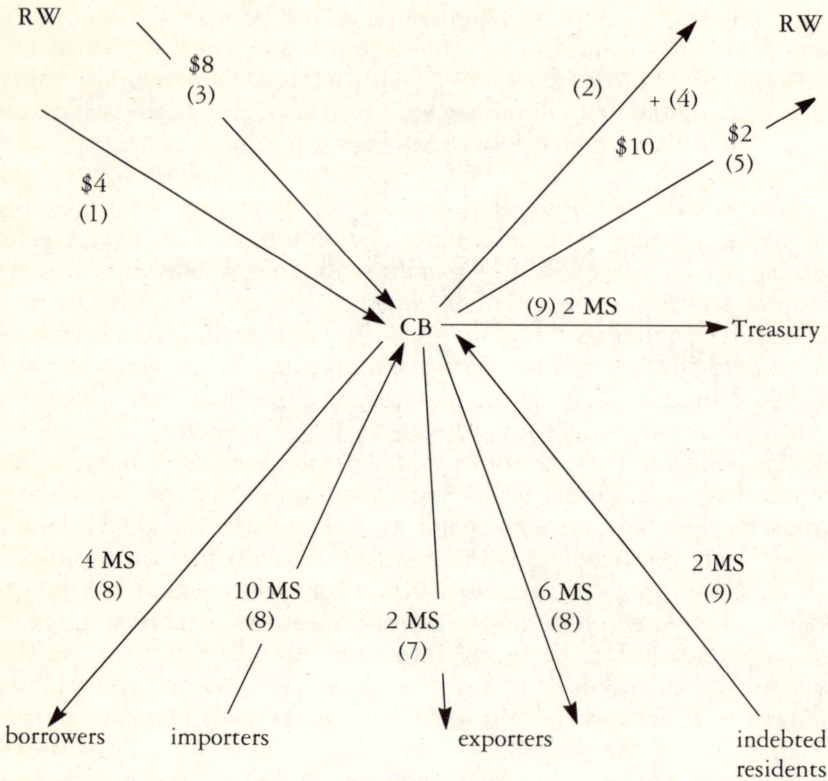

Figure B

The operations are the following:

(1) New loan of 4 dollars from the rest of the world.
(2) Imports financed through the loan of 4 dollars.
(3) Commercial exports equal to 8 dollars.
(4) Commercial imports equal to 6 dollars.
(5) External debt servicing of 2 dollars.
(6) Transfer to the Central Bank's first department of the gain obtained from the decrease in the external debt carried by country *S*.
(7) Monetization in country *S*'s domestic currency of the gain due to positive debt servicing and partial payment of *S*'s exporters.
(8) Payment in money S carried out by the country's importers and transfer of this amount to the residents who have borrowed from the rest of the world (4 units of MS) and to the exporters (6 units of MS).

(9) Payment in money S carried out by the indebted residents of country *S* and transfer of the sum to the Treasury.

Table 14.4

CENTRAL BANK

External department II

	Liabilities (MS)		Assets (MS)	
	External debt	X	Imported goods	X - y
			Reserves	y
(1)	Capital	4	Reserves	4
(2)	Reserves	4	Capital	4
(3)	Capital	8	Reserves	8
(4)	Reserves	6	Capital	6
(5)	Reserves	2	Capital	2
(6)	Department I	2	External debt	2

The only difference with the previous case (A) is that this time the external loan is equal to 4 dollars. Otherwise all the payments are carried out in the same way and the external debt servicing brings the Treasury a gain equivalent to the decrease in the country's accumulated external debt. The book-entries are as follows.

CENTRAL BANK

Department I

depart. II in $ l.	a.	transfer from depart. II l.	a.
(7) $2	$2 (6)	(6) $2	

depart. II

l.	a.
	2 MS (7)

importers

l.	a.
	10 MS (8)

exporters

l.	a.
(8) 6 MS (7) 2 MS	

borrowers

l.	a.
(8) 4 MS	

indebted res.

l.	a.
	2 MS (9)

Treasury

l.	a.
(9) 2 MS	

clearing

l.			a.		
	$	MS	$	MS	
(7)		2	2		(7)

CENTRAL BANK

Department II

accumulated external debt

l.	a.
$X $(X + i)	
	$2 (6)

reserves

l.	a.
	$y
(2) $4	$4 (1)
(4) $6	$8 (3)
(5) $2	

imports

l.	a.
	$X - y

capital

l.	a.
(1) $4	$4 (2)
(3) $8	$6 (4)
	$2 (5)

CB dep. I

l.	a.
(6) $2	

borrowers

l.	a.
	$4 (1)

new external debt

l.		a.
(1) $4		

TREASURY

transfer from CB

l.		a.
(9) 2 MS		

CB dep. I

l.		a.
		2 MS (9)

INDEBTED RESIDENTS

external debt

l.		a.
$X		$2 - i (9)

CB dep. I

l.		a.
(9) 2 MS		

interests on external debt

l.		a.
$ i		$ i (9)

clearing

l.	$	MS	$	MS	a.
(9)	2 - i			2 - i	(9)
(9)	i			i	(9)

IMPORTERS

CB dep. I

l.		a.
(8) 10 MS		

imported goods

l.		a.
		$10 (8)

clearing

l.	$	MS	$	MS	a.
(8)	10			10	(8)

EXPORTERS

CB dep. I

l.	a.	
	2 MS	(7)
	6 MS	(8)

exported goods

l.		a.
(7)	2 MS	
(8)	6 MS	

BORROWERS

CB dep. II
external debt

l.		a.
(1)	$4	

CB dep. I

l.	a.	
	4 MS	(8)

clearing

l.	$	MS	$	MS	a.
(8)		4	4		(1)

Case C

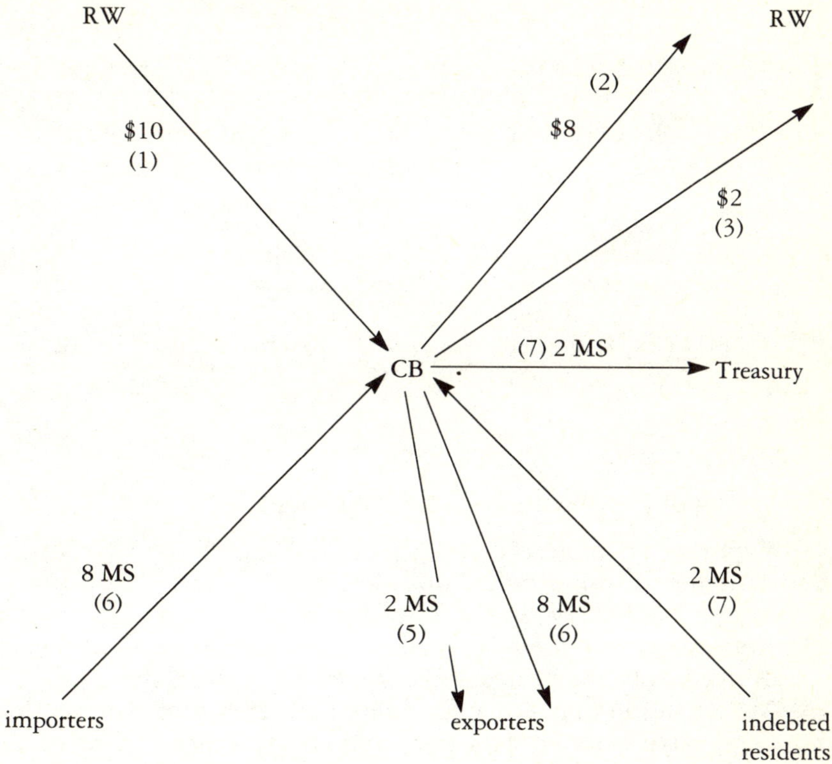

Figure C

Analytical Accounting

Table 14.5

CENTRAL BANK

Internal department I

	Liabilities (MS)		Assets (MS)	
(5)	Exporters	2	Department II	2
(6)	Exporters	8	Importers	8
(7)	Treasury	2	Indebted residents	2

Table 14.6

CENTRAL BANK

External department II

	Liabilities ($)		Assets ($)	
	External debt	X	Imported goods	X - y
			Reserves	y
(1)	Capital	10	Reserves	10
(2)	Reserves	8	Capital	8
(3)	Reserves	2	Capital	2
(4)	Department I	2	External debt	2

The meaning of the operations is the following:

(1) Exports of commercial goods of 10 dollars.
(2) Commercial imports of 8 dollars.
(3) External debt servicing of 2 dollars.
(4) Transfer to the Central Bank's first department of the gain derived from the decrease in country *S*'s external debt.
(5) Monetization in country *S*'s domestic currency of the gain due to positive external debt servicing and partial payment of *S*'s exporters.
(6) Payment in money S carried out by the country's importers and transfer of this sum to the country's exporters.
(7) Payment in money S carried out by the indebted residents of country *S* and transfer of the sum to the benefit of the Treasury.

Unlike the previous cases, no new loan is required here since the country's net commercial exports provide the amounts of foreign currencies necessary to pay for its imports and to carry out its external debt servicing. On the other hand, the decrease in the country's external indebtedness guarantees the Treasury an equivalent inflow of domestic money which it can use to relieve, for example, the burden of the country's public debt.

Relative to this last case the book-entries are as follows.

CENTRAL BANK

Department I

transfer from depart. II

l.	a.
(4) $2	

depart. II in $

l.	a.
(5) $2	$2 (4)

depart. II

l.	a.
	2 MS (5)

importers

l.	a.
	8 MS (6)

exporters

l.	a.
(6) 8 MS	
(5) 2 MS	

indebted res.

l.	a.
	2 MS (7)

Treasury

l.	a.
(7) 2 MS	

clearing

l.	l. $	l. MS	a. $	a. MS	a.
(5)		2	2		(5)

CENTRAL BANK

Department II

accumulated external debt

l.	a.
$ X	
$ (X + i)	
	$2 (4)

reserves

l.	a.
	$ y
(2) $8	$10 (1)
(3) $2	

imports

l.	a.
	$ X - y

capital

l.			a.
(1)	$10	$8	(2)
		$2	(3)

CB dep. I

l.			a.
(4)	$2		

TREASURY

transfer from CB

l.			a.
(7)	2 MS		

CB dep. I

l.			a.
		2 MS	(7)

INDEBTED RESIDENTS

external debt

l.			a.
	$ X	$2 - i	(7)

CB dep. I

l.			a.
(7)	2 MS		

interests on external debt

l.			a.
	$ i	$ i	(7)

clearing

l.				a.		
	$	MS		$	MS	
(7)	2 - i				2 - i	(7)
(7)	i				i	(7)

IMPORTERS

CB dep. I

l.			a.
(6)	8 MS		

imported goods

l.			a.
		$8	(6)

clearing

l.					a.
	$	MS	$	MS	
(6)	8			8	(6)

EXPORTERS

CB dep. I

l.	a.
	2 MS (5)
	8 MS (6)

exported goods

l.	a.
(5) 2 MS	
(6) 8 MS	

Notes

Introduction

1. The necessity of establishing a multi-currency standard was already stressed at the Bretton Woods conference by central bankers and was later theorized, among others, by Lutz, Roosa, Zolotas and Wallich.

2. As results from the following quotation, the main distinction between inter-regional and international transactions is often reduced to a difference of degree of substitution between financial claims. 'Nobody doubts that regions do run current-account surpluses (or deficits) in trade with each other; some regions find it becoming relatively easier or more difficult to sell their goods and services in inter-regional (national) markets; that marked regional disparities in wealth, incomes and unemployment develop between regions and that large net regional migrations take place. Yet despite such signs of balance-of-payments problems, it is often claimed that in inter-regional transactions — as compared and contrasted with international transactions — there are no balance-of-payments problems, or at least that these are of a qualitatively different kind. What this actually means is that the portfolio adjustments required to *finance* a current-account surplus/deficit can be much more smoothly and easily arranged in inter-regional transactions, indeed so simply facilitated that they may pass virtually unnoticed' (Goodhart 1975: 264).

3. Among them, Robert Triffin is probably the theorist who has most consistently opposed the use of a national currency as international money.

Chapter One

1. They are also out of balance when *A* spends less than he earns but in this case there is no need to finance any deficit and a new equilibrium can easily be reached through an increase in financial assets.

2. See, for example, B. Schmitt (1984a) and A. Cencini (1988).

3. Except those which can pay for their imports by sending abroad their own national currency.

4. This conclusion should, obviously, not be taken to mean that prolonged regional trade deficits are not to be seriously analysed since they do not end up with an inter-regional debt. On the contrary, the lack of dichotomy between expenditure-flows and asset-stocks shows that the analysis of current-account deficits cannot be constrained within the rigid limits of the false couple deficit-debt.

Chapter Two

1. For a detailed analysis of money creation see R. S. Sayers (1958), B. Schmitt (1984a) and A. Cencini (1988).

2. It is only after a further development of the analysis that it will be shown that, in reality, this assumption is too restrictive and can easily be disposed of.

3. Interesting results have already been obtained in this respect (Schmitt 1984b and 1989) and it has been proved convincingly that the solution to the external debt payment can be successfully implemented by any single country, irrespective of the system followed by all the others (see Part III of this work).

Chapter Three

1. From a modern point of view Ricardo's analysis of the gold standard can be seen also as a rigorous atempt to prove that international payments can be carried out only through the circular flow of gold. Used as international currency, gold would act as a vehicular money allowing for the constant equilibrium of the balance of payments. For more details see Bernard Schmitt's introduction to *Scritti monetari di David Ricardo*, 1984, Istituto dell'Enciclopedia Italiana, Rome.

2. Among these economists we find Triffin, Rueff and Kindleberger.

3. See Sayers (1958), Cencini (1984, 1988) and Schmitt (1966, 1975, 1984a).

4. It has to be noted that, in their famous paper, Despres, Kindleberger and Salant asserted a different point of view.

5. E. Despres, C. P. Kindleberger, W. S. Salant (1966).

Chapter Four

1. The modern revival of the monetary approach to the balance of payments can be ascribed mainly to Meade (1951), and, among others, to Hahn (1959), Pearce (1961) McKinnon (1968) McKinnon and Oates (1966).

2. See Cencini (1984, 1988) and Schmitt (1975, 1984a).

Chapter Eight

1. The multilateral clearing system advocated by Schumacher (1943) differentiates from Keynes's Clearing Union mainly because no international standard is supposed to be needed in order to vehiculate international transactions. 'It will be clear that the International Clearing Office requires no finance of its own, nor does it have to create a new international currency' (p.153). In his attempt at avoiding monetary payments between countries, Schumacher considered multilateral clearing as a kind of multi-currency system. By claiming that 'In this way, one might say, every national currency is made into a world currency, whereby the creation of a new world currency becomes unnecessary' (p.154) , he was explicitly assuming that, to be effective, payments had to be carried out in kind. Yet, his solution is still too rigid, the lack of monetary circulation having as a corollary the need to achieve balance in the trade of every country. 'No matter what is the technical set-up, every country must ultimately pay for what it buys, which means, in the long run, that it must achieve a position in which it can supply as much in goods and services to the rest of the world as it receives' (p.155).

2. Important suggestions as to the way internal payments can be related to (but not interrelated with) international transactions can be found in Schumacher's proposals for the institution of a multilateral clearing house. His solution implies the creation, in each country, of a Clearing Authority to receive payments, in domestic money, from national importers and to make payments, in domestic currency, to national exporters. 'Each National Clearing Fund thus receives and disburses only national currency: it receives such currency from the home importers and disburses it to the home exporters' (1943: 151).

Given the absence of any international currency in Schumacher's plan, the separation between national and international monetary circuits is a problem which does not even arise here, it is true, yet the mechanism based on the particular role played by the Clearing Authorities is a valuable step towards the internalization of external transactions which, in a system where money still plays an essential role, remains a fundamental requirement for the correct solution of the international debt problem.

3. For more details see Schmitt (1973, 1977, 1984b, 1988).

Bibliography

Allsop, C. and Joshi, V. (1986) 'The Assessment: The International Debt Crisis', *Oxford Review of Economic Policy*, Spring.

Altman, O. L. (1963) 'Professor Triffin on International Liquidity and the Role of the Fund', in *World Monetary Reform: Plans and Issues*, ed. H. G. Grubel, Stanford University Press: Stanford.

Angell, J. (1963) 'The Reorganization of the International Monetary System: An Alternative Proposal', in *World Monetary Reform: Plans and Issues*, ed. H. G. Grubel, Stanford University Press: Stanford.

Arrow, K. J. and Boskin, M. J. (eds) (1988) *The Economics of Public Debt: Proceedings of a Conference held by the International Economic Association at Stanford, California*, Macmillan: London and Basingstoke.

Baranzini, M. (ed.) (1982) *Advances in Economic Theory*, Blackwell: Oxford.

Baranzini, M. and Cencini, A. (eds) (1987) *Contributi di analisi economica*, Edizioni Casagrande: Bellinzona.

Belassa, B. (1964) 'The Purchasing Power Parity Doctrine Reexamined: A Reappraisal', *Journal of Political Economy*, Vol. 72.

Bergsten, C. F. (1975) *Toward a New International Economic Order: Selected Papers of C. Fred Bergsten, 1972–1974*, Lexington Books: Lexington Mass.

Bernal, R. L. (1987) 'Resolving the Global Debt Crisis', *Economia Internazionale*, May-August.

Bernstein, E. M. (1963) 'Proposed Reforms in the International Monetary System', in *World Monetary Reform: Plans and Issues*, ed. H. G. Grubel, Stanford University Press: Stanford.

———(1978) 'The Economics of Fluctuating Exchange Rates, in *Exchange Rate Flexibility*, eds. J. S. Dreyer, G. Haberler and T. D. Willet, American Enterprise Institute: Washington.

——— (1980) 'Back to the Gold Standard?', *Brookings Bulletin*, Brookings Institution, Vol. 17.

——— (1988) 'The Search for Exchange Stability: Before and After Bretton Woods', paper presented at a conference on *The Future of the International Monetary System* at Glendon College, York University, Toronto, June.

Berthélèmy J. C. (1987) 'Endettement international et théorie des transferts', *Revue d'économie politique*, Vol. 97, n. 3.

Bhagwati, J. N. (ed.) (1977) *The New International Economic Order: the North–South Debate*, The MIT Press: London and Cambridge Mass.

Bhagwati, J. N., Jones, R. W., Mundell, R. A. and Vanek, J. (eds) (1971) *Trade, Balance of Payments, and Growth*, North Holland: Amsterdam.

Bloomfield, A. I. and Ethier, W. (1977) 'Developments in International Economics', in *Modern Economic Thought*, ed. S. Weintraub, Blackwell: Oxford.

Bourquinat, H. and Mistral, J. (eds) (1986) *La crise de l'endettement international, acte II*, Economica: Paris.

Bradlow, D. D. (ed.) (1986) *International Borrowing: Negotiating and Structuring International Debt Transactions*, International Law Institute: Washington.

Brunner, K. and Meltzer, A. H. (1972) 'Money, Debt and Economic Activity', *Journal of Political Economy*, September/October.

Byé, M. (1965) *Relations économiques internationales*, deuxième édition, Dalloz: Paris.

Caigdon, T. (1988) *The Debt Threat*, Blackwell: Oxford.

Calleo, D. P. (ed.) (1971) *Money and the Coming World Order*, New York University Press: New York.

Carli, G. *et al.* (1972) *A Debate on the Euro-dollar Market*, Ente Einaudi: Roma.

Cencini, A. (1984) *Time and the Macroeconomic Analysis of Income*, Pinter Publishers: London and New York.

——— (1987) 'L'attuale non-sistema dei pagamenti internazionali: una diagnosi', in *Contributi di Analisi Economica*, eds. M. Baranzini and A. Cencini, Edizioni Casagrande: Bellinzona.

——— (1988) *Money, Income and Time*, Pinter Publishers: London and New York.

Chipman, J. S. (1974) 'The Transfer Problem Once Again', in *Trade, Stability, and Macroeconomics*, eds. Horwich and Samuelson, Academic Press: New York.

Claudon, M. P. (ed.) (1986) *World Debt Crisis: International Lending On Trial*, Ballinger Publishing Co.: Cambridge Mass.

Cline, W. R. (1976) *International Monetary Reform and the Developing Countries*, Brookings Institution: Washington.

——— (1983) *International Debt and the Stability of the World Economy*, Institute for International Economics: Washington.

——— (1985) *International Debt*, The MIT Press: Cambridge Mass.

——— (1988) 'International Debt: Progress and Strategy', *Finance and Development*, June.

Coakley, J. and Harris, L. (1983) *The City of Capital*, Blackwell: Oxford.

Cohen, B. J. (1978) *Organizing the World's Money: the Political*

Economy of International Monetary Relations, Macmillan: London and Basingstoke.

——— (1988) 'LDC Debt: Toward a Genuinely Cooperative Solution', paper presented at a conference on *The Future of the International Monetary System*, at Glendon College, York University, Toronto, June.

——— (1989) *Developing-country Debt: a Middle Way*, International Finance Section Department of Economics, Princeton University: Princeton.

Connolly, M. B. and Swoboda, A. K. (eds) (1973) *International Trade and Money*, Allen & Unwin: London.

Cooper, R. N. (1972) 'Eurodollars, Reserve Dollars and Asymmetries in the International Monetary System', *Journal of International Economics*, no. 2.

——— (1987) 'The Evolution of the International Monetary System Toward a World Central Bank', in *The International Monetary System, Essays in World Economics*, MIP Press: Cambridge Mass. and London.

Davidson, P. (1982) *International Money and the Real World*, Macmillan: London and Basingstoke.

Dell, S. (1986) 'The World Debt Problem: A Diagnosis, Report to the Group of Twenty-Four', UNCTAD document, UNCTAD/MFD/TA/33.

——— (1988) 'The Future of the International Monetary System', paper presented at a conference on *The Future of the International Monetary System*, at Glendon College, York University, Toronto, June.

Dembinski, P. H. (1989) *L'endettement international*, Presses Universitaires de France: Paris.

Despres, E., Kindleberger, C. P. and Salant, W. S. (1966) 'The Dollar and World Liquidity: A Minority View', *The Economist*, February.

Dicke, D. C. (ed.) (1986) *Foreign Debts in the Present and a New International Economic Order*, Presses Universitaires de Fribourg: Fribourg (Switzerland).

Dornbusch, R. (1985a) 'Dealing with Debt in the 1980s', *Third World Quarterly*, 7.

——— (1985b) *Purchasing Power Parity*, Working Paper, National Bureau of Economic Research, Cambridge Mass.

——— (1986) 'Purchasing Power Parity', *New Palgrave Dictionary of Economics*.

——— (1987) *Dollars, Debts and Deficits*, Leuven University Press: Leuven and The MIT Press: Cambridge Mass. and London.

Dornbusch, R. and Fischer, S. (1986) 'The World Debt Problem: Origins and Prospects', *Journal of Development Planning*.

Ellyne, M. J. and Flinch, H. (1990) 'Issues in the Measurement of

External Debt', *Finance and Development*, March.

Ethier, W. J. and Marston, R. C. (eds) (1985) *International Financial Markets and Capital Movements: a Symposium in Honor of A. I. Bloomfield*, International Finance Section, Department of Economics, Princeton University: Princeton.

Fellner, W. (1972) 'The Dollar's Place in the International System', *Journal of Economic Literature*, September.

Fellner, W., Machlup, F., Triffin, R. and eleven others (1966) *Maintaining and Restoring Balance in International Payments*, Princeton University Press: Princeton.

Fiorentini, R. (1986) 'Parità del potere di acquisto', *Giornale degli economisti*, November/December.

Fleming, J. M. (1971) *Essays in International Economics*, Harvard University Press: Cambridge Mass.

——— (1974) *Reflections on the International Monetary Reform*, Princeton Essays in International Finance no. 107, Dept. of Economics, Princeton University: Princeton.

Floyd, J. E. (1969) 'Monetary and Fiscal Policy in a World of Capital Mobility', *The Review of Economic Studies*, October.

——— (1973) 'A Reply', *The Review of Economic Studies*, April.

Fraga, A. (1986) *German Reparations and Brazilian Debt: A Comparative Study*, International Finance Section Department of Economics, Princeton University: Princeton.

Fraser, R. (1987) *The World Financial System*, A Keesing's Reference Publication, Longman: Harlow (Essex).

Frenkel, J. A. (1971) 'A Theory of Money, Trade and the Balance of Payments in a Model of Accumulation', *Journal of International Economics*, May.

——— (1981) 'The Collapse of Purchasing Power Parity During the 1970's', *European Economic Review*, May.

Frenkel, J. A. and Johnson, H. G. (eds) (1974) *The Monetary Approach to the Balance of Payments*, Allen & Unwin: London.

Friboulet, J-J. (1988) 'Ressources et emplois dans la comptabilité du commerce extérieur', Working Paper, Centre d'Etudes Monétaires et Financères, Université de Bourgogne, Dijon.

Frieden, J. (1984) 'Endeudamiento y fuga de capital', *Investigacion economica*, Mexico, no. 170, October/December.

Friedman, M. (1953) *Essays in Positive Economics*, Chicago University Press: Chicago.

Giovannetti, G. (1987) 'Testing Purchasing Power Parity as a Long Run Equilibrium Condition', *Giornale degli economisti*, September/October.

Gnos, C. and Rasera, J-B. (1985) 'Circuit et circulation: une fausse analogie', *Cahiers de la Revue d'économie politique*, Sirey: Paris.

Goodhart, C. A. E. (1975) *Money, Information and Uncertainty*,

Macmillan: London and Basingstoke.

Griffith-Jones, S. (ed.) (1988) *Managing World Debt*, St. Martin's Press: New York.

Griffith-Jones, S. and Sunkel, O. (1989) *Debt and Development Crises in Latin America: The End of an Illusion*, Clarendon Press: Oxford.

Grubel, H. G. (ed.) (1963) *World Monetary Reform: Plans and Issues*, Stanford University Press: Stanford.

——— (1965) 'The Case Against an International Commodity Reserve Currency', *Oxford Economic Papers*, Vol. 17.

——— (1971) 'The Demand for International Reserves. A Critical Review of the Literature', *Journal of Economic Literature*, December.

——— (1977) *The International Monetary System*, Penguin Books: Harmondsworth.

Gutowski A., Lutz, F. A. and Machlup, F. (1972) *International Monetary Problems*, American Enterprise Institute for Public Policy Research: Washington.

Haberler, G. (1965) *Money in the International Economy*, Harvard University Press: Cambridge Mass.

——— (1976) 'Review of J. A. Frenkel and H. G. Johnson (eds.) *The Monetary Approach to the Balance of Payments*', *Journal of Economic Literature*, December.

Habermeier, W. O. (1979) 'The SDR as an International Unit of Account', *Finance and Development*, March.

Hahn, F. H. (1959) 'The Balance of Payments in a Monetary Economy', *Review of Economic Studies*, February.

Haq, K. (ed.) (1985) *The Lingering Debt Crisis: North South Roundtable*, North South Roundtable: Islamabad.

Harrod, R. (1963) 'Liquidity', in *World Monetary Reform: Plans and Issues*, ed. H. G. Grubel, Stanford University Press: Stanford.

——— (1965) *Reforming the World's Money*, Macmillan: London and Basingstoke.

Hart, A. G. (1968) 'The Case For and Against International Reserve Currency', *Oxford Economic Papers*, Vol. 18.

Hart, A. G., Timbergen, J. and Kaldor, N. (1964) 'The Case for an International Commodity Reserve Currency', in N. Kaldor, *Essays on Economic Policy*, Duckworth: London.

Hawtrey, R. G. (1932) *The Art of Central Banking*, Longman: London.

Hirsch, F. (1969) *Money International*, Penguin Books: Harmondsworth.

——— (1973) *An SDR Standard: Impetus, Elements, and Impediments*, Essays in International Finance, no. 99, Princeton University Press: Princeton.

IMF (1974) *International Monetary Reform: Documents of the*

Committee of Twenty, IMF: Washington.
——— (1979) *Survey*, September, IMF: Washington.
——— (1985) *Survey*, July, IMF: Washington.
Jacobson, P. (1963) 'The Two Functions of an International Monetary Standard: Stability and Liquidity', in *World Monetary Reform: Plans and Issues*, ed. H. G. Grubel, Stanford University Press: Stanford.
Johnson, H. G. (1956) 'The Transfer Problem and Exchange Stability', *Journal of Political Economy*, June.
——— (1963) 'International Liquidity-Problems and Plans', in *World Monetary Reform: Plans and Issues*, ed. H. G. Grubel, Stanford University Press: Stanford.
——— (1969) 'The Case For Flexible Exchange Rates', *Federal Reserve Bank of St Louis Review*, June.
——— (1972) 'The Monetary Approach to Balance-of-Payments Theory', in H. G. Johnson, *Further Essays in Monetary Economics*, Allen & Unwin: London.
——— (1974) 'Towards a General Theory of the Balance of Payments', in *The Monetary Approach to the Balance of Payments*, eds. J. A. Frenkel and H. G. Johnson, Allen & Unwin: London.
Johnson, H. G. and Swoboda, A. K. (eds) (1973) *The Economics of Common Currencies*, Harvard University Press: Cambridge Mass.
Kahn, R. (1973) 'The International Monetary System', *American Economic Review*, May.
Kaldor, N. (1983) 'The Role of Commodity Prices in Economic Recovery', *Lloyds Bank Review*, July.
Keynes, J. M. (1923) *A Tract on Monetary Reform*, Macmillan: London.
——— (1929a) 'The German Transfer Problem', *The Economic Journal*, March.
——— (1929b) 'A Rejoinder', *The Economic Journal*, June.
——— (1929c) 'A Reply by Mr. Keynes', *The Economic Journal*, September.
——— (1972) *Essays in Persuasion*, Macmillan: London and Basingstoke.
——— (1973) *The Collected Writings of John Maynard Keynes*, ed. D. Moggridge, Macmillan: London and Basingstoke.
Kindleberger, C. P. (1953) *International Economics*, Richard D. Irwin: Homewood.
——— (1966) *Europe and the Dollar*, MIT Press: Cambridge Mass.
——— (1981) *International Money*, Allen & Unwin: London.
——— (1988) *The International Economic Order: Essays on Financial Crisis and International Public Goods*, Harvester-Wheatsheaf: New York and London.
Kindleberger C. P. and Shonfield, A. (eds) (1971), *North American*

and Western European Economic Policies, Macmillan: London.

Laughlin, J. L. (1903) *The Principles of Money*, Scribner: New York.

Lutz, F. A. (1963) 'The Problem of International Liquidity and the Multiple Currency Standard', in *World Monetary Reform: Plans and Issues*, ed. H. G. Grubel, Stanford University Press: Stanford.

McDonald, D. C. (1982) 'Debt Capacity of Developing Country Borrowing: A Survey of Literature', *IMF Staff Papers*, Vol. 29, no. 4.

Machlup, F. (1943) *International Trade and the National Income Multiplier*, Blakiston: Philadelphia.

——— (1963) 'Reform of the International Monetary System', in *World Monetary Reform: Plans and Issues*, ed. H. G. Grubel, Stanford University Press: Stanford.

——— (1964a) *Plans for Reform of the International Monetary System*, rev. edn., Princeton University Press: Princeton.

——— (1964b) *International Payments, Debts and Gold*, Charles Scribner's Sons: New York.

——— (1970) *International Monetary Economics*, Allen & Unwin: London.

Machlup, F., Salant, W. and Tarshis, L. (eds) (1972) *International Mobility and Movement of Capital*, National Bureau of Economic Research, Columbia University Press: New York.

McKinnon, R. I. (1968) 'Portfolio Balance and International Payments Adjustment', in *Monetary Problems of the International Economy*, eds. R. A. Mundell and A. K. Swoboda, University of Chicago Press: Chicago.

——— (1969) 'Private and Official International Money: The Case for the Dollar', *Essays in International Finance*, no. 74, Princeton University Press: Princeton.

——— (1984) *An International Standard for Monetary Stabilization*, Institute for International Economics: Washington.

——— (1988) 'Monetary and Exchange Rate Policies for International Financial Stability: A Proposal', *Journal of Economic Perspectives*, February.

McKinnon, R. I. and Oates, W. E. (1966) 'The Implications of International Economic Integration for Monetary, Fiscal and Exchange Rate Policy', *Princeton Studies in International Finance*, no. 16.

McKinnon, R. I. and Ohno, K. (1988) 'Purchasing Power Parity as a Monetary Standard', paper presented at a conference on *The Future of the International Monetary System*, at Glendon College, York University, Toronto.

Magee, S. P. and Rao, R. K. S. (1980) 'Vehicle and Non-Vehicle Currencies in International Trade', *American Economic Review*, no. 70.

Masera, R. S. (1972) 'Deposit Creation, Multiplication and the Eurodollar Market', in G. Carli *et al.*, *A Debate on the Euro-dollar Market*, Ente Einaudi: Roma.

Meade, J. E. (1951) *The Balance of Payments*, Oxford University Press: London.

——— (1963) 'The Future of International Payments', in *World Monetary Reform: Plans and Issues*, ed. H. G. Grubel, Stanford University Press: Stanford.

Meheran, H. (ed.) (1985) *External Debt Management*, International Monetary Fund: Washington.

Meier, G. M. (1982) *Problems of World Monetary Order*, Oxford University Press: London.

Milivojevic, M. (1985) *The Debt Rescheduling Process*, Pinter Publishers: London and New York.

Mill, J. S. (1893) *Principles of Political Economy*, 5th edn, Appleton: New York.

Mundell, R. A. (1961) 'A Theory of Optimum Currency Areas', *The American Economic Review*, September.

——— (1968) *International Economics*, Macmillan: London.

——— (1971) *Monetary Theory*, Goodyear: Pacific Palisades.

——— (1973) 'Uncommon Arguments for Common Currencies', in *The Economics of Common Currencies*, eds. H. G. Johnson and A. K. Swoboda, Harvard University Press: Cambridge Mass.

Mundell, R. A. and Polak, J. J. (eds) (1977) *The New International Monetary System*, Columbia University Press: New York.

Mundell, R. A. and Swoboda, A. K. (eds) (1969) *Monetary Problems of the International Economy*, University of Chicago Press: Chicago.

Nowzad, B. (1990) 'Lessons of the Debt Decade: Will We Learn', *Finance and Development*, March.

OCDE (1986) *Financement et dette extérieure des pays en développement: étude*, OCDE: Paris.

——— (1988) *External Debt: Definition, Statistical Coverage and Methodology*, OCDE: Paris.

Ohlin, B. (1929a) 'Transfer Difficulties, Real and Imagined', *The Economic Journal*, June.

——— (1929b) 'Mr. Keynes' Views on the Transfer Problem: A Rejoinder', *The Economic Journal*, September.

Pearce, I. F. (1961) 'The Problem of the Balance of Payments', *International Economic Review*, January.

Pigou, A. C. (1932) 'The Effect of Reparations on the Real Ratio of International Interchange', *The Economic Journal*, Vol. 42.

Poulon, F. (1985) 'Le débat de 1919-29 sur les transferts internationaux de revenu: point de départ de la révolution keynesienne', *Communication au colloque de l'Association C. Gide pour l'Etude de la Pensée Economique*: Montpellier.

Reisen, H. and Trotsenburg van, A. (1988) Developing Country Debt: The Budgetary and Transfer Problem, OECD Development Centre Studies: Paris.

Ricardo, D. (1811) *Reply to Mr. Bosanquet's Practical Observations on the Report of the Bullion Committee*, reprinted in Vol. III of *The Works and Correspondence of David Ricardo*, Cambridge University Press: Cambridge.

——— (1951-5) *The Works and Correspondence of David Ricardo*, ed. P. Sraffa, 11 vols., Cambridge University Press: Cambridge.

——— (1985) *Scritti monetari*, Introduction by B. Schmitt, Istituto della Enciclopedia Italiana: Roma.

Rockefeller, D. (1963) 'International Monetary Reform and the New York Banking Community', in *World Monetary Reform: Plans and Issues*, ed. H. G. Grubel, Stanford University Press: Stanford.

Roosa, R. V. (1963) 'Assuring the Free World's Liquidity', in *World Monetary Reform: Plans and Issues*, ed. H. G. Grubel, Stanford University Press: Stanford.

Rueff, J. (1929) 'Mr. Keynes' Views on the Transfer Problem: A Criticism by M. Jacques Rueff', *The Economic Journal*, September.

——— (1963) 'Gold Exchange Standard a Danger to the West', in *World Monetary Reform: Plans and Issues*, ed. H. G. Grubel, Stanford University Press: Stanford.

——— (1980) *Oeuvres complètes*, Plon: Paris.

Sachs, J. D. (1986) 'Managing the LDC Debt Crisis, *Brookings Papers on Economic Activity*, no. 2.

——— (1989) *New Approaches to the Latin American Debt Crisis*, International Finance Section Department of Economics Princeton University: Princeton.

Salama, P. (1989) *La dollarisation: essai sur la monnaie, l'industrialisation et l'endettement des pays sous-développés*, Ed. La Découverte: Paris.

Salant, W. S. (1972) 'Financial Intermediation as an Explanation of Enduring "Deficits" in the Balance of Payments', in *International Mobility and Movement of Capital*, eds. F. Machlup W. Salant and L. Tarshis, Columbia University Press: New York.

Samuelson, P. A. (1952) 'The Transfer Problem and Transfer Costs: the Terms of Trade When Impediments are Absent', *The Economic Journal*, Vol. 62.

——— (1954) 'The Transfer Problem and Transfer Costs II: Analysis of Effects of Trade Impediments', *The Economic Journal*, Vol. 64.

——— (1971) 'On the Trail of Conventional Beliefs About the Transfer Problem', in *Trade, Balance of Payments, and Growth*, eds. J. N. Bhagwati, R. W. Jones, R. A. Mundell, and J. Vanek, North Holland: Amsterdam.

Sayers, R. S. (1958) *Modern Banking*, Oxford University Press: London.

Schmitt, B. (1966) *Monnaie, salaires et profits*, Presses Universitaires de France: Paris (reprinted 1975 ed. Castella: Albeuve, Switzerland).

——— (1973) *New Proposals for World Monetary Reform*, Castella: Albeuve (Switzerland).

——— (1975) *Théorie unitaire de la monnaie, nationale et internationale*, ed. Castella: Albeuve.

——— (1977) *La monnaie européenne*, Presses Universitaires de France: Paris

——— (1984a) *Inflation, chômage et malformations du capital*, Economica: Paris and Castella: Albeuve.

——— (1984b) *La France souveraine de sa monnaie*, Economica: Paris and Castella: Albeuve.

——— (1985) *Les pays au régime du FMI*, Economica: Paris and Castella: Albeuve.

——— (1988a) *L'ECU et les souverainetés nationales en Europe*, Dunod: Paris.

——— (1988b) 'External Debt — Eternal Debt', paper presented at a conference on *The Future of the International Monetary System* at Glendon College, York University, Toronto.

Schumacher, E. F. (1943) 'Multilateral Clearing', Economica.

Schvarzer, J. (1985) 'Deuda externa: un enfoque no ortodoxo desde la perspectiva del deudor', *El Bimestre*, Marzo-Abril, Buenos Aires.

Simonsen, M. H. (1985) 'The Developing Country Debt Problem', in *International Debt and the Developing Countries*, eds. G. Smith and J. Cuddington, World Bank: Washington.

Singer, H. W. and Sharma, S. (eds.) (1989) *Economic Development and World Debt*, Macmillan: London and Basingstoke.

Smith, A. (1978) *The Wealth of Nations*, Pelican Classics: Harmondsworth (first published 1776).

Smith, G. and Cuddington, J. (eds) (1985) *International Debt and the Developing Countries*, World Bank: Washington.

Solomon, R. (1977) *The International Monetary System 1945-76*, Harper & Row: New York.

Sprinkel, B. W. (1986) 'Challenges Facing the World Economy', in *International Banking Symposium* [1986, Lugano], Haupt: Bern and Stuttgart.

Stamp, J. (1963) 'The Stamp Plan — 1962 Version', in *World Monetary Reform: Plans and Issues*, ed. H. G. Grubel, Stanford University Press: Stanford.

Sweeney, R. J. and Willet, T. D. (1976) 'Eurodollars, Petrodollars, and World Liquidity and Inflation', *Journal of Monetary Economics*, North Holland: Amsterdam.

Swoboda, A. K. and Dornbusch, R. (1973) 'Adjustment, Policy and Monetary Equilibrium in a Two-Country Model', in *International*

Trade and Money, eds. M. B. Connolly and A. K. Swoboda, Allen & Unwin: London.

Tarshis, L. (1987) 'German Reparation and the Debt of the LDCs' (mimeo).

——— (1988) 'A Return Visit to the International Debt Problem of the LDCs', paper presented at a conference on *The Future of the International Monetary System*, at Glendon College, York University, Toronto.

Tobin, J. (1966) 'Adjustment Responsibilities of Surplus and Deficit Countries', in *Maintaining and Restoring Balance in International Payments*, eds. W. Fellner, F. Machlup, R. Triffin and eleven others, Princeton University Press: Princeton.

——— (1978) 'A Proposal for International Monetary Reform', *The Eastern Economic Journal*, Vol. 3, July/October.

Tower, E. (1972) 'Monetary and Fiscal Policy in a World of Capital Mobility: a Respecification', *The Review of Economic Studies*, July.

Tower, E. and Willet, T. (1976) *The Theory of Optimum Currency Areas and Exchange-Rate Flexibility*, Department of Economics, Princeton University Press: Princeton.

Triffin, R. (1961) *Gold and the Dollar Crisis*, Yale University Press: New Haven.

——— (1963) 'After the Gold Exchange Standard?', in *World Monetary Reform: Plans and Issues*, ed. H. G. Grubel, Stanford University Press: Stanford.

——— (1964) 'The Evolution of the International Monetary System: Historical Reappraisal and Future Perspectives', *Princeton Studies in International Finance*, no. 12, June.

——— (1969) *Le système monétaire international*, Ed. Clé: Paris.

——— (1987) 'Lo *SMI* (*Sistema ... Scandalo?* Monetario Internazionale) e lo *SME* (*Sistema* Monetario Europeo)', *Moneta e Credito*, September.

——— (1988) 'The International Monetary System and the Paper-Exchange Standard', paper written for a conference on *The Future of the International Monetary System*, Glendon College, York University, Toronto.

Turay, A. M. and Hamdar, B. (1989) 'The New International Debt Strategy for Indebted Nations: A Problem of Liquidity', *Economia Internazionale*, August/November.

Viner, J. (1937) *Studies in the Theory of International Trade*, Harper: New York.

Wachtel, P. (ed.) (1982) *Crisis in the Economic and Financial Structure*, Lexington Books: Lexington Mass.

Wallich, H. C. (1963) 'Cooperation to Solve the Gold Problem', in *World Monetary Reform: Plans and Issues*, ed. H. G. Grubel, Stanford University Press: Stanford.

Weintraub, S. (ed.) (1977) *Modern Economic Thought*, Blackwell: Oxford.

Wicksell, K. (1918) 'International Freights and Prices', *Quarterly Journal of Economics*, February.

Willett, T. D. (1971) 'Statement of Thomas D. Willett' in *The Balance-of-Payments Mess* Hearings before the Subcommittee on International Exchange and Payments of the Joint Economic Committee, 92nd Congress, June.

Williamson, J. H. (1976) 'The Benefits and Costs of an International Monetary Nonsystem', in *Reflections on Jamaica*, *Essays in International Finance*, no. 115, Department of Economics, Princeton University, April.

——— (1977) *The Failure of World Monetary Reform 1971-74*, New York University Press: New York.

Yeager, L. B. (1963) 'The Triffin Plan: Diagnosis, Remedy and Alternatives', in *World Monetary Reform: Plans and Issues*, ed. H. G. Grubel, Stanford University Press: Stanford.

Zolotas, Z. (1963) 'Towards a Reinforced Gold Exchange Standard', in *World Monetary Reform: Plans and Issues*, ed. H. G. Grubel, Stanford Universtiy Press: Stanford.

Subject Index

Author Index